Victory Faust

To Jeff:

May good luck and Charley
Faust stay with you!

Gabriel Schechter

VICTORY FAUST

The Rube Who Saved McGraw's Giants

Gabriel Schechter

Charles April Publications
Los Gatos

To my parents,

Harold and Tanya Schechter,

who taught me to love baseball and words

Designed by Jennie Kaufman.
Set in Electra type by à la page, Brooklyn, New York.
Printed in the United States of America by United Graphics, Mattoon, Illinois.

Library of Congress Cataloging-in-Publication Data

Schechter, Gabriel.
　　Victory Faust : the rube who saved McGraw's Giants / Gabriel Schechter — 1st ed.
　　p. cm.
　　Includes bibliographical references and index.
　　LCCN: 99-91481
　　ISBN: 0-9675221-0-2
　　1. Faust, Victory.　2. Baseball players—United States—Biography.
　　3. New York Giants (Baseball team)—History.　I. Title.
　　GV865.F3S34 2000　　　　　　　　　　　　　　　796.357/092
　　[B]　　　　　　　　　　　　　　　　　　　　　QBI99-1844

10 9 8 7 6 5 4 3 2 1

Contents

Foreword

Lawrence S. Ritter

I REMEMBER as though it was only yesterday the day when I first heard the now-familiar name of Charles "Victory" Faust. It was on August 25, 1963, in Ventura, California, while I was sitting in Fred Snodgrass's living room along with Fred, his wife, my son Steve, and my girlfriend Barbara.

Fred Snodgrass was himself the victim of man's inhumanity to man. Centerfielder on the National League–champion New York Giants in 1912, he dropped an easy fly ball in that year's World Series, an error for which the world never forgave him. When Fred passed away in 1974, sixty-two years after the event, the New York *Times*'s obituary headline read FRED SNODGRASS, 86, DEAD; BALLPLAYER MUFFED 1912 FLY.

But what goes around comes around, and in 1963 Fred atoned for that grievous error by reintroducing Charlie Faust to the world. Charlie had died tragically in 1915, in his mid-thirties, and with the passage of time had been completely forgotten. By the 1950s most baseball aficionados, including serious baseball historians, were totally unaware of the name Charles Victory Faust. The strange and unusual circumstances that surrounded his intriguing role in major league baseball had been completely obliterated by the shifting sands of time.

And then came that fateful day in 1963 when Fred Snodgrass casually mentioned the name in passing. Did I remember Charlie Faust, Fred asked during a pause in the conversation. No, I had never heard of him. Fred's eyes sparkled and his face broke into a broad grin: he had hooked a live one!

For most of the next hour we were regaled with Fred's version of the Charles Victory Faust saga. Printed in *The Glory of Their Times* (Macmillan 1966, Morrow 1984, Quill Books 1992, HighBridge Audio 1998), the Charlie Faust story fascinated whole new generations of baseball fans.

Among them, fortunately, was Gabriel Schechter, by profession a poker dealer, who embarked on practically a lifelong research project devoted to separating fact from fiction in received doctrine regarding Charlie Faust.

Schechter's two-decades-long obsession with Charlie Faust may have turned his own life upside down, but it has been a blessing for baseball fans and historians. We finally learn the true story, the whole story, behind the Victory Faust legend. Moreover, Schechter knows how to tell a tale, as you will discover once you turn the page.

New York City
April 1999

Acknowledgments

IT WAS THE BASEBALL HISTORIAN John Holway more than anyone else who got the ball rolling on this book. After showing me the ropes at the Library of Congress microfilm room in 1992, he turned me loose and shared my glee at the daily discoveries. At some point he commented that I was going to have enough material for a book about Victory Faust. I hadn't thought it possible given the initial scarcity of Faust material, and without John's early encouragement and guidance it still would not have happened.

I spent innumerable hours at libraries all over the country, and each hour increased my esteem for the people who work in libraries. Nowhere is this more true than at the National Baseball Library in Cooperstown, whose able assistance has been acknowledged in hundreds of baseball books. Especially helpful to me were Bill Deane, Dan Bennett, Pat Kelly, and the late Gary Van Allen. My most intense research was at the Library of Congress, where Darryl Jones and others patiently handled my flood of microfilm requests.

Other significant library research was done at the University of Nevada, Las Vegas; the New York State Library, Albany; the Carnegie Library, Pittsburgh; the New York State Historical Society, Cooperstown; the University of Cincinnati; public libraries in St. Louis, Boston, and Tacoma; Kansas State University; and the University of Oregon.

I am particularly grateful to the hospitality of Phyllis Melton, Lorraine Hadsell, and Bud Pierce of the Marion County (Kansas) Historical Museum. They made me feel welcome and special during my visit to Faust's hometown.

Lawrence Ritter, who revived the Faust story in the first place, encouraged my enthusiasm for Faust and offered timely help, as did Thomas Busch, Bart Ripp, Richard Raddon, Tom Heitz, Richard Scheinin, Albert DeCirce, Ron Visco, Danny Peary, Eddie Frierson, Larry Mansch, Alvin Hall, and Don Reddick. Many friends have provided moral support over the years, but none more than George Steedle, Stew Baskin, and Tim Carson. I would also like to thank the hundreds of people to whom I have told the Faust tale and whose responses helped convince me that the story deserved a wider telling.

Every writer yearns for an ideal editor, one with a compatible temperament, sound judgment, and a commitment to making every word and sentence count. I got lucky to find such an editor in Dan Heaton. His perspectives and suggestions were invaluable, as was the design and typesetting expertise of Jennie Kaufman. Their advice and efforts helped me through every stage of this project.

Finally, I thank Judy for helping me get this far, for standing by me during the years when writing the Faust story was just a good idea, and for appreciating how much this quest has meant to me.

Introduction

TELLING THE TRUE STORY of Charles "Victory" Faust is like putting together a jigsaw puzzle without the box; there is no total picture to work toward, no pattern to fill in. Despite collecting several hundred pieces of that puzzle, unearthed one or two at a time in libraries all over the country, I don't know how many undiscovered pieces are still out there. Saying it's a baseball story gives us the general outline but no hint of the rich detail. The outlandish events happened in 1911, and nothing like it has been seen in the major leagues since, even though most men have dreamed of doing something like it. Victory Faust was a once-in-a-lifetime phenomenon, a below-average man thrust into the spotlight of extraordinary circumstances, a real-life Forrest Gump.

The trickiest thing about putting the story together is that some of the pieces turn out to belong to other puzzles. Like most people of my generation, I first came across Charles Victor Faust in Lawrence Ritter's *The Glory of Their Times*. His tale was told by Fred Snodgrass, the centerfielder on John McGraw's New York Giants in 1911, when Faust joined the team and became—for a while—the most infallible good-luck charm in baseball history, helping the Giants win more than one pennant. Although Snodgrass vividly conveyed the truth of Faust's amazing adventure, he was a half-century removed from events, and many of his facts don't hold up.

One misleading piece from the wrong puzzle was Snodgrass's statement that Faust spent three years with the Giants. It turns out that he came and went within a much shorter period. Therefore, Snodgrass had to have been wrong when he said that Faust performed in vaudeville during his third season. So when *was* Faust in vaudeville? Where was that piece of the puzzle? It turned up at the Library of Congress five minutes before closing time one night. After going cross-eyed for eleven hours of scanning microfilm, I caught a two-paragraph item on the bottom of page 5 of the New York *Morning Telegraph*. Finding that large piece of the Faust puzzle raised questions that led to more discoveries, until that part of the picture was exhilaratingly clear. Other sections fell into place along the way, while more always beckoned—elusive, deep mysteries.

I have been obsessed by the story of Victory Faust for more than twenty years. In 1977 I reread Ritter's book in preparation for teaching a course in baseball literature at the University of Montana. Faust's improbable feat grabbed me, and within six months I wrote a novel based on Faust. I modernized it, called him Invincible King instead of Victory Faust, and gave him to the Cubs, who then as always seemed in dire need of some supernatural force to bring them a pennant. The novel had its moments, but it went unpublished.

It sat for many years while I invented ways to jazz up the story. By the time I hatched a workable rewrite plan, it was 1991 and I was prepared to hand Faust/King over to the Boston Red Sox and see how he'd fare against the "Curse of the Bambino." Searching for inspiration, I checked the Charles Victor Faust file at the National Baseball Library in Cooperstown and found just enough clues to send me scurrying to the nearest microfilm machine. Before long, it was obvious that the true adventures of Victory Faust were much more fascinating than the ones I was trying to invent for Invincible King. Exit King.

By luck, I soon met John Holway, one of two people who had done significant research on Faust. He acquainted me with the other, Thomas Busch. Like members of an obscure cult, we compared our separate findings and agreed that they raised more questions than they answered. Encouraged to explore further, I found many of the answers. Not all of them, but enough to use inference, extrapolation, and educated guesswork to piece the available parts of the puzzle into a portrait of Faust that makes sense.

In the past decade, Victory Faust has become something of a cult figure among SABR members and other explorers of baseball history.

Lots of people have heard something about him. His name crops up more often each year, a brief mention here, a short listing in a reference work there, always variations on the same basic account. As in the party game "telephone," however, a message that is clear at the start becomes increasingly garbled and inaccurate the more times it is repeated. In Faust's case, the original account was inaccurate, multiplying the problem down the line.

The ironic result is that while more people hear about Faust all the time, what they hear is wrong. Not only wrong, but improbably diminished, contrary to all principles of mythic exaggeration. The capsule summaries don't do justice to Faust's real achievements. In the companion book to the comprehensive Ken Burns baseball documentary on PBS, for instance, Burns and coauthor Geoffrey Ward included a six-paragraph box on mascots. Three short paragraphs repeated the basic Faust myth, three harmless-looking paragraphs which nevertheless contained seven factual errors and treated Faust's presence on the Giants as merely incidental. This is not to condemn Burns and Ward. Eyewitness accounts of Faust by some of the greatest baseball writers frequently contradicted each other, and many of those scribes couldn't remember a year later how many games Faust really pitched. Those conflicting reports formed the first links in a chain of misinformation that makes reconstructing the puzzle such a beguiling exercise.

But when we connect the pieces, the picture that emerges does not place Charley Faust at the fringe of John McGraw's Giants. Faust did not simply happen to be there while the Giants won. In his heyday, he became a central member of McGraw's squad, in some ways indispensable to their success. This is the story told by the men who saw it happen, by the writers and the players who watched it unfold one amazing day after another. The story is far richer, funnier, and more poignant than can be imagined from a second-hand summary.

1

One Giddy Weekend

MANAGER JOHN McGRAW was in a rotten mood as his New York Giants rode a train across the endless fields of Indiana and Illinois near the end of July 1911. It did not take much to disturb the volatile McGraw, but this time he had ample excuse for gloom. Come morning, the Giants would be in two places that genuinely distressed him: third place and St. Louis.

Awful things happened in St. Louis, the perilous western outpost of the major leagues. During their June visit, the Giants had lost two players when McGraw's entire squad numbered only eighteen. Shortstop Al Bridwell got wobbly and weak-kneed before breaking down completely, felled by malaria blamed on bad drinking water. Fear of the perils of water may have cost them Bugs Raymond as well. A fine spitball pitcher when sober, Raymond fell off the temperance wagon in St. Louis with such a thud that he never climbed on again.

It wasn't just the Giants who came to dread venturing to St. Louis. On July 26, the second-place Philadelphia Phillies, making their first pennant run in years, lost catcher-manager Red Dooin in a collision at home plate. Dooin's broken leg shattered the Phillies' pennant hopes, and the news of this fresh calamity reminded McGraw that there was no safe haven across the Mississippi River. The Cardinals were managed by Roger Bresnahan, a McGraw protégé who had taken second-division talent and raised them to within two games of the Giants and five games of the first-place Chicago Cubs.

McGraw wondered what might happen this time in St. Louis, though things couldn't get much worse. July had been a disaster from the start, when the Giants dropped from first place to third by losing four straight games in Philadelphia during a brutal heat wave. The continuing hundred-degree heat slowed their running attack all month and sapped their pitchers' stamina. The Giants staggered through July playing listless .500 ball.

McGraw tried desperately to ignite the needed spark. He brought back the most popular player from his 1905 champions, batting star Mike Donlin, who had "retired" to go on the stage in 1908 after marrying vaudeville star Mabel Hite. Bringing back Donlin succeeded only as a publicity boost. Donlin got plenty of headlines and ovations, but only four hits. Later in July, McGraw shook up his infield by trading the popular but weakened Bridwell to Boston for Charlie Herzog, a hardnosed ex-Giant. The new alignment had not jelled yet, as the Giants lost two of the last three games in Cincinnati before boarding the train for St. Louis.

When nothing else worked, McGraw went berserk, his preferred motivational tool. The scourge of National League umpires, McGraw chalked up three ejections and one suspension in July. The first to toss him was old nemesis Hank O'Day, who had made the fateful decision on "Merkle's Boner" that cost the Giants the 1908 flag. The day after O'Day nailed him, McGraw was bounced again, this time by Bill Finneran. Finneran still sported the scars of a pummeling three days earlier by Phillies outfielder Sherry Magee, an all-purpose slugger. McGraw stopped short of assaulting the rookie umpire but berated him all the way to the clubhouse, a long, loud walk.

Those eruptions made small blips on the screen compared with McGraw's big blowup in Cincinnati on July 25. It began with an argument at the plate, McGraw claiming that a Reds runner veered out of the baseline to avoid a tag. It continued when the Giants came to bat and McGraw went out to coach third base. Few umpires could stomach the sight of McGraw, five feet, seven inches of rabid competitive fury, barking at them from such close range. When umpire Jimmy Johnstone had heard his fill and ejected him, McGraw went nuts, screaming at Johnstone for five minutes before consenting to leave the field. Everyone in the ballpark heard McGraw accuse Johnstone of being "drunk all summer." Fuming in the clubhouse, McGraw fired off a letter to N.L. President Thomas Lynch, accusing Johnstone of bragging to players that he was "going to get" the Giants. Lynch, a former umpire who had just suspended Magee for the season for his attack on Finneran, probably felt he was letting McGraw off easy with the customary three-day suspension, his second of 1911. Like all suspensions of that era, it was effective immediately, with appeals rare.

McGraw began his suspension the last day in Cincinnati. Popular wisdom regarded the Giants as helpless without the "Little Napoleon" leading them, and games like this proved why. With McGraw banished to the bleachers, team captain Larry Doyle was the acting manager as the Giants took a 4–2 lead to the seventh inning. Pitcher Louis Drucke fell apart and was sabotaged further by a trio of infield misplays. Second baseman Doyle acted like an innocent bystander, leaving Drucke in so long that he not only blew the game but also blew out the tender shoulder he had nursed all summer. Doyle accepted the blame, but the damage was done; Drucke remained sidelined until October and never won another major league game.

Hurtling toward St. Louis, McGraw agonized over how to shore up his collapsing pitching staff. Drucke was through, and Raymond wasn't coming back. That left only five pitchers. McGraw had not used a five-man staff since the days when Joe "Iron Man" McGinnity stood alongside Christy Mathewson as the only teammates in this century to win thirty games in the same season—and they did it twice. This 1911 crew could not handle a load like that. The ace, Mathewson, was past his prime and looked increasingly mortal, with four losses already in July. Two veterans, Red Ames and Hooks Wiltse, were cold-weather horses who wilted in the summer heat. The workhorse relief specialist, Doc Crandall, was suffering from recurring headaches, courtesy of a Red Dooin line drive that nailed him on the forehead and literally knocked him out of the Fourth of July disaster in Philadelphia.

Reluctantly, McGraw had to rely more often on the staff's youngest pitcher, twenty-one-year-old Richard "Rube" Marquard. A lefty phenom with a high price tag, the erratic Marquard got his big chance when Raymond was jettisoned. Starting regularly for the first time, Marquard prospered, doubling his win total from five to ten during July. Still, the jury was out on the wry-necked kid dubbed "the $11,000 Lemon," whose reputation for falling apart under the slightest pressure overshadowed the flashes of brilliance that made him Mathewson's heir apparent.

Only Marquard and Mathewson could start more than once a week. The staff was full of part-timers and question marks. McGraw needed pitching help—lots of it and right away, wherever he could find it. He tried all month to make a trade for a pitcher. Rumors dangled and disappeared, as the other clubs saw McGraw's dilemma and asked for more than he could bring himself to give. Frustrated, he turned to the minor leagues. In St. Louis he announced the signing of Birmingham ace Bert Maxwell. But Maxwell would not report until Birmingham's season ended in September. McGraw needed another arm right away. He kept looking. The Giants had just won a court judgment against a team from Marion, Ohio, which now owed McGraw a player. Maybe he'd get lucky there.

Indeed, there was a lucky pitcher from Marion waiting for the Giants at Robison Field in St. Louis that Friday, though McGraw didn't know it. This pitcher was from Marion, but not the one in Ohio. His home was a farm outside the little town of Marion in the middle of Kansas, and he had hopped a train for his first trip to the big city, just to meet John McGraw. Giants centerfielder Fred Snodgrass described the first appearance of the stranger who approached them during batting practice: "Out of the grandstand walked a tall, lanky individual in a dark suit, wearing a black derby hat. He walked across the grass from the grandstand to the bench, and said he wanted to talk to Mr. McGraw. So some of us pointed McGraw out, and he went over to him. 'Mr. McGraw,' he said, 'my name is Charles Victory Faust. I live over in Kansas, and a few weeks ago I went to a fortune-teller who told me that if I would join the New York Giants and pitch for them that they would win the pennant." The desperate McGraw could hardly wait to give Faust a tryout.

The truth dawned quickly: Faust, despite elaborate signals and a furious windmill windup, had only one speed—slow. McGraw soon tossed off his glove and caught Faust barehanded, simmering at this waste of his valuable time. What was that fortune-teller crap? Was this somebody's idea of a prank, or did this nut really think he was a ballplayer? McGraw needed a hurler, not a slowball twirler. It was a bad joke, and someone would pay for it.

McGraw plotted a swift revenge on the unsuspecting farmer. He told Faust to take batting practice and run the bases, then sent instructions around the infield. The plan worked better than he imagined. After a flurry of pathetic swings, Faust connected with a slow pitch and sent a soft roller toward shortstop. Heeding McGraw's shouts, he took off for first base, lumbering up the line. The shortstop launched the first of several deliberate overthrows that chased Faust around the bases. At second base, the gawky Faust attempted a slide, bouncing along the pebbly dirt, biting the dust until a chorus of yells propelled him toward third base. McGraw raced across the infield to spur Faust onward, almost following him. This riled up the gathering crowd, and as Faust sprawled across third and hauled himself up again, he was surrounded by laughter and cheering. One more wild throw sent him staggering home, with frenzied voices telling him to slide one more time. When he tumbled across the plate with his make-believe run, his Sunday clothes torn and dusty, the crowd roared, and everyone had a big belly laugh at his expense. For the first time in weeks, the Giants saw their manager smile.

McGraw's mood turned dark again during the game, the second of his suspension. The Giants played their sloppiest game of the season, committing five errors to undermine Mathewson and cost him a tough 5–2 loss. "Matty got non-support of the sort that a bunch of hucksters selling strawberries might give Caruso at the Metropolitan Opera House," wrote Sid Mercer in the New York *Globe*. Another apparent blunder by acting manager Doyle in the eighth inning multiplied McGraw's disgust. Trailing 5–0, Doyle let Mathewson bat, then pinch-hit for leadoff man Josh Devore. The move may have been punishment for Devore, who had dropped an easy fly ball in left field and later heaved another ball into the stands to cap Mathewson's nightmare. It was all the same to McGraw. The whole performance stank. Nobody could remember Matty losing five games in a month, but there it was. Worse yet, nobody could remember how to play ball in McGraw's absence, and one more day remained in his suspension.

Next day at Robison Field, the Giants found Charles Victor Faust lurking again. Undaunted by his failed audition, he repeated his intention of pitching the Giants to the pennant. The players welcomed this comic relief, found him a uniform, and perpetrated more pranks on the determined gate-crasher during practice. The spectacle of Faust attempting to play baseball caused such a sensation that after only his

CHARLEY FAUST looked like any pitcher posing for a baseball card in this still photo. McGraw, however, measured Faust's energetic windup against his lack of velocity and quickly figured him to be ludicrous. (Brace Photo)

second day of action, the St. Louis *Post-Dispatch* noted that "Charley Faust, the Hector (Kan.) farmer boy, again amused with his awkward batting, fielding, and base running." That hustling awkwardness soon became his trademark.

No matter how much the Giants tormented him, he took it all with a goofy lopsided grin. In fact, his good cheer buoyed the slumping players so much that they let him sit on the bench during the game. Inspired by his hyperactive pregame romp, the Giants ran wild, winning 8–0 before a huge crowd. They stole nine bases, leaving the Cardinals infielders dizzy and demoralized. The rampage made life easy for Rube Marquard, who didn't need much help. His four-hitter was the first shutout of Marquard's career, and Faust cheered every pitch, savoring his closeness to the team of his destiny.

Faust returned on Sunday, which greatly resembled Saturday. The Giants ran roughshod over the Cardinals, embarrassing the home team again. With McGraw back directing traffic from the coaching box at third base, the Giants piled up fourteen hits and five more stolen bases to win 6–0. Hooks Wiltse eclipsed Marquard's performance. After the Cardinals loaded the bases in the first inning, Wiltse stifled them completely, retiring the last twenty-five batters.

For Charley Faust, it was a day he would never forget. He cavorted on the field in his Giants uniform, performing his already familiar baseball stunts to the acclaim of twenty-eight thousand fans, the biggest crowd in St. Louis baseball history. Just before the game began, players from both teams formed a circle near the plate for a ceremony, and Faust was summoned to their midst. Cardinals outfielder Steve Evans made a presentation. "On behalf of the fans of St. Louis," Evans intoned, "who thoroughly appreciate your great work since becoming a member of the New York team, I present this slight token to you and hope you will continue to succeed in your chosen profession."

After this touching speech, Evans handed a jewel box to the wide-eyed Faust, who bowed and doffed his cap to the cheering crowd. A moment later, persuaded that the real "token" was inside the box, Faust opened it and found a pocket watch. Encouraged to open the watch, Faust did so. That's when the trick watch exploded like a pistol-shot, the parts scattering as quickly as the players who had perpetrated the prank, while Faust gawked at his empty watch chain.

The Giants, indulging Faust's claim to be a pitcher, got him to warm up during Wiltse's first-inning difficulties, telling him to get ready in case Wiltse needed his help. Picture Wiltse gazing toward the outfield, where the eager but weak-armed Charles Victor Faust prepared to rescue him. No wonder Wiltse refused to allow a base runner the rest of the way; he was afraid to.

The series ended Monday, and accounts conflict over Faust's presence. The St. Louis *Post-Dispatch* reported that "things were dull . . . because Charley was missing. He simply dropped off the earth and the players know not what happened to him." But according to the New York *Globe*, "Faust worked out every day with the Giants in St. Louis," though he refused to put on a uniform Monday. "He says the old player won't give the young fellows a chance." This was not the first time a budding star complained about veterans stifling new talent by such means as muscling them out of their batting-practice swings. Ty Cobb had felt victimized by the same thing when he broke in, using it to justify his aloofness from even his own teammates. But Charley Faust? Did Faust expect McGraw to put him in the game?

Maybe if he had been left-handed McGraw would've given him a chance. Wiltse and Marquard, his only lefties, had smothered the Cardinals on six hits in two games. On Monday, McGraw brought Marquard back on one day of rest, doubting that the vulnerable Cardinals would put much pressure on him. The move worked. Marquard scattered five hits and won 3–2, keying both scoring rallies himself with singles. His seventh win of July moved the Giants back into second place.

Suddenly McGraw's outlook brightened. Three days after their sluggish arrival in St. Louis, the Giants were revived. Five more stolen bases made a total of twenty-three in the series. The offense was alive, the new infield looked better, Marquard was blossoming, and Matty would have four days of rest when he opened the series in Pittsburgh. For the first time in weeks, McGraw relished the showdown with the Cubs in Chicago that would conclude the road trip.

Then McGraw did something stupid. He got rid of Charley Faust. Mathewson told the tale in his book *Pitching in a Pinch*, written after the 1911 season. Faust met the team at the St. Louis train station, "ready to go along. 'Did you get your contract and transportation?' asked McGraw, as the lanky Kansan appeared. 'No,' answered Charley. 'Pshaw,' replied

McGraw. 'I left it for you with the clerk at the hotel. The train leaves in two minutes,' he continued, glancing at his watch. 'If you can run the way you say you can, you can make it and be back in time to catch it.' It was the last we saw of Charley Faust for a time—galloping up the platform in his angular way with that contract and transportation in sight. 'I'm almost sorry we left him,' remarked McGraw as Charley disappeared into the crowd," and the train left without him.

A superstitious man in a superstitious age, McGraw knew that he risked feeling sorry indeed. Good-luck charms and mascots, those stray freaks of human fate, came and went with some frequency (though Connie Mack of the Athletics kept one mascot, a hunchback dwarf, for the better part of a decade). Winning gave credibility to each new talisman, until losing inevitably blew his cover. But Faust was undefeated, and it could be bad luck to discard him while his jinxing power remained potent.

McGraw was willing to take his chances. He didn't need a fortune-teller to know that it would take pitching help for the Giants to win the pennant. This unathletic hayseed, no pitcher at all, could not be the answer to his prayers. There was no denying that the Giants had won three straight games convincingly with Faust on the bench, but what was McGraw supposed to do, pay the bumpkin's fare to Pittsburgh so that he could hang around with the team until they lost? On the basis of three games?

John McGraw managed the New York Giants, professional ball-players about to engage in fierce battles of baseball skill with the power-houses of the National League, the Pirates and Cubs. Faust, with no baseball skills, was irrelevant, an aberration, a nut whose clowning had kept the team loose during one giddy weekend in St. Louis. Nothing could have made McGraw hold the train while Faust chased that wild goose. McGraw could not help expressing a twinge of doubt as he wondered how he got himself in this spot, but he couldn't even have imagined then that Faust would indeed help the Giants win the pennant. How could he? He hardly believed it after it happened.

2

Hope Goes Up in Flames

The lid was off the Polo Grounds,
  The April sun shone bright,
And some were shivering with cold,
  And others with delight.
Long months had fled since last the fans
  Had felt the baseball thrill,
And now they trembled in their seats,
  Prepared to get their fill.
A hum of deep, expectant bliss
  Swept over all the grounds,
And for a moment, more or less,
  Obscured all other sounds.
A moment thus, each fan alert
  To hear the welcome call,
And then, like music to their ears
  The umpire yelled "Play Ball!"
          W. J. Lampton, New York *Times*, April 13, 1911

LINED UP OUTSIDE the gates of the Polo Grounds six hours before game time, the fans of the New York Giants could hardly wait for the 1911 season to begin. Never mind the wintry chill in the April air. The Polo Grounds was the center of the New York universe, the only place to be. Manhattan was filled with empty offices and clubs, Broadway nearly deserted as the theater crowd made its annual spring pilgrimage to the best show in town.

The fortunate few drove their automobiles up Eighth Avenue to 158th Street, where the massive Polo Grounds sat overlooking the Harlem River. Most fans arrived by subway or elevated trains, and one of the first things they noticed was a new fence atop the grandstand, a new fence that blocked the customary view into the ballpark. This new fence dealt a terrible blow to the many Giants fans who could not or would not pay their way in. For years, they had congregated on the heights of Coogan's Bluff, partylike gatherings from which they could watch some of the action, catch the rest from hand signals passed by fans inside the park, and bet on almost everything. Now their anxious eyes could make out only a sliver of the diamond. The fence "puts Coogan's Bluff out of business," declared Heywood Broun in the New York *Morning Telegraph*.

To entice those fans into the park, the Giants restored twenty-five-cent seating for the first time in years. So what if you could hardly see the action from the two-bit section in center field? The price was right, and fans lined up early to grab those precious tickets. The game wouldn't start until four o'clock, the gates didn't even open until one, but thousands were there before noon, eager for their first look at the 1911 Giants. This had to be their year!

The pennant had eluded the Giants since 1905, and their fans could not understand how. In the five seasons since, the Giants won sixty percent of their games, averaging ninety-two wins a season. They were good, but not good enough to get more than a glimpse of the flag, finishing within a dozen games of first place only once in those bittersweet years. That was in 1908, the year when "Merkle's Boner"—a rookie's failure to run from first to second base on a game-winning single—helped cost the Giants the title. The Chicago Cubs nitpicked their way to the pennant with a sore-loser stunt, a frantic appeal of Fred Merkle's lapse. Umpire Hank O'Day called it an out on a technicality, league president Henry Pulliam backed O'Day and ruled it a tie game, and the Giants and their fans went insane. When the teams finished the season tied, the replay of that protested tie amounted to a one-game playoff for the N.L. championship. McGraw and the Giants refused at first to play the game, insisting that the pennant was already theirs and could not be stolen from them on a technicality. Finally they played, and they lost. Chicago's Three Finger Brown outdueled Christy Mathewson, and the pennant vanished as darkly as a glittering lode of gold in a mine cave-in.

The citizens of New York have never suffered this kind of outrage lightly. Second place never sat well with them, this time in particular. The Giants were owed a pennant, and nothing else mattered until they squared things with the Cubs, the league, and Fate.

The next two seasons brought 183 wins for the Giants but no revenge, as the Pirates and Cubs each won their fourth pennant since 1900. The Giants finished third, then second, as McGraw engineered a major overhaul. After using the oldest lineup in the league for years, McGraw gradually dumped his veterans and handed their jobs to youngsters even greener than Merkle, who was only nineteen when he lost his way. By the end of 1911, only one regular from 1908 remained, and that was Doyle, the twenty-four-year-old captain. Four of McGraw's prospects—outfielders Fred Snodgrass and Josh Devore, catcher John "Chief" Meyers, and first baseman Merkle—became regulars in 1910, and their expected improvement gave Giants fans hope for gaining their long-awaited justice in 1911.

It all hinged on the pitching, which had changed little since 1908. McGraw did unload Iron Man McGinnity, considering him washed up at thirty-seven (a hasty judgment, as McGinnity went on to win more than two hundred games in the minors). To replace McGinnity, McGraw rescued Bugs Raymond from last-place St. Louis, and Raymond won eighteen games for him in 1909. Eighteen more in 1910 would have put the Giants ahead of the Cubs, but Raymond started drinking again and slipped to a dismal 4–11 record and an uncertain future. Rube Marquard, seemingly still traumatized by his failed 1908 debut, when he lost a key game with the pennant up for grabs, made no progress in 1910 and won only four games. A dozen wins by rookie Louie Drucke were not enough to make up the difference, and the Giants were no threat to Frank Chance's Cubs, who topped one hundred wins for the fourth time in five years.

How was McGraw going to beat the Cubs? That's what Giants fans wanted to learn as they scoured the sports pages from mid-February to

April for spring training propaganda. The Giants trained at Marlin, Texas, a quiet mineral springs resort near Waco, and the only news New Yorkers got of those distant doings came from the city's thirteen newspapers. Several papers sent reporters to Marlin to satisfy the fans' wintertime need for gossip about their favorites and for early dope on coming stars.

There was plenty of both in 1911, and most of it concerned the pitching question marks. Raymond topped that list, and the papers carried one glowing report after another of Bugs's reformation. When he signed in January, the *Times* reported that "Mr. Raymond has been sojourning in a sanitarium in Dwight, Ill., an institution which endeavors to further the use of Lithia water as a thirst quencher. 'Bugs' had the high average among a large class of inmates." In Marlin, W. W. Aulick found Raymond "in better condition than New Yorkers have ever seen him" and pitching "as steady as a clock."

Aulick was less excited about the rest of McGraw's staff, Mathewson excepted. "Wiltse is going back, Ames is erratic, Crandall is effective only against Boston, and Marquard should get in some other profession. Drucke may improve greatly over last year." The rumor mill had Marquard going back to the minors, probably to Newark. McGinnity was managing there, and when he broke his arm in March, his old buddy McGraw promised him a pitcher or two. Marquard was a likely candidate.

There were other possibilities. McGraw always brought a promising stable of pitching colts to spring training. Of the 1911 class, only two—Jeff Tesreau and Dick Rudolph—went on to the majors, carving out decent careers over the next decade. (Tesreau started helping McGraw in 1912.) The biggest of the 1911 flops was J. W. Jenkins, a twenty-eight-game winner in the minors in 1910. Jenkins started well in Marlin, living up to the bold claims in letters that had deluged the Giants offices when they signed him in January. After a rash of mid-March drubbings, however, he was ready to go back to terrorizing the Illinois-Missouri League.

Few managers took spring training as seriously as McGraw. After training for years in Los Angeles, McGraw decided that there were too many distractions there. He herded his men to this dusty town in the middle of Texas and set up a Spartan operation there beginning in

1908. There was nothing for the players to do in Marlin but play, talk, and think baseball. In 1911 the grateful Marlinites, hosting the Giants for the fourth spring, presented McGraw with the deed to the ballpark. The Giants wound up training there for ten years, until World War I travel restrictions ended the association.

For 1911 McGraw brought in his old Baltimore Orioles teammate, catcher Wilbert Robinson, to work with the pitchers. Robinson made Marquard his special project and attempted to convince the youngster that throwing strikes would prolong his career. Practices were long and hard and twice a day, as McGraw quickly conditioned his men for the all-out running attack he planned to unleash on the National League. Various Giants squads played two or three games a day. McGraw, retired with bad legs but only thirty-eight years old, played in some of the games himself, stealing bases and leading the way in competitive hustle.

In an unprecedented move, McGraw even brought his own umpire to Texas in 1911. The theory was that inconsistent native umpiring impeded the players' pursuit of baseball excellence; by providing one steady umpire for intrasquad and exhibition games, McGraw showed his commitment to winning. C. L. Hansell, an aspiring ump who had worked some Polo Grounds exhibitions, signed on for this dubious assignment, which he soon regretted. McGraw limbered up his vocal chords early that spring, haranguing Hansell at every opportunity, and the players followed his example. On March 11 McGraw and Chief Meyers double-teamed Hansell, and two days later Hansell walked off the field. After arguing with the whole team, he "said if Manager McGraw was going to allow his men to question decisions and kick on such plays he would refuse to umpire any more practice games." What straw broke Hansell's back? Nothing much, just a safe call at first base— in an intrasquad game! On these Giants, kicking was in and Hansell was out, working only one more game that spring.

The fans back in New York knew that "McGraw's own umpire" was an oxymoron and could laugh at the account of Hansell's retreat. Events in Atlanta shocked and alarmed them, however. On March 30 an Atlanta fan, one Erskine Brewster, called Chief Meyers a "nigger." The Giants jumped to the defense of their proud Indian catcher, and pretty soon Christy Mathewson was grabbing Brewster, who "quickly threw 'Big Six' over his head" and decked Meyers. When McGraw and other Giants kept after Brewster, the situation got scary. According to the *Times*, Brewster "started after McGraw, the latter retreating, when Bridwell jumped in and the two exchanged blows, the Giants' shortstop getting the worst of the argument. He was cut about the mouth and bled profusely. Mathewson again took a hand, grabbing Brewster while he was scrapping with Bridwell, and nearly choking the life out of the Atlanta man. This conduct on the part of Mathewson aroused the ire of Third Baseman Odell of the Atlanta team, who grabbed a bat and started for Mathewson, threatening to kill him. Managers McGraw and Jordan then interfered, stopping hostilities." When the New York fans read that, they didn't know which image was more shocking: Matty the gentleman choking somebody, or Matty the savior bludgeoned by some maniacal southerner.

It didn't end there. The next day the Giants steered clear of Brewster, but not of trouble. Third baseman Art Devlin got in a brief scuffle with Odell, and later Merkle and Marquard were ejected for arguing. McGraw, showing up the home team, pitched the last few innings himself and stole three bases before getting caught trying to steal home with a 9–1 lead. Lynching would have been too good for McGraw in some locals' eyes, but the Giants managed to get out of town with their limbs intact. McGraw had his team in a frenzy, and it was still March!

The Giants worked their way north without further mayhem and arrived in New York four days before the April 12 opener. They opened the Polo Grounds with the Yale exhibition game, customarily a happy reunion for the fans and their darlings. But two things put a damper on the 1911 inaugural. One was that the team arrived two weeks before spring, and the frigid weather kept all but the diehards away, though the *Times* noted that "2,000 fans who sat shivering in the cold greeted [the Giants] like lost relatives." They were still freezing three days later when the Giants polished off Joe McGinnity's Newark team on the eve of the opener, and good baseball weather remained but a daydream.

Bad weather was an annoyance to the baseball community, but a downtown tragedy had outraged the entire city. On March 25 a fire raced through the top three floors of the unfortunately named ten-story Asch Building, near Washington Square. It was late Saturday afternoon, almost quitting time for the seven hundred workers at the Triangle

Shirtwaist Company, when the fire started on the eighth floor. The building was fireproof, but piles of shirtwaists and fabrics quickly ignited the crowded factory, and the whole interior burned in a nightmarish half-hour. The workers, mostly young women and teenage girls, did not know it, but their lone sure escape route was via the roof. The only working elevator took one load of tenth-floor office workers to safety and never returned. The stairs were blocked within minutes, and those who made their way to the building's solitary fire escape found the door bolted, dooming them. Many others found faster death by jumping, and arriving firemen had to dodge falling bodies to set up their ladders. Inside, they found piles of bodies burned beyond recognition, a pyre of perished hopes.

Nearly 150 died, and it could have been much worse. A crowd of fifty thousand gathered outside the Asch Building, stunned by the carnage. Their outrage spread as rapidly and powerfully as the fire. Factory fires were common, and only a week earlier, fire commissioner Rhinelander Waldo had issued new orders regarding fire prevention and protection. Waldo had visions of sprinklers in factory ceilings and stairwells, among other radical ideas. The Manufacturers Association had called a hasty meeting to organize opposition to this fresh attempt by government to tell honest businessmen how to spend their money. Disdain and negligence were bad enough, but the bolted fire escape door defied understanding. Soon it came out that the Triangle Shirtwaist Company owners, Max Blanck and Isaac Harris, had escaped the fire by leading tenth-floor workers to a boxed-off stairway that the shrieking girls below did not even know existed.

Action accelerated on all fronts. Other factory workers came forward to tell about firetrap working conditions, and an engineer claimed that the new library on Fifth Avenue was no better. Legislators proposed a bill strengthening fire escape laws. A Fire Sufferers' Fund topped $50,000 by March 29, the same day that a $5 million fire nearly destroyed the state capitol in Albany. Fire awareness multiplied, and factory workers began regular fire drills. On April 5, 120,000 people marched along Fifth Avenue, paying solemn tribute to the fire victims.

The next day, a grand jury began considering charges against Blanck and Harris. They were indicted on April 11, charged with manslaughter because of the bolted door, and held on $25,000 bail.

The public outcry continued. It was December before the trial began, but bitterness remained so strong that when the defendants entered the courtroom, some spectators shouted "murderers!" and attacked them. Blanck and Harris were acquitted but disgraced.

In the long run, this scandalous fire led to much-needed reforms in fire prevention and safety. On April 12 New Yorkers read about the indictments, relieved by the glimmer of justice though far from satisfied. Grim reality could not be ignored, but Giants fans could seek shelter for the day at the Polo Grounds. Maybe they would witness the first win in the Giants' march toward reclaiming the stolen 1908 pennant, their own form of justice. So the people flocked to the ballpark that day, more than thirty thousand of them, a new Polo Grounds attendance record. They got there early, eager to have their spirits lifted.

They got one break when stadium officials wisely opened the gates early, a little after noon. A mad rush ensued until unreserved sections were filled; one paper estimated that twenty thousand fans were inside the great wooden horseshoe two hours before game time. Despite the sunshine, many already regretted not having brought overcoats or sweaters. Players drifted onto the field to warm up, every move cheered by thousands of their neighbors, intoxicated by baseball's renewal ritual.

After an hour or so of practice, the players were warm and the fans were bored and restless. To fight off the chill, fans began pelting each other with newspapers and bags of peanuts. The barrage was high-spirited at first, as newcomers were given the treatment, but when more people tried to jam into the unreserved sections, Pinkerton guards were called on to keep the peace. Some people (the New York World called them "the simian semblances to human creatures that always invade public assemblages") couldn't help themselves, like children waiting for a tardy teacher. Even when the bags of peanuts and newspapers were nothing more than shells and wads of paper, they kept throwing them, making sure that the late-arriving society gentlemen and their lady companions got theirs, too, on the way to the field boxes.

A band began playing near the Giants bench at three o'clock, about the time the Broadway stars made their grand entrances. Among the celebrities were George M. Cohan, Eddie Foy, DeWolf Hopper (the popularizer of "Casey at the Bat"), and producer Sam Harris. The Morning Telegraph, the theater-oriented daily, published a list of one hundred ninety-four notable attendees, including the usual run of politicians and authors (Booth Tarkington and James Whitcomb Riley), as well as former boxing champ Jim Corbett. The baseball delegation couldn't be topped, starting with both league presidents (Thomas Lynch and Ban Johnson) and pioneer Albert Goodwill Spalding. Giants owner John T. Brush and family hosted two other owners, Charles Ebbets of Brooklyn and Charles Comiskey of the Chicago White Sox. Even former Giants owner Andrew Freedman, much despised during his tenure, attended.

Shortly before four o'clock, the man they were all waiting for arrived. Mayor William Gaynor entered through the right field gate, leading his entourage across the field. He shook hands with Larry Doyle and outfielder Red Murray on the way to his third base box, hounded by photographers. Sid Mercer wrote that Gaynor "was shot eighty-six times by still photographers, but rallied bravely. One picture man hung by his toes from an adjoining box and in this heroic pose waited five minutes for the mayor to take his wind-up and pitch the first ball." Then, at last, it was time to play ball.

Manager McGraw waited until the last minute to name his starting pitcher, a manager's privilege at that time. He had Red Ames and Rube Marquard both warm up, though Ames was the expected starter. What about Christy Mathewson? McGraw usually spared him the cold spring weather, saving him for the hot midsection of the season. Ames liked cool April days and had started four of the past five openers. Besides, Matty could draw a bigger crowd on his own tomorrow. McGraw, who owned shares in the Giants, always minded the turnstiles.

Some fans yelled at McGraw to give Marquard the nod over Ames, the traditional choice. The problem was that Ames had developed into a traditional loser after winning his first opener in 1906. In fact, his misfortune had its own identity: the Ames Hoodoo. Most pitching staffs have one guy who seems to catch all the bad luck: the better he pitches, the less support he gets. For the Giants, it was Leon K. Ames, whose frustration multiplied with each opening-day debacle. It began in 1907, when the Giants offense manufactured exactly one hit and Ames trailed 3–0 after eight innings. Many fans, in their haste to escape this cheerless debut, cut across the field. Umpire Bill Klem refused to let play continue with fans on the diamond, while those still in the stands

LEON "RED" AMES was nicknamed Kalamity because of his notorious bad luck, a trend confirmed early in 1911. By September, Ames had a lucky tie, a winning streak, and a firm faith in the invincibility of Victory Faust. (Transcendental Graphics)

refused to wait any longer. When a thousand fanatics stormed the field, Klem declared a forfeit. Welcome to opening day.

Mathewson won the 1908 opener, a hint McGraw ignored when he went back to Ames in 1909, the most heartbreaking opener ever for a pitcher. Ames pitched the game of his life yet couldn't beat the lowly Brooklyn Superbas. Ames started the season with nine hitless innings, but the Giants were almost as helpless against Irvin "Kaiser" Wilhelm, who gave up only two hits himself before extra innings. Whitey Alperman broke up Ames's no-hitter with a tenth-inning double, but the

Giants couldn't touch Wilhelm. The scoreless tie lasted until the thirteenth inning, when the Superbas rallied for three runs. Instead of everlasting fame for tossing the first opening-day no-hitter, Ames had nothing to show for his brilliance but one loss and an asterisk in the record book.

Later in 1909 Ames pitched an agonizing twenty-seven consecutive shutout innings without getting a win, including a seventeen-inning tie at Boston. The 1910 opener, also in Boston, convinced Ames that he was jinxed no matter how well he pitched. He barely fell short of his 1909 gem, settling for seven hitless innings to start his season. The Giants led 2–0 when Boston got its first hit in the eighth, scoring once on a Bridwell fumble. In the bottom of the ninth, Ames got the first two batters, but a walk and a pair of singles tied the game. The Giants offense stalled, and again Ames went to extra innings opening the season. He suffered a numbing demise in the tenth inning on a two-out error by Devlin that sent the winning run across the plate. Ames didn't even get an asterisk for a martyred no-hitter this time, just another brutally routine loss.

After wasting twenty-three innings of great pitching in two openers, Ames's luck had to change in 1911. Or so McGraw reasoned, figuring he owed Ames a chance to break the jinx and silence the spreading rumor that his middle initial stood for Kalamity. Leon Kessling Ames never did live down that nickname despite a seventeen-year career. The encyclopedias dutifully list Kalamity as Ames's nickname, and April 12, 1911, cemented that destiny. Once again he took a no-hitter to the seventh inning, and once again he lost.

The villains were the Philadelphia Phillies, major culprits in the Giants' 1908 collapse. The Giants would have overcome the Merkle incident except for three shocking late-season losses to the Phillies. Harry Coveleski won all three games, raising his career win total to four and earning himself the sobriquet Giant Killer. McGraw avenged himself by ferreting out Coveleski's emotional weak spot and razzing him out of the league by 1910. Still, the Phillies somehow always played better against the Giants than New Yorkers figured they should.

The 1911 Phillies had a much-touted rookie pitcher named Grover Cleveland Alexander, but the opening-day assignment went to Earl Moore, a wild righty called Crossfire. Moore walked eight Giants but was as unhittable as Ames. Doyle singled in the first inning, and the hometown fans got another chance to cheer in the eighth, when Devore singled. In between there were nothing but outs dotted with walks, not the action-packed battle the fans anticipated. The scoreless tie left the overeager fans cold in every sense, as W. J. Lampton noted in the *Times:* "When the ninth opened there was a feeling that it was time for somebody to do something or everybody would go home. Forty or fifty innings can be stood for in warm weather, but nine is the limit when the temperature is down."

Both pitchers entered the ninth with two-hitters, so what chance did Ames have? Alone against his hoodoo, he got in trouble on two singles, one a weak infield tap. He fought unaided and almost survived, until a two-out double by Fred Luderus scored both runners. Moore's two-hitter held up, and Ames lost 2–0.

Nobody could believe that it had happened to Ames three years in a row. The fans went home numb and mystified, but the writers loved the angle. Everybody rehashed the "Ames Hoodoo," even the *American's* Damon Runyon, who had seen neither Ames nor the Polo Grounds before and was reporting his first major league game. The *Herald* milked the most out of it, John Wheeler mentioning it ten times in his game account, every time something went wrong for the Giants. Wheeler capped his coverage with a poignant postgame speech, purportedly delivered by Ames to McGraw: "Mac, if I was to wear a uniform trimmed with four leaf clovers and a horseshoe in my glove, I couldn't win an opening game. This morning I walked under a ladder before I noticed what I was doing, and the conductor on the car which started to bring me to the grounds was No. 13. I jumped off as soon as I made his figures, but it was too late."

Whether Ames actually spoke those words was not as important as that Wheeler reported it. The Ames Hoodoo reached full bloom, and McGraw learned his lesson. Next season, he opened with Marquard, sparing Ames further torture. Was Ames the problem? No, the Giants were the problem. Spared the burden of trying to support Ames, they relaxed enough to score eighteen runs for Marquard. That's all it took.

Frigid weather held the crowd down to ten thousand for the second game of 1911, even with Mathewson pitching. His opponent, Jack Rowan, should have had no chance. Mathewson already had three seasons where he won as many games as Rowan was to win in his whole career. The mismatch on the field equaled the mismatch on paper, except that the wrong side dominated. The Phillies ripped Mathewson for fifteen hits and six runs, a profound pounding. Fred Luderus had two singles and a double. So did the Giants.

Rowan, who struck out only one, did not have to overpower anybody. The overeager Giants popped the ball up all day and looked flat and lifeless, losing 6–1. In two games, their offense had totaled one run and five hits. The biggest ovation of the day came when Phillies centerfielder Dode Paskert snared a long drive by Fred Snodgrass with his bare hand. Aside from that, the crowd remained subdued, waiting for the real Giants to emerge.

While the huddled masses shivered through defeat at the Polo Grounds, another disaster was averted downtown. A fire broke out at the Manhattan Soap Company, whose owners had instituted fire drills after the Triangle tragedy. Preparedness paid off, with more than sixty girls and young women following the drill route to safety as flames filled the factory.

But nothing could prepare New Yorkers for what happened that night. Not long after midnight, a fire started in the Polo Grounds grandstand between home plate and first base. Piles of peanut shells and newspaper littered the ground under the stands, and most likely a dropped match or cigar smoldered for hours before igniting. The flames spread rapidly through the twenty-one-year-old wooden structure, long recognized as a firetrap. Some sparks jumped from the left field stands to a storage yard for Interborough elevated trains, where at least eight trains burned. The first horse-drawn fire wagons reached the scene within a half-hour, and the firemen quickly realized that they could not save the grandstand. They had their hands full just saving the center field bleachers and clubhouse, separated from the grandstand by a gap in left-center.

Despite the late hour, a huge crowd gathered to watch, drawn by the brilliant blaze visible all over the city. More than ten thousand people overran Coogan's Bluff, hampering firemen trying to reach the fire. Elevated train service was shut off twenty blocks south of the stadium, but cabs brought people who wanted to get close to the spectacle. The fire drew a bigger audience at two o'clock in the morning than Mathewson had brought the previous afternoon, and they got a better show.

John McGraw was shooting pool at the downtown billiard parlor he owned when he got the word, and he sped to the scene. There he found Mathewson, Marquard, Ames, Raymond, Meyers, and Merkle amid the mournful throng that watched their beloved Polo Grounds burn. Some of the visiting Phillies were also there, equally helpless.

The *Herald* reported the only amusing note of the grim night. "Superstitious fans will see an omen in the fact that after the firemen had salvaged the tarpaulin which is spread over the diamond after every game, a spark ignited the second base bag. As it flared up there came from the edge of the field one lone, loud cheer from Fred Merkle. 'They can't say it wasn't touched that time,' he chuckled, as he witnessed the passing of his hoodoo."

By daylight, only the bleachers and part of the left field stands remained. The damage exceeded $250,000, but the emotional loss was greater. While the Triangle fire kicked the public in the guts, the Polo Grounds fire fluttered their hearts. Damon Runyon's elegy in the *American* painted the Polo Grounds as baseball's mecca and New York's hub. "It means the Big Town; it means the Big City club; it is all the lights of Broadway and the lure of Gotham summed up in two words. To those who analyze it is, perhaps, just a baseball park of some beauty, as baseball parks go, which, on baseball days becomes a bowl of howling humanity in a rather grimy setting beneath Coogan's euphoniously named bluffs; to the rest of us it is the home of excitement; of some romance, and much baseball glory and achievement; it is a place of surpassing magnificence, sparkling beneath the silver sun like a great green jewel, and best of all, it is the abiding place of the Giants!" Runyon continued in the same vein for nearly a dozen paragraphs, stopping just short of proposing a national day of mourning.

Once the smoke cleared, fire chief Richard Croker had a less sentimental reaction. "I am glad it is gone," he declared. "If it had caught fire when a game was under way and 25,000 or 30,000 persons were crowded into the place, the loss of life might have been great. Under such circumstances a panic would have been inevitable, and hundreds might have been trampled to death. It is a good thing it did as it did and when it did." Indeed, the specter of the Triangle fire multiplied by the size of a Giants crowd sobered many observers. A *Tribune* editorial stated that "the fire at the Polo Grounds, disastrous as it was and embarrassing to the players and devotees of one of the most popular of games, was really very fortunate. . . . It is appalling to think of what might and probably would have happened if it had broken out in mid-afternoon. . . . The crowd is a disorganized and undisciplined mob, and it is with the view of assuring the largest possible measure of safety to such a mob in an emergency that such places of assemblage must be designed and built."

The Polo Grounds, which opened in 1890 to host the New York Giants of the short-lived Players League, was one of the last wooden ballparks. Many had burned down, including League Park in Washington, destroyed in March of 1911. These firetraps were gradually replaced with steel-and-concrete structures like Pittsburgh's Forbes Field, which opened in 1909 and ushered in the era of classic ballparks. After the Polo Grounds burned, the New York Board of Coroners ruled that unless the new stadium was built of fireproof material, the owners would be legally liable for any deaths resulting from fire.

The day after the fire, it was too soon to make rebuilding plans. The Giants had more immediate worries, like where to play today's scheduled game. There was one encouraging piece of news about the fire damage: their bats, those miserable slabs of wood which had produced only five hits in two games, also perished in the fire. The Giants had lost two games and their home, but at least there was hope for their offense.

3
Exile and Return

APART FROM THE POLO GROUNDS burning down, April 14 was a pretty good day for the Giants. For one thing, fire damage spared them a third showdown with the Phillies, and they used their free afternoon to scour the sporting goods houses for the bats with the hits in them. Even better, by the end of the day they had a place to play.

Charles Ebbets, owner of the Brooklyn Superbas, offered the Giants the use of his park. There were several dates on which both teams had home games scheduled, though, so that plan was not feasible. Instead, the Giants accepted help from the last place where John McGraw wanted it: the American League. The New York Highlanders (already called the Yankees by some) had no home dates that conflicted with the Giants. Their owner, Frank Farrell, was in Atlantic City when he heard about the fire, and he immediately wired the Giants that they could use the Highlanders' Hilltop Park as long as needed.

Farrell's offer, which would not have been made a few years earlier, marked a turning point in New York baseball. For McGraw it signaled the end of his long-standing feud with the American League, which began a decade earlier with the mess in Baltimore. McGraw was the star third baseman and rabblerouser of Ned Hanlon's championship teams in the 1890s. The original Orioles were the most feared and despised squad in a tough sport, an intimidating group that fought and argued its way to the top. Its standards for nasty play have never been equaled, not even by McGraw's Giants. The National League abandoned Baltimore after the 1899 season, and when Ban Johnson, president of the Western League, renamed his circuit the American League for 1901, he resurrected the Baltimore franchise with many of the same players. McGraw, the Orioles' twenty-eight-year-old manager, soon got in hot water with Johnson, whose vision of making his league a showcase of gentlemanly competition clashed directly with McGraw's combativeness.

McGraw made his American League debut on April 28, 1901, and before the month ended Johnson tagged him with the first of several suspensions. It soon became apparent that Johnson intended to crack down on exponents of the McGraw style, starting with McGraw himself. With his pit bull personality, McGraw thrived in the doghouse, continuing to terrorize umpires and opponents. Johnson kept suspending him and vowing to eliminate rowdyism from baseball.

Midway through the 1902 season, it dawned on McGraw that Johnson could and inevitably would expel him from the league. So he took the offensive, conspiring with two National League owners—New York's Andrew Freedman and Cincinnati's John T. Brush (then preparing to buy the Giants)—to sabotage the Baltimore franchise and wreck the fledgling American League. Their plot almost worked. They bought a controlling interest in Baltimore and released most of the Orioles, who signed with N.L. teams. Those who signed with the Giants, including McGraw, formed the nucleus of their 1905 World Series championship team. Baltimore was left with only five players, but Johnson salvaged the season by patching together a roster.

Johnson's revenge came after the season, when he moved the Baltimore franchise to New York to compete directly with the Giants. McGraw and Brush became the sworn enemies of Johnson and his league. That's why they refused to play the 1904 World Series after McGraw won his first pennant, even though the American League was clearly here to stay.

The Highlanders posed little threat to the Giants' supremacy during those early years, and their smaller Hilltop Park never saw the kind of crowd that packed the Polo Grounds to see what outrage McGraw and company would commit next. Still, once each major league had a team in the neighborhood, New Yorkers began debating the relative merits of their teams. With each year, fan pressure increased to settle the debate on the field by staging a city championship. Each year, McGraw and the Giants said no thanks.

City championships were nothing new, and these postseason series gained some success in two-team cities like Chicago and St. Louis even though nothing was at stake except bragging rights and some extra cash for the winners. New York hadn't had a city championship since 1886, when the Giants lost to the Brooklyn Trolley Dodgers. In 1910 the Giants finally said okay and let the fans have their wish. The teams had almost identical records, both finishing second, and New Yorkers turned their attention away from the upcoming World Series and toward the burning question of whether Christy Mathewson, 27–9 in 1910, would prevail over the Highlanders' Russ Ford, 26–6. Nearly twenty-five thousand fans jammed the Polo Grounds for the opener and Mathewson's answer, an emphatic 5–1 win. Neither team lost at home in the best-of-seven series, and the difference was Matty's three wins and a save at the Polo Grounds. Though bad weather kept the last two crowds down, the series generated money and goodwill all around. The winning Giants made $1,110 apiece at a time when their full-season salaries averaged only two or three times that amount. The clubs made money, the fans confirmed that Matty was indeed the king of New York baseball, and McGraw got tossed out of only one game.

That cooperative effort paved the way for Farrell's role in helping the Giants survive the Polo Grounds fire. Brush returned the favor tenfold after the 1912 season, when the Yankees abandoned Hilltop Park. For the next decade, the two teams shared the Polo Grounds. Yankee Stadium may be "The House That Ruth Built," but Babe Ruth never hit more homers there in one season than the thirty-two he hit in 1921 at the Polo Grounds.

Playing that city championship paid early dividends for the Giants in 1911, when they wound up playing twenty-eight home games at the Hilltop. Their three-game peek at the quirky Hilltop gave them a head start on their National League opponents. McGraw learned early about the park's two dangerous spots. Right field was not only much larger than in the Polo Grounds, it was also the most notorious sun field in the majors, the wicked glare turning singles into triples. McGraw moved Red Murray to left field, switching Josh Devore, a faster, better fielder, to right. Infielders had a tougher adjustment to make on the harder Hilltop ground. Grounders gathered more topspin, quickly skipping past unsuspecting infielders, especially at shortstop. The Giants knew what to expect, but their visitors never could adapt fully. Those small edges added up to a big Giants advantage, and McGraw put his troops through extra fielding practice to maximize it.

The schedule gave the Giants another big break. They played fifteen of their next seventeen games against the two weakest teams in the league, Brooklyn and Boston. In addition, they would not make a western trip until June. The tougher teams played in the West, notably the Cubs and Pirates. The Giants were the class of the eastern quartet, and for the first six weeks of the season they ventured no farther than Philadelphia, Boston, and Brooklyn. By the time the Giants had to spend the night in a Pullman car, the season was one-fourth over.

HILLTOP PARK HAD fifteen thousand seats, not nearly enough for the Giants' April 15 game against the Brooklyn Superbas. Several thousand more fans were herded into the outfield to stand behind ropes, the custom of the time. The fans didn't mind standing on such a beautiful day—sunny, with no chilling wind—the first real baseball weather of the season.

"The situation brought about by Thursday night's fire caused much speculation as to how the Giants would be received on the Hilltop," read the *Times*. "All doubt was removed yesterday afternoon. The reception which was accorded them was as hearty as if they had been playing on their home field, their loyal rooters turned out in force, and if there were any of the overloyal Yankee supporters on hand to pull for the defeat of the Giants they kept their feelings to themselves. . . . For the first two innings there was a noticeable stillness in the ranks, but the volleys of noise which were unloaded after the third inning left nothing to be desired. It evidently required that short time for the Polo Grounders to shake off their shyness in the strange quarters."

It took a short time because the Giants offense awoke slowly. They didn't score until the third inning, when Doyle's ground-rule triple into the overflow crowd helped them to a 2–1 lead. Brooklyn regained the lead in the fourth inning against a shaky Louie Drucke, who left for a pinch hitter as the Giants tied the game 3–3 in their half of the fourth. At that point the game turned in the Giants' favor, thanks to the rescue work of Doc Crandall.

James Otis Crandall was McGraw's one-man bench, arguably the most versatile substitute in baseball history. An Indiana farmboy, he joined the Giants in 1908 at age twenty and quickly became one of

McGraw's favorites. He could pitch, hit, and play almost any position on the field. A solid starting pitcher, he was molded by McGraw into one of baseball's first relief specialists. Sid Mercer dubbed him "Doc" because he was the "healer of sick games," saving the Giants again and again. Control and stamina were his strong suits. In 1910 he told an interviewer that he developed his control on the farm. "I have shucked corn all day with my head down and never once missed a target on the sideboard with every ear. I'd have a circle about a foot in diameter as a mark, and I got so I didn't even have to aim at it." That year, Crandall had a won-lost record of 17–4 and batted .342, emerging as McGraw's all-around star.

The party ended for the Superbas once Crandall entered the game. He shut them out on two hits over the last five innings, and he got the two key hits that won the game. In the sixth inning he tripled into the crowd to drive in the go-ahead run. In the eighth he tripled in another run with a blast past the centerfielder. The Giants had their first win of the season. "Burning grandstands may be expensive business, but it seems to be successful," asserted Heywood Broun in the *Morning Tele-graph.* "President Brush has always desired a winner at any price, so we may expect frequent conflagrations at the Polo Grounds."

Winter reprised at the Hilltop the next day, and fewer than ten thousand fans braved the raw wind blowing in from the Hudson River. Hooks Wiltse started but lasted only four batters. John Hummel led off the second inning with a shot up the middle that Wiltse tried to snag with his pitching hand. His wrist got nailed, ending his day early. McGraw had Rube Marquard and Bugs Raymond warm up before giving Raymond the first official test of his temperance campaign.

Arthur "Bugs" Raymond was the only import on the 1911 Giants staff. McGraw usually developed his own pitchers, but he had a fondness for reclamation projects. He gave second and even third chances to men found incorrigible elsewhere. Maybe he identified with their bad reputations or sensed that they'd be doubly loyal to him, the way a stray dog attaches himself to anyone whose first move isn't to kick him. McGraw saw something in Raymond, obtaining him, along with Red Murray, after 1908 in exchange for future Hall of Famer Roger Bresnahan. Bresnahan was McGraw's protégé and wanted to manage; McGraw was decades away from stepping aside, so he found Bresnahan a managing spot with the Cardinals.

McGraw met his match when he took on Raymond, who enjoyed pitching but loved drinking more. He ended both the 1909 and 1910 seasons under suspension and was fined so often that McGraw took to forwarding the fine money to Raymond's wife behind his back. One suspension came when McGraw sent Raymond out behind the bleachers to warm up. Raymond kept on going, out of the ballpark to a nearby saloon. He traded the baseball for whiskey and returned to the Polo Grounds in no condition to pitch. Some people believed his spitball danced so much because it was drunk, too.

Raymond's well-publicized sobriety coming into 1911 made Giants fans optimistic that he could join Mathewson in anchoring the staff. They could not know the publicity was a sham. After his winter "cure," Raymond fell off the wagon back in Marlin, setting up a hilarious scene in which McGraw put Raymond on trial before the New York reporters. Confronted with a detective's report showing that he had visited numerous bars and consumed several dozen beers plus eight Bermuda onions, Raymond protested, "It's a lie—I ain't et an onion in seven months!" McGraw hoped to embarrass Raymond into sobriety by getting the reporters to let him slide one last time. Raymond's first outing in 1911 justified McGraw's high hopes. Though some of his spitballs froze on the way to the plate, he kept the Brooklyn bats colder, holding them to one hit from the second inning until the ninth, when they got one run. He held on for a 3–1 win that brought rave reviews. "Even saloon keepers cheered," declared the *Herald*.

The reviews were better still for Rube Marquard in the third Brooklyn game. He cruised to a 7–1 win, allowing only four hits. "Marquard Finally Breaks Long Hoodoo," read the *American*'s headline, while the *Globe*'s Sid Mercer wrote a deliciously ornate account under the heading "Select Society Welcomes Debutante Marquard." In part, Mercer wrote that

> one of the most brilliant affairs of the post-Lenten season took place yesterday afternoon at the beautiful country place of Frank Farrell of Washington Heights. The sole topic of conversation this morning in select baseball circles is the successful debut of Richard Marquard, the famous $11,000 beauty. . . . Mr. Marquard is one of the younger set of whom much has been heard. For three years the fame of this fair debutante has been heralded in the soci-

ety columns, and the presentation of such a popular and promising candidate for a high place in exclusive circles has been impatiently awaited. Fandom at large, after yesterday's triumph, admits that Mr. Marquard has "arrived." . . . It was an afternoon of unalloyed pleasure, eclipsing even the official return of Mr. Arthur Raymond to the ranks of the "400." Now that Mr. Marquard has flashed on the social horizon he no doubt will be ardently wooed by good fortune. . . . His versatility was freely commented on. Just before the guests departed for their homes Mr. Marquard gave a demonstration of his remarkable talent just to show that he has not forgotten the tricks that kept him on the waiting list so long. In the ninth stanza he filled the bases by walking three of the Brooklyn boys, but struck out the side and was not scored on. . . . It was feared that Mr. Marquard might become nervous and spoil everything, but he bore up grandly, and in his boudoir after the excitement had subsided accepted numerous congratulations.

After the Giants polished off Brooklyn a fourth time behind Red Ames, they traveled to Philadelphia. Two of the four games there got rained out, and that was the good news. Earl Moore stifled them again in the opener, allowing only a bloop single by Fred Snodgrass and beating Crandall 3–0. McGraw refused to accept that anybody could hold his offense to three hits in two games, so he took up the attack himself the next afternoon. Arguing a close call at the plate, McGraw was banished to the bench by umpire Jim Johnstone. On the way, McGraw passed Moore, coming out to coach first base, and took his anger out on his latest nemesis. They yapped at each other even after McGraw reached the bench. Moore soon wearied of McGraw's verbal assault and charged toward the Giants dugout. McGraw picked up a bat, intent on showing his team a different way of hitting Moore, but the umpires and police kept them apart. This aggressiveness inspired the Giants to a nine-hit explosion against the Phillies, but they lost anyway and were happy to get out of town without having to bail their manager out of jail.

BACK IN NEW YORK, McGraw got his first glimpse of the real Giants offense. The Giants had led the National League in scoring and batting average in 1910 with the same young lineup that began 1911, so he knew that they were overdue. McGraw relied on a regular lineup,

JOHN "CHIEF" MEYERS, left, and RICHARD "RUBE" MARQUARD were two of the four 1911 Giants interviewed in the 1960s by Lawrence Ritter for *The Glory of Their Times*. The others were Fred Snodgrass and Al Bridwell, the short-stop who was traded to Boston shortly before Faust joined the Giants. (National Baseball Hall of Fame Library & Archive, Cooperstown, N.Y.)

and these eight starters, like interchangeable parts, fit the McGraw mold of smart hitters and aggressive runners. McGraw didn't need sluggers or stars in his offense; when Bresnahan left after 1908, McGraw won four pennants in ten years without so much as a Hall of Fame candidate in his lineup (until Ross Youngs came up to stay in 1918). The lineup:

	1910	1911	Lifetime	1911 Age
Devore, lf	.304	.280	.277	23
Doyle, 2b	.285	.310	.290	24
Snodgrass, cf	.321	.294	.275	23
Murray, rf	.277	.291	.270	27
Merkle, 1b	.292	.283	.273	22
Bridwell, ss	.276	.270	.255	27
Devlin, 3b	.260	.273	.269	31
Meyers, c	.285	.332	.291	30

They did not have much power. Red Murray managed to lead the National League in homers in 1909—with seven, his career high. Only Larry Doyle had a higher one-season total before 1911, a whopping eight in 1910. Only Murray had ever driven in more than seventy runs in a season. None of that mattered to McGraw or his followers. The Sunday papers listed sacrifice bunts and stolen bases for each player, not homers and runs batted in. With his pitching staff, the Giants needed only to manufacture a few runs a game to win most of the time.

Manufacturing runs was McGraw's specialty, the legacy of those 1890s Orioles, who had originated the hit-and-run play and other ploys that McGraw fine-tuned as a manager in the dead-ball era. Speed keyed the offense. No manager ever valued stolen bases as much as McGraw, whose 1904–13 Giants amassed seven of the top fourteen all-time one-season stolen base totals. Catcher Chief Meyers was a tortoise on the basepaths, but everyone else ran wild. In 1910 they stole 282 bases; Murray led the way with 57, Devore had 43, Doyle 39, Snodgrass 33, and five others were in double figures.

In 1911 the Giants topped themselves, setting the all-time record with 347 steals. But speed meant more to McGraw than stolen bases. The Giants always tried to take the extra base, and even if two or three runners were thrown out in a game, the constant pressure on the defense paid off in the long run. Pressure meant exposing the defense's weaknesses. If the pitcher was slow getting off the mound, McGraw made everyone bunt. If the catcher made a weak throw, he soon found his throwing arm tested again. McGraw schooled his men in making the opposition pay for any inadequacy and every lapse.

Boston and Brooklyn led the National League in inadequacies, and the Giants stole thirty-one bases in two weeks against them, averaging more than six runs a game and winning eight of eleven. In Boston on May 6 the running mayhem peaked in the wildest game of the year. Forget the dead ball. The teams combined for twenty-six hits, thirteen walks, nine errors, four hit batters, ten stolen bases, and four ejections. The Giants prevailed 15–9 largely thanks to nine stolen bases, including two each by Doyle, Snodgrass, and Merkle. Boston's catcher, veteran Peaches Graham, had enough by the third inning and got himself tossed out of the game.

The Giants spent the last three weeks of May entertaining at the Hilltop, every team appearing except Boston. The home stand began with the season's first games against the Chicago Cubs, their most bitter rivals. So far, the Cubs were not the same powerhouse that won 104 games in 1910 for their fourth pennant in five years. Two pitching mainstays, Jack Pfiester and Orvie Overall, went from a combined eighteen wins in 1910 to zero in 1911, and their Hall of Fame infield was in shambles. Second baseman Johnny Evers suffered a nervous breakdown after an automobile accident in which a friend was killed, and he was resting back home in Troy, New York. Third baseman Harry Steinfeldt had been traded to Boston, and first baseman–manager Frank Chance's skills were eroding monthly from the cumulative effect of some three dozen beanings. Still, they were the Cubs, the main obstacle to a Giants pennant and the one team they could never intimidate.

The series opened on May 9, the same day construction began on the new Polo Grounds, a two-deck structure of steel and reinforced concrete that would seat at least ten thousand more fans than the old stadium. John T. Brush could only daydream about the crowd that might have gathered there to watch this marquee matchup between Mathewson and Chicago's Hall of Fame ace, Mordecai "Three Finger" Brown. This marked their eighteenth head-to-head battle, Brown holding an 11–6 edge so far.

Not even driving rain could prevent this fitting start to the season series. Nine thousand people sat in the Hilltop's open stands, enduring the downpour to watch the two best pitchers in the league. The slippery conditions caused three errors on each side and limited the Giants to one stolen base, but Mathewson went the route to win 5–3. Hooks Wiltse beat the Cubs the next day before the visitors rebounded to take the final two games, handing Red Ames his third straight loss. Ames, who had walked ten in an embarrassing loss in Boston, had better control against the Cubs but was hit freely and lost his spot in the starting rotation to Louie Drucke.

One month into the season, the baseball world buzzed with talk of the dynamic rise in run production. In 1911 the major leagues introduced the cork-center baseball, which was noticeably livelier than its predecessors. Pitchers still doctored the ball with a wide variety of substances, but when hit it traveled farther than anyone could remember. On May 11 eight games yielded an eyepopping 126 runs and 177 hits, including scores of 20–6 and 19–10. The 1911 season was an anomaly, a big offensive year amid the dead-ball doldrums that dominated baseball until 1920. More damage occurred in the American League, where Cleveland rookie Joe Jackson hit .408 yet lost the batting title to Ty Cobb by a dozen points.

The Giants contributed to the offensive explosion on May 13, setting a scoring record against St. Louis. In the first inning the first ten Giants scored in what the *Times* called "a parade of Giants around the bases." Snodgrass tripled in two runs, Merkle drove home three with an inside-the-park homer, Meyers escaped a rundown, Mathewson singled in a run, and when Merkle hit a bases-loaded double his second time up, the score reached 12–0. McGraw capped the merciless inning by calling for a double steal that scored Merkle to make it 13–0. Did McGraw kick his opponents when they were down? The Giants stole four more bases en route to a 19–5 rout, including thefts by Crandall and reserve catcher Grover Hartley.

The only person McGraw spared was Mathewson, who got the day off after pitching one inning (yet still got credit for the win according to 1911 rules). In a shrewd move more significant than the scoring binge, McGraw let Rube Marquard pitch the rest of the game. After his "debutante" win over Brooklyn, Marquard had been knocked out by Boston, shattering his confidence. Relegated to mop-up duty, he logged only fifteen innings in the first month. Now, with a safe lead, McGraw turned Marquard loose. Pitching without pressure for the first time, Marquard showed a blazing fastball and sharp curve. He allowed a dozen hits, but he fanned fourteen Cardinals, tops in the National League that season. For the first time, he got the idea that he could overpower major league hitters, and it marked a turning point in his career.

McGraw enjoyed that romp, but he shouldn't have picked on his protégé Bresnahan's team. He paid with five straight days of bad news, even the two winning days. Louie Drucke beat the Cardinals, but before the game his lawyer announced that the pitcher was suing the IRT subway for $25,000. In October 1910 Drucke was a straphanger on a train that derailed. According to the *Times*, "the lurch threw him against a stanchion, breaking a rib and spraining his arm to an extent that will probably impair permanently his success as a baseball pitcher." Drucke, added his lawyer, "had found the use of his arm very painful, and . . . yesterday a specialist who examined it gave him slender hope for the future." Drucke pitched poorly despite winning 10–6, and clearly his days with the Giants were numbered. He hoped to make more from his lawsuit than McGraw would ever pay him, and who was McGraw to argue with that specialist?

Matters got much worse the next day, on two fronts. McGraw had to wonder about the future of Bugs Raymond, who suffered through his third straight bad outing. Raymond got knocked out in the second inning, giving up two walks and two triples without retiring anybody. He was more than matching this dismal performance off the field. Still, Raymond lasted longer than McGraw did that afternoon. McGraw got into trouble with umpire Bill Finneran, who neglected to call what McGraw and Raymond insisted was a third strike on Steve Evans in the top of the first. Finneran kicked McGraw out of the game, but McGraw didn't realize it until he went out to coach in the second inning. Finneran told him to leave, proving to McGraw's satisfaction his case that Finneran was blind: why hadn't he noticed the Giants manager coaching in the first inning? McGraw raved at Finneran for more than ten minutes before leaving the field.

For this overacting, McGraw drew an immediate three-game suspension, though that was not enough for one writer. Heywood Broun, a recent Harvard dropout who had landed on the Giants beat at the *Morning Telegraph,* could not tolerate McGraw's tirades, which Broun considered a waste of everyone's time (particularly beat writers anxious to finish work). After each McGraw tantrum, Broun editorialized against the man he termed "the most fearful of baseball bores." With Puritan distaste, Broun wrote that "if we can win a pennant only by the tiresome dilatory tactics of the so-called Muggsy, by all means let us pass up the championship. Very few spectators would complain if President Lynch suspended the tiresome little person for life. If there were anything in the remotest degree picturesque about McGraw's kicking it would have some reason to exist. It has no reason to exist. Manager Mack wins games without having them delayed by endless kicking; Manager Chance is only an occasional offender; Manager Clarke knows when to stop. Then why McGraw?"

The Giants lost the first two games of McGraw's suspension, and even their third-game victory cost them dearly. Devore suffered a bad spike wound in his leg and was hobbled for a week. More seriously, Hooks Wiltse again tried to catch a smash through the box with his pitching hand. This drive tore his hand open, and he left the field with blood streaming down his fingers. He feared that one finger was broken and was lucky to miss just over two weeks.

Hot pitching helped the Giants win nine of their last eleven games at the Hilltop. On May 24, in his first start since the fourteen-strikeout breakthrough, Rube Marquard pitched a brilliant 2–1 win that moved the Giants into first place for the first time in 1911. Marquard allowed the Reds two first-inning hits, then held them hitless the rest of the way. He got two hits himself, his bunt single leading to the winning run. Maybe he would turn into an $11,000 beauty after all.

A record crowd of nearly thirty thousand packed the Hilltop on May 27 to see Mathewson face the Phillies, the league leaders since Earl Moore had two-hit the Giants on opening day. Now the teams were tied after a Mathewson win in relief the day before. The expected duel was scoreless when Larry Doyle singled in the fifth inning, went to second on Moore's wild pitch, stole third as Snodgrass walked, and raced home on a double steal. That's what it took for the Giants to get their first run off Moore in twenty-three innings. Matty wasn't about to waste it.

The Phillies fought back in the sixth inning—literally. Harry Welchonce hit a roller down the first base line and bore down on Mathewson, who was waiting to tag him. Mathewson struck first, tagging Welchonce with a shoulder to the ribs that knocked him down. Sherry Magee, the next batter, told Welchonce that he was supposed to spike Mathewson, then demonstrated his point with a feet-first slide into Fred Merkle on a routine grounder. That almost started a brawl, but the umpires intervened. Mathewson took care of business after that, shutting the Phillies out 2–0 for his eighth win of the season.

On May 30 the first-place Giants played their last games at the Hilltop, a Memorial Day doubleheader. As Heywood Broun put it, "The Giants played Brooklyn twice yesterday on the Hilltop and won on both occasions. Brooklyn is something like baseball, only much easier." The sweep gave the Giants nine straight wins over the hapless Superbas. The only sour note came when Bugs Raymond left the afternoon game while pitching shutout ball in the fifth inning. The papers carried tongue-in-cheek reports that Raymond had suffered a sudden case of ptomaine poisoning from "bad ice cream" he had for lunch. Nobody had ever suspected Raymond of being a secret ice cream eater; if anything, he fell victim to bad ice in his liquid lunch.

The Giants ended their Hilltop exile with twenty wins in twenty-eight games, but they gladly packed up and didn't look back. Construction on the new Polo Grounds had progressed swiftly, and everyone expected the Giants to play there when they returned from their first western swing in late June, even if the grandstands were unfinished. All they had to do was survive four weeks on the road. Most of them did.

THE JUNE ODYSSEY began in Chicago, the most hostile city in the league. In years past the Giants frequently traveled from their hotel to the ballpark with police escorts while being pelted with rocks and garbage. These days, Chicago fans seemed content to taunt Fred Merkle by asking him for directions to second base.

Even with Chance and Evers sidelined, the Cubs trailed the Giants by only one game when the series began. The Giants were missing McGraw, detained in New York by a family illness but expected any day in Chicago. He never made it, and Mathewson and Doyle handled the decisions in his absence. Doyle did a perfect imitation of the Little

Napoleon by getting ejected from two of the first three games and sus-pended for the fourth.

McGraw missed four of the most exciting games of the year. Bugs Raymond talked his way into starting the opener but got drilled for five runs in two innings. Ames relieved and held the Cubs to one run the rest of the way. "The jinx did not quite land on him," wrote Sid Mercer. "Must have got lost en route from New York." The hoodoo landed on the Cubs this time as they blew a 6–0 lead. Four walks and an error handed the Giants a seven-run gift inning, and Ames held on for the 7–6 win that quieted the Chicago fans—for a day.

The opener was the tamest game of the week. McGraw missed a near-riot in the second game, as the biggest West Side Park crowd of the season witnessed five ejections. Three Finger Brown got a quick heave-ho in the first inning for arguing a tag at the plate. After a similar play in the third inning, three Giants got tossed. The Cubs got the best of the exchange. Ed Reulbach relieved Brown and shut the Giants out the rest of the way. Tied 4–4 in the eighth inning, Rube Marquard loaded the bases and had to face Frank "Wildfire" Schulte, Chicago's best hitter. Schulte, who in 1911 became the first player in the twentieth century to hit twenty homers in a season, already had two doubles in the game, but McGraw wasn't there to rescue Rube from facing this scourge again. Schulte picked out a fat pitch and deposited it in the right field bleachers for a grand slam that handed Marquard his first loss of the season.

Chicago, St. Louis, and Cincinnati were the only N.L. cities that permitted Sunday baseball, and the third Chicago game marked the Giants' Sunday debut for 1911. The Cubs delivered a Sunday punch. Hooks Wiltse made his first start since splitting his hand open, and the Giants got him an early 5–2 lead against Brown. But Wiltse ran out of luck in the eighth inning. For a rail-thin guy he made a great target, and this time Joe Tinker smacked a line drive off Wiltse's chest. Shaken, he gave up three more hits, and suddenly it was 5–5. He got in trouble again in the bottom of the ninth on a pair of one-out singles. That gave the Cubs fourteen hits off Wiltse, who finally came out. Why did he take all that punishment? McGraw was still in New York, Mathewson, whose religious devotion made him shun Sunday ball, wasn't in uni-form, and Doyle's ejection left the team leaderless—so leaderless that

Louie Drucke, coaching third because nobody else wanted to stand out in the hot sun, forgot to send a runner home on a two-out single. Wiltse could have used that run. Instead, Ames belatedly relieved Wiltse and gave up a game-ending single to the first batter. The Giants and Cubs were tied for first place.

On Monday word came from New York that McGraw would definitely rejoin the team in Pittsburgh, and from league headquarters in Cincinnati that Doyle was suspended for three games. That left it up to Mathewson, making his first start in nine days. The game was scoreless until the seventh inning, when Schulte doubled and went to third on a bunt single. The Cubs launched a double steal, and Meyers made a low throw which Mathewson tried to intercept for a throw home. The ball glanced off his glove, and Schulte scored easily. Cubs pitcher Harry McIntyre took that 1–0 lead to the ninth inning before the Giants hauled themselves up off the mat, exploding for seven runs for the second time in the series. Fred Merkle tripled to start the rally and doubled to cap it.

That last-minute rally salvaged a split in a series as intense as an October pennant showdown. Both teams felt that they deserved to sweep, and they were right. Certainly the Giants were sunk without those seven-run outbursts. Sid Mercer pinpointed their problem. Without McGraw they had no killer instinct, coasting on slim leads that disappeared when tired pitchers weren't replaced in time. McGraw would have to rejuvenate them in Pittsburgh.

Not that McGraw had been idle back in New York. He tried to trade for a pitcher and took steps to revive Mike Donlin's career. Donlin, a brilliant player with an erratic personality, was one of McGraw's favorite reclamation projects. Their association had begun in 1901, when Donlin played for McGraw's Baltimore team. McGraw brought him to the Giants in 1904, and Donlin was the star centerfielder of the 1905 championship team. By then he had a reputation as a drinker and a roughneck, having been jailed in 1902 for assaulting a woman in Baltimore. When Giants owner Brush cut his salary for 1907, Donlin sat out the whole year. Signed again for 1908 and named team captain by McGraw, "Turkey Mike" responded by leading the team with a .334 average, 106 RBI, and 30 stolen bases. His rowdy nature had been tamed thanks to his marriage to actress Mabel Hite, a Christian Scientist. The handsome, merry Donlin had always been popular; once sober and upright, he became the toast of New York. But when Brush again denied his salary demands for 1909, he cashed in his celebrity downtown, joining Mabel's act.

Donlin's stage career blossomed, thanks to his ability to avoid upstaging his more talented wife. Yet whenever the Giants' offense dipped, there was talk of bringing him back. Nobody knew where he'd play, for McGraw was happy with his young outfield of Devore, Snodgrass, and Murray. Still, Donlin was a lifetime .334 hitter, and if McGraw couldn't fit him into his lineup, he could always use him as trade bait.

Donlin was signed and reinstated while the Giants were in Chicago and joined them in Pittsburgh, but Bugs Raymond almost didn't. When the Giants met McGraw at the Hotel Schenley there, they reported that Raymond had disappeared en route. Raymond eventually wandered in and explained that he had spent the last few hours visiting an old friend, the train's engineer. No doubt the engineer had access to the best ice cream on board.

A skeptical McGraw let Raymond start the Pittsburgh opener as scheduled, but both men suffered that afternoon. Raymond pitched indifferently and left after five innings, sabotaged by two fielding muffs that put him behind 4–0. He never started another game in the majors. McGraw, outraged by a call at first base that kept the Giants from tying the game, got no consolation from the postgame admission by Pirates shortstop Honus Wagner that the umpire had blown the call. The loss dropped the Giants back to second place, behind the Cubs.

As if guilt-ridden over their tainted victory, the Pirates surrendered the next three games to the Giants, who went on to split four games in Cincinnati. There they learned of a seven-player trade between Boston and the Cubs, who unloaded longtime catcher Johnny Kling. There was talk around the league about outlawing trades during the season, but McGraw kept shopping Donlin. One rumor had Donlin going to Philadelphia for Earl Moore, McGraw's sparring partner.

Mathewson won the Cincinnati finale to gain the split, his eighteenth straight victory over the Reds. In a brief burst of cockiness fueled by press claims of his invincibility, Matty told the *Times* afterward that he "could have been hit for twenty-five safeties, yet could have trimmed them." Matty paid for that boast; in his next start, in St. Louis, he threw a two-hitter and lost. That tough loss marked only part of the Giants' nightmare in St. Louis. The series began well enough, with a Doc Crandall shutout, but turned ugly the following day, June 16. Drucke started but lasted only long enough to walk the first three batters. McGraw, seething, sent Drucke directly to the doghouse to trade places with Raymond. Bugs was no better. He let all three runners score, and in the fifth inning he blew sky-high. Two walks, a hit batter, and three hits led to four runs, the difference in the 8–4 loss. Six walks in six innings of work provided the conclusive evidence in McGraw's case against Raymond's pretense of remaining a functioning, sober-enough pitcher. McGraw fined Raymond $200 and suspended him indefinitely.

"Raymond Falls From Grace in St. Louis," read the *Globe*'s headline, and there was no chance for redemption. McGraw, who was legendary for helping needy ex-players on the sly, ignored Raymond's pleas for reinstatement, and within days the crushed Bugs was negotiating to pitch in semipro games for beer money. He never pitched in the majors again and met a swift demise. Just over a year later, while he argued with an umpire in a game near Chicago, a fan threw a brick at him. He threw it back at a second fan, who charged onto the field to attack him. During the struggle, somebody grabbed a bat and swung it, nailing Raymond in the head. Raymond staggered back to his room but died several days later from cerebral hemorrhaging. Knowing only baseball and booze, he was done in by both at age thirty.

On June 17, a torridly hot Saturday, a different kind of weakness cost the Giants: the offense managed only three hits off Cardinals ace Bob Harmon. Mathewson suffered an Ames-like fate, taking a no-hitter to the seventh inning and losing. Two hits cost him a 2–1 loss, his only June setback, and the Giants needed the final game just to salvage a split for the series.

More significant in the long run was the growing weakness of the Giants infield, in particular at shortstop. Terrible all month in the field, wobbly at the plate, Al Bridwell broke down completely in St. Louis, sidelined for a week by malaria. His replacement, Art Fletcher, suffered a bad charley horse and missed two weeks. Undermanned, McGraw slipped all-purpose Doc Crandall into the lineup, batting sixth and playing shortstop. Crandall survived his week in the infield but was

CHRISTY MATHEWSON, right, the team leader, appreciated the dual role of Faust on the Giants as good-luck charm and as comic relief to balance the harshness of manager JOHN McGRAW. (Transcendental Graphics)

hardly the solution to McGraw's problems. In seven starts, he hit .208, drove in one run, and committed four errors.

The Giants gained the split in St. Louis behind Wiltse's 5–4 win. Red Murray burned his ex-teammates with a spectacular catch and a two-run double in the ninth inning. Traveling halfway across the country from St. Louis to Boston, the Giants contemplated one more week on the road before returning home to the not-nearly-finished Polo Grounds. Depleted as they were, they remained very much alive, within two games of the first-place Cubs.

Al Bridwell didn't make it to Boston. His stomach "completely knocked out by the St. Louis heat and water," Bridwell stayed in bed the whole trip. Unable to eat for his fourth day, he clung to his Pullman berth and tried to survive the constant movements of the train. At Albany he left the team and took a train to New York to recover at home, hoping to rejoin the club in Brooklyn. This idleness probably gave him time to realize that his Giants career was in jeopardy.

In Boston, the Giants won the first two games behind Marquard and Mathewson. Rube's win was his fourth, matching his 1910 total and earning praise from some scribes; Matty's win was his twelfth. But the series finale ruined the visit. The Giants led 4–2 until Louie Drucke collapsed in the seventh inning. A five-run inning continued the countdown on his New York tenure; he didn't start again for three weeks despite being part of a slim six-man staff. "McGraw has given Drucke every opportunity to get started this season," wrote Sid Mercer, "but the Texan hasn't had the confidence and is disheartened." His chances were better with that IRT lawsuit—eventually settled out of court after the injury did indeed end Drucke's career.

McGraw had had all summer to prepare for Drucke's demise, but the ninth-inning nightmare, an unexpectedly perverse finish, hurtled him into the kind of temporary insanity he so enjoyed sharing with everyone else in the ballpark. The Giants trailed 7–6 when Merkle launched a long blast that according to McGraw curled into the stands just fair. Umpire Bill Finneran called it foul, and McGraw led a pack of Giants in protest. Merkle made their arguments moot by blasting the next pitch a little farther to the right for the game-tying home run. In the bottom of the ninth, reliever Marquard's first pitch sailed off the bat of Harry Steinfeldt, heading to the area where Merkle's shots had landed. This time the Giants were certain that it hooked foul, but Finneran called it fair. That ended the game and began the rhubarb of the week, which police broke up just as it appeared that McGraw and his players would physically assault Finneran. As they had all month— indeed as they did throughout McGraw's heyday—the Giants fled another city with the citizenry virtually at their heels.

The good news was a four-game detour to Brooklyn on the way home to stomp their cousins the Superbas. The Giants took three of four there, winding up the four-week road trip with a 14–9 mark. Now they played nineteen of their next twenty-four games at home. Even better, after ten weeks of exile, home meant the Polo Grounds. True, half the construction remained unfinished, and what stood there was being called Brush Stadium, but the Giants and their fans savored the serenity of being home again.

"THE NEW STADIUM will be faced with a decorative frieze in the facade containing a series of allegorical treatments in bas-relief in polychrome, and the box tiers are designed upon the lines of the royal boxes of the Colosseum in Rome, and pylons in the Roman style will flank the horseshoe on either side." So read the prospectus concocted by Giants secretary Bill Gray to tease the cultured class into paying seventy-five cents for a seat in the new grandstand. On June 28, when the Giants hosted Boston there, it looked more like an ongoing construction area with a ballgame nearby.

Two months' work had finished half the job, and the park was not completed until the Giants returned from their second western trip in mid-August. By then, nobody pretended any more that it would be known as Brush Stadium; everyone used the old sacred name Polo Grounds. Eventually the seating exceeded fifty thousand and the bas-relief flourished, but at the end of June you could only imagine what that magnificent second deck would look like perched above the new concrete-and-steel grandstand. Never mind that, thought New Yorkers on the morning of the 28th, pondering a more immediate problem. The so-called Brush Stadium lacked a roof, and a hot early sun promised a long afternoon at a shadeless ballpark.

Only something as basic as killing heat could keep Giants fans away from their team's return home. Away they stayed. Estimates of the crowd ranged from six to twelve thousand. Every one of them suffered. Management hastily attached large canvas sheets to the back of the grandstand, but they provided only a symbolic barrier between the baseball fanatics and a "pitilessly" beating sun. Leave it to Damon Runyon to put the heat in perspective: "A fellow named Dante, who made a scouting trip through the Inferno League a long time back, has always contended that the sunfield there was the hottest place in the world for a ball player, next to Yuma, Arizona, but some of the 12,000 fans who sweltered on the concrete beneath Judge Coogan's bluffs yesterday are inclined to take issue with this contention." Those intrepid enough to attend managed to overcome the heat and whoop it up. For them, more annoying was the presence of concrete under their heels. Conditioned for decades to stamp their feet on resounding wood, they were quieted by the concrete and faced a quick adjustment to extra cheers and applause.

The Giants provided plenty to cheer about on this gala occasion. The game itself drew no more than third billing, topped also by the Polo Grounds return of Mike Donlin. A pregame ceremony honoring Donlin was accompanied by what the *Herald* calculated as "flowers enough to give three popular Aldermen decent funerals." It took ten people to carry in all the flowers. Photographs and speeches followed, umpire Hank O'Day accepted some posies from Larry Doyle, and only after the debris was cleared did the ballgame commence.

The game took little longer than Donlin's tribute, as Christy Mathewson mowed down the Boston Rustlers (as the Braves were called that year) 3–0 in one hour and thirty-five minutes. What a perfect way for the Giants to christen this latest incarnation of the Polo Grounds! The outlook was sunny, roof or no roof. Mathewson's record stood at a stellar 14–3, the Giants had a two-game grip on first place, and Boston was staying for three more games.

Despite losing one of those games, the Giants took a 41–24 record into July, leading the Cubs and Phillies by two games. McGraw had weathered enough of the travails of a long season to enjoy the view from the top of the roller coaster while he could. The view would have been spoiled had he known how quickly the Giants would plunge into third-place limbo.

4

Summer Daze

THE HEAT ON JUNE 28 provided a mere preview of miseries to come. The worst heat wave in more than a decade seared the eastern half of the country for the first two weeks of July. In a time when electric fans were scarce and air conditioning still a theory, heat killed. More than a thousand people died in the first ten days in July, including at least two hundred in New York and twice that in Chicago, while thousands were more prostrated. The New York *Times* published daily lists of local casualties and collapses, listed by borough. The band of suffering stretched from Maine to the western edge of Kansas, where Junction City recorded a high of 113 degrees on July 5. July 2 was the hottest day in New York City in a dozen years, and two days later it was eight degrees hotter!

There was no escape from the sun, little relief even at night, and no help from a public official's suggestion that overheated people should visualize subfreezing winter days to block out the debilitating truth that they were boiling over right now. After the heat wave broke, forest fires began in areas that had been scorched. Devastating fires in Michigan, Maine, and Ontario killed hundreds more, burning uncontrolled for days.

Nobody had to tell people in 1911 about survival of the fittest in a perilous world. Disasters and accidental deaths occurred at a much higher rate than they do now. Forces of nature could not be stopped, but an appalling multitude of manmade tragedies filled the daily newspapers. Any kind of vehicle seemed doomed to crash into something. Witness this sampling from July 1911: More than thirty people died in four major train wrecks, including the Boston Flyer, which went over an embankment in Connecticut at 3:30 AM. A dozen people died and several dozen were injured; the passengers included the St. Louis Cardinals, who escaped unhurt and were highly praised for their rescue efforts. Two shipwrecks killed more than sixty people, and a steamer carrying more than eleven hundred passengers foundered off Coney Island, causing a brief panic. Aviation, only a few years old, consisted of a succession of pioneers setting records until they crashed. The month's most prominent casualty was Bud Mars, one of the first aviators to tour the globe. Mars died when his "aeroplane" crashed in front of a crowd of thousands in Erie, Pennsylvania.

No activity was safe, not even a day at the beach. On the Sunday before July 4, twenty-seven people drowned, seven in New York City. On the Fourth, twenty more drowned just around New York. Leaving home required grave vigilance lest death fly around the corner and find you. Automobiles, trolley cars, and horse-drawn wagons turned pedestrians into moving targets, and being inside the vehicles didn't guarantee survival either. The great terror in 1911 was railroad crossings, too often unlit, unmarked, on grades or curves, and thoroughly deadly. A New York *Times* editorial late in July cited these statistics for 1911 to date: in New York, New Jersey, and Connecticut, collisions with trains had killed fifty-nine people, seriously injured seventy-six, killed twenty-two horses, and destroyed thirty-two horse-drawn vehicles and fourteen automobiles. Automobile travel was so new that the obvious dangers of railroad crossings were only then becoming apparent.

Wherever you looked—the sky, the air, the water, the ground in front of you—something could rip a hole in your fate. Life was a cruel struggle, and the heat wave made it more oppressive. With nighttime temperatures hovering around 80 degrees, refreshing rest eluded most people, making the next day that much more unbearable. So it continued for weeks, with an occasional false hope of lurking rain or cooler air.

THE DEVASTATING HEAT made people miserable from the northeast to the nation's center. Some of the worst heat struck Kansas, which could least withstand it. The only outdoor refuge from the sun was shade, and Kansas suffered from its annual shortage of shade. After the hottest, driest June on record, Kansas withered in early July. Topeka faced a record high temperature five days in a row, and Junction City, sixty miles west of Topeka, reached an unthinkable peak of 113 degrees on July 5.

"Heat May Be Responsible for Some Insane Cases," read a headline in the Topeka *Daily Capital* on July 2, with seven more degrees of heat still on the way. "The expression about going 'crazy with the heat' is a common one, but it is a fact that the extreme heat in Kansas for the last month has affected the head gear of a good many people." Both state hospitals for the insane were already overcrowded, and sixty-six new applications arrived in June, mainly for older people. Presumably younger people had stronger physical resistance to sunlight and thus remained free to roam the planet despite being addled by the heat. The newspapers carried daily reports of missing people who wandered off in the heat and were found days and miles away. Usually their dementia departed with the heat. In Massachusetts, a man recuperating from being hit by a baseball drifted away from his nurse and thence out to sea in a small boat. In Manhattan, a banker's wife disappeared for four days, disoriented and lost. Heat was blamed for at least one suicide. And so on.

In Kansas, one person about to break loose from the tethers of reality was a farmer's son in Marion, sixty miles south of Junction City. Charles Victor Faust was born on October 9, 1880, the eldest of six children of John and Eva Faust. John Faust was born in 1843 in Danzig, Germany, and his firstborn inherited his thick German accent. Eva came from Woonsocket, Rhode Island, and was thirteen years younger than the immigrant farmer who married her and took her west to establish a family. They settled along the Cottonwood River near the county seat of Marion County in east-central Kansas.

Located along the Santa Fe Trail, Marion County was first settled in the 1850s. In 1860 five covered wagons full of homesteaders, pointed toward an area described by a government surveyor as the "best place I've seen," founded Marion Centre, later Marion, one year before Kansas became a state. Like many midwestern settlements, it was named for Revolutionary War general Francis Marion. The first settlers were Swedes and Bohemians, followed in the 1870s by Mennonites and Germans. Several thousand people inhabited the area by the time John Faust and his young bride found Marion in the late 1870s.

After Charles's arrival, five more Faust children came along in the 1880s. The parents outlived four of their six children; they were survived only by John and George, the next two after Charles. Freddie, born in 1885, died in infancy, and Fred, the youngest, died in 1908 at age eighteen. John Faust Sr. was a hard man. When four-month-old Freddie died during the autumn harvest, the father declared that there was no time for a funeral and had Freddie buried in the field he was working at the time. He kept his only daughter, Louise, in virtual servitude in the house, which explains why the girl escaped when she found a chance. A traveling salesman swept her off her feet, got her pregnant, and took her to Oklahoma to marry her. Her spiteful father cut her down to a $1 bequest in his will, but her death in Oklahoma at age thirty-two made the matter moot.

No doubt John Faust expected his oldest son to succeed him in running the farm, and it had to disappoint him to discover that Charley could not meet that responsibility. Instead, John Jr. wound up taking over the farm when his father died in 1921; John Jr. never married and apparently never learned to read or write, but he managed the Faust farm until he died in 1949, the last of the Marion Fausts. The Faust homestead is still there, a couple of miles west of town, the farmhouse now covered by yellow aluminum siding. Marion has changed little in the century since Charley Faust grew up there. It has survived several floods and the Depression, remains the county seat, and maintains a rigidly obeyed 20 mph speed limit through its entire 1.1-mile length.

Almost nothing is known about Charles Victor Faust's life before the summer of 1911. There is no way of estimating the exact limitations of his intellect except by examining his known behavior, which suggests that he was at best slow-witted and gullible. He endured life on the farm and fared no better in town. There were two baseball teams in Marion, and both did without Faust's services. Apparently he would hang around when the teams practiced and was sometimes allowed to participate, but he never pitched competitively before presenting himself to John McGraw as a pitcher. His prospects in Kansas would likely remain bleak, and at the age of thirty he resolved to do something about it.

According to S. Carlisle Martin, a St. Louis *Post-Dispatch* reporter who interviewed Faust in 1911, Faust fled the farm and went to Wichita early that spring. There he found a fortune-teller who informed him that his destiny was to become a great pitcher, lead the New York

Giants to the championship, and meet Lulu, the girl of his dreams. Unarmed with the wits to see through the theatrics of this fantastic vision, Faust took it to heart. He went back to Marion and pondered this portentous future through the first half of the baseball season and the first Giants visit to St. Louis in June. An alternative theory is that he visited the fortune-teller in June or July, possibly at a county fair (the nearest were in Hutchinson and Peabody, southwest of Marion and closer than Wichita), and acted soon after getting a vivid glimpse of his glorious future.

In any case, the July heat wave spelled the end of Charley Faust's life on the farm in Marion, Kansas. Did he tell anybody about the prophecy that he would pitch the Giants to the title? If he did, was he ridiculed, his dreams scoffed at to the point where he became doubly determined to make them real? Did anyone imagine that he would actually act on something a fortune-teller told him? We know only the facts. Sometime in July, with nobody telling him, "Whoa, Charley, don't be such an idiot," Faust left Marion and made his way to St. Louis to rendezvous with the Giants and meet his destiny.

THE GIANTS BEGAN this hellish month by playing five games in three days in Philadelphia, where they found temperatures over 100 degrees, not to mention a torrid Phillies team. They hit Christy Mathewson early and hard, piling up thirteen hits to take the first game 7–3. A record Monday crowd of eighteen thousand went wild over every Phillies hit in a victory that brought them within one game of the Giants, with two doubleheaders to follow.

The Phillies continued to batter Giants pitching through the Fourth of July doubleheader, sweeping them 11–7 and 7–5. In the second game, Doc Crandall surrendered fourteen hits, including nine for extra bases. To cap his ordeal, he fielded a liner by Red Dooin on his forehead. The blow opened a gash, knocked Crandall unconscious for a nine-count, left a large welt, and caused him recurring headaches all month. He pitched only four innings in the next two weeks at a time when McGraw was so short-staffed that Rube Marquard relieved in both July 4 losses and started a game the next day.

Intense heat prevailed again during the July 5 doubleheader, exacting its biggest toll on Mathewson, who started the opener with only one day of rest. This time the Phillies got fourteen hits off him, beating him for the third time in 1911 by a 6–4 score. That added to up thirty-one runs and four straight wins for the upstart Phillies over Gotham's Goliaths. McGraw, stunned, couldn't even protest hard enough to get himself ejected. The Giants did manage to win the finale 10–1 behind Marquard, who earned his first victory against a first-division team. McGraw's battered troops retreated back to New York in third place, behind the Phillies and Cubs. Sid Mercer described them as "a most wretched bunch of athletes" on the ride home. "They felt as if they had been put through a wringer. . . . The Philadelphia experience just melted the vitality out of them and wore their dispositions to a frayed edge."

In this condition, they opened a four-game series at the Polo Grounds against the hated Cubs, who had their own problems, starting with manager Frank Chance. After the latest of innumerable beanings, persistent dizzy spells dogged Chance, and when he collapsed in Cincinnati near the end of June, team doctors ordered him sidelined. He wasn't ready to admit it, but his playing career was essentially over, his future holding only two dozen scattered appearances. Defying the doctors, he accompanied his team to New York to match wits with McGraw, though he looked feeble and was too groggy to leave the bench. Johnny Evers worked out with the Cubs and expected to play soon, but he also seemed drained of his former pep.

Indeed, July was rough on all the National League contenders. On July 2, Pirates manager Fred Clarke was beaned by Slim Sallee of St. Louis and carried off the field on a stretcher. Clarke, a player-manager since 1897, was thirty-three years old in 1911 and slowing down, but the beaning hastened the end of his career. This was big news. First Chance gone, and within days Clarke, too, the rivals who had deprived McGraw of so many pennants over the past decade. When the Phillies' Red Dooin broke his leg late in the month, it left McGraw as the only first-division manager to escape July without a key player maimed.

While the Giants labored in Philadelphia, construction workers began building the second deck of the Polo Grounds. After that would come the roof, touted as utilizing the latest fireproof asbestos design by Johns Manville. But on July 6 Brush Stadium offered no protection from the sun, and with the temperature once again over 100 degrees, a sparse crowd attended the start of the season's biggest series so far. About five thousand diehards witnessed a dull effort by the sluggish Giants, who lost 6–2.

Relief came on Friday, when the New York high reached only 92 degrees. Black clouds threatened rain all day but kept the sun at bay, and a breeze blowing in from the Harlem River made fans almost comfortable. Red Ames made them excited again about their team. The Giants' "cold weather" pitcher spun a walkless five-hit shutout and drove in the first two Giants runs with a triple. The lifetime .141 hitter added a single later, sailing to a 5–0 win.

Saturday belonged to Rube Marquard, the new workhorse of the staff. He trailed 2–1 until the sixth inning, the Giants run coming on the only home run of Marquard's career. He pitched in and out of trouble, getting three key strikeouts off Wildfire Schulte, whose grand slam had burned him in Chicago. The Giants gave Marquard a four-run sixth inning, all the support he needed to show off in front of twenty-five thousand fans who cheered the Giants back into first place.

The Monday finale was the most exciting game of the series, with Mathewson facing Lew Richie on a cloudy, bearable day. Mathewson pitched well enough to win, but the Giants defense betrayed him. Errors by Larry Doyle and Art Fletcher handed the Cubs a 2–1 lead, but Fletcher redeemed himself with a game-tying inside-the-park homer. The Giants did no further damage, mainly because they stole no bases, a rare 1911 speed failure. Richie singled leading off the tenth inning, and the Cubs made Matty pay. With a runner on third, Al Bridwell kicked a grounder, and the third Cub of the game crossed the plate on an error. This fumble, Bridwell's second of the game, proved fatal, and Matty suffered his third loss in early July.

The Cubs reclaimed first place in the tightest midseason pennant race in memory. Only three games separated the Cubs from the fifth-place Cardinals; the standings shifted daily. On this same Monday, however, Sherry Magee of the Phillies, the defending National League batting champion, charged rookie umpire Bill Finneran and decked him with a punch to the mouth that sent Finneran to the hospital for stitches. League president Thomas Lynch hurried to Philadelphia to investigate and soon suspended Magee for the season. By the time Lynch lifted the suspension in mid-August, Red Dooin's leg was in a cast and the Phillies' pennant hopes were gone.

Fourth-place Pittsburgh visited the Polo Grounds for four games starting July 11, another brutally hot day that wilted Hooks Wiltse more than anybody. The Pirates stormed Wiltse and two relievers for nineteen hits (four by Honus Wagner) in a 13–4 win. The lethargic Giants, who committed three more errors and failed to steal a base for the third straight game, were booed by their boiling fans, whose main target, Josh Devore, struck out weakly three times. Perhaps the Giants deserved this rare razzing by their loyal followers. With the defense leaking runs, the offense dragging, and only Marquard pitching well, no wonder they had plunged to third place.

In this topsy-turvy month, the doldrums lasted no longer than the triumphs. Two days later, the Giants reached first place again, yet their next loss dropped them back to third place. Marquard got the first win with another complete game, giving him four of the Giants' five July wins. Louie Drucke followed with his first start in three weeks. According to the *Herald's* John Wheeler, a behind-the-scenes drama precipitated Drucke's return, not the obvious factor that McGraw's other five pitchers had all pitched their limit in the past three days. Wheeler revealed the lingering jealousy between the unheralded Drucke and the underachieving Rube Marquard. Drucke's lawsuit was based on the premise that his arm was shot, and his terrible June outings seemed to prove it. "Then suddenly Marquard made good," Wheeler continued, "and came so fast that Drucke could hardly see him disappearing over the baseball horizon. This irritated Drucke as acutely as fleas do a hairless terrier. The idea of that long 'Rube' putting him in the penumbra!" The day after Marquard's fourth straight complete-game win, Drucke talked McGraw into giving him another chance. The result was a 9–4 Giants win, but Drucke hardly sparkled. He gave up a dozen hits in what turned out to be his final major league victory. Still, McGraw welcomed this timely effort, and his staff got even more rest when the final game of the series was rained out.

On Saturday the Cincinnati Reds came to town, and Mathewson celebrated with his nineteenth straight win over his patsies. Fred Merkle broke up a 1–1 game with a three-run home run in the sixth inning, and Mathewson held off a ninth-inning Reds rally to win 4–3. It was his fifteenth win of the season but his first in July, leaving twenty thousand Polo Grounds fans extremely relieved on the first cool baseball day all month.

The Giants seemed to catch more luck when Sunday's off-day was followed by another rainout. By playing only once in four days, the heat-drained Giants rested their weary legs and arms. Meanwhile, the Phillies won six in a row to grab first place; the Giants, tied with the Phillies on July 14, did not see first place again until Charles Victory Faust brought them there.

On July 18 the Giants came back flat, losing 8–2 as the Reds ripped Marquard for a dozen hits. The Giants made three errors and stole no bases, but did provide the hometown fans with one gratuitously sublime moment. Mike Donlin pinch-hit for Marquard and drilled a home run into the right field bleachers. That was the sole high point of his Giants comeback, which lasted exactly twelve at-bats. Apart from that one happy event, the fans booed their team's careless defense, prompting a lecture from Fred Lieb, the rookie reporter of the New York *Press*. "Brush and McGraw," Lieb advised, "should endeavor to squelch the cheap element which always is ready to abuse the Giants when they are losing."

In that day's New York *American*, Damon Runyon presented a more optimistic outlook. "As the season waxes and wanes," Runyon wrote, "and some of the clubs which were supposed to explode about now consistently fail to do so, the local fans are becoming more and more convinced that the 1911 decision will depend in a large measure on luck, with the Giants looking just about as lucky as anybody else in the grand scramble. They have had their share of the bad luck so far in more ways than one, and as the popular theory of luck anyway is that it has got to change, they are about scheduled for some of the smiles of fickle fortune right now."

The Giants took the final game from the Reds but lost the opener to the Cardinals when Mathewson was knocked out in the second inning. True to the what-have-you-done-for-me-lately mentality of base-ball, Mathewson found himself second in the league in wins yet the subject of wide public speculation that his skills were shot and he might be washed up. The *Herald*'s John Wheeler, Mathewson's ghostwriter, called it "the passing of an idol or at least the temporary hesitation of one." It turned out to be the latter.

On July 21 McGraw finally pulled off the kind of deal he had wanted to make for weeks. Though it didn't bring the needed pitching help, it did enable McGraw to field a lineup even faster than the one he envisioned when the season started. He traded Al Bridwell and third-string catcher Hank Gowdy to the Boston Rustlers and reacquired Buck Herzog, then playing shortstop but a better third baseman. McGraw liked the young Art Fletcher's work since he had taken Art Devlin's spot at third base, but Fletcher was a better shortstop, so he got Bridwell's old job.

Herzog was hitting .310 for the Rustlers and stood fourth in the league in stolen bases, a blossoming star who had just turned twenty-six. A week before the trade, Herzog "quit" the Rustlers after being fined $300 by manager Fred Tenney for not hustling in a series against the Giants. The Giants players saw no problem with ex-teammate Herzog's play and thought Tenney had given him a raw deal. Herzog took it personally, too, and went on strike, refusing to pay the fine. The Rustlers began entertaining trade offers. McGraw gave them Gowdy, who became a solid catcher for them for a dozen years, but the Giants got what they needed now.

John McGraw controlled the levers on the roller-coaster careers of many major leaguers, but none more than Charles Lincoln "Buck" Herzog, the quintessential McGraw player. In the first ten years of his career, the pugnacious Herzog got himself traded five times—three times away from McGraw and twice back to him. McGraw once said, "I hate his guts, but I want him on my team." No wonder, considering how well the Giants did with Herzog in their lineup.

Herzog's exiles and returns illustrate McGraw's conflicting impulses of expediency and loyalty in making roster changes. Most of his deals involved expediency, and he never hesitated to trade a popular, senior player if he thought the move would address a pressing need. After the 1909 season, McGraw felt a pressing need to be far away from Herzog. After a promising .300 rookie season in 1908, Herzog struggled at .185 in 1909, and he and McGraw spent most of the season crabbing at each other. So McGraw exiled him to last-place Boston. The 1911 deal saw McGraw trade the popular Bridwell for a player who had essentially been run out of town, but McGraw knew what he was doing. Herzog's speed jump-started the Giants offense, and he became a mainstay in the infield for three consecutive pennant-winning teams; in 1912 he became the first player to get a dozen hits in a World Series.

Yet the Giants traded Herzog to Cincinnati in December 1913. The Giants, yes, but not McGraw. While McGraw and a large group of major leaguers crossed the Pacific Ocean to begin an around-the-world tour, Herzog was traded for a speedy outfielder named Bob Bescher. It was a hasty deal arranged by new owner Harry Hempstead, the managing partner of the group who inherited ownership after the death in 1912 of John T. Brush, Hempstead's father-in-law. Hempstead knew that McGraw coveted Bescher and hated Herzog. Moreover, Cincinnati owner August "Garry" Herrmann would satisfy Herzog's oft-declared urge to manage. When he learned of the deal, McGraw pitched a small fit at being denied his customary final say in deals and declared that he liked Bescher but hated giving up Herzog.

In 1914 the Giants missed Herzog sorely. They finished second to the "Miracle" Braves, and the shock hurtled the Giants into last place in 1915, one game behind Herzog's Reds. McGraw dismantled his team, unloading Snodgrass, Murray, and Marquard late in the 1915 season, Meyers that winter, and Doyle and Merkle late in 1916, when the Giants finished fourth. Doyle was the defending National League batting champion but got swept aside in the housecleaning.

That didn't include the biggest deal of all, in which McGraw packaged three future Hall of Famers for—that's right, Buck Herzog. The price tag on Herzog was not quite as extravagant as it sounds. The three immortals included Bill McKechnie, enshrined as a manager, Edd Roush, who played less than one season for the Giants before blossoming with the Reds, and Christy Mathewson, whose pitching skills had faded away. Mathewson wanted to manage but, like so many a McGraw protégé, would not get the chance in New York. McGraw, as he had done for Roger Bresnahan and later did for others, found Mathewson a team to manage. Herzog had worn out his welcome in Cincinnati by 1916, so Mathewson got Herzog's job.

McGraw put Herzog at second base in 1917, and the Giants won the pennant. Herzog, however, ended the season under suspension for refusing to make the last road trip. McGraw lifted the suspension before the World Series, then grew skeptical of Herzog's defensive effort. So he traded him a third time, this time for good, back to Boston for pitcher Jesse Barnes and Larry Doyle, exiled only briefly before giving McGraw three more solid seasons. Yet without Herzog it took the Giants four seasons to win another pennant.

What made Herzog so valuable to McGraw? More than any other Giant, he reminded McGraw of the scrapping player he had been in Baltimore, which happened to be Herzog's hometown. Herzog hated the opposition, fought for everything, and was particularly aggressive on the bases. He even followed his mentor's example of starting fights as the underdog. Indeed, Herzog is most famous for his 1917 brawl with Ty Cobb, dubbed by columnist Joe Williams "the Louis-Schmeling fight of baseball." It began with a pregame shouting match and turned serious when Cobb stole second base spikes-first and clipped Herzog on the thigh. That started a fight in which Cobb was grinding Herzog's face in the dirt when Jim Thorpe, then a Giants outfielder, broke it up. Cobb was ejected, but for Herzog that was not enough. That evening, he went to Cobb's hotel room and challenged him, leading to a brutal fight inside the room that lasted half an hour. "I got hell kicked out of me," a bloodied Herzog told teammates later, "but I knocked the bum down, and he'll never get over the fact that a little guy like me had him on the floor."

One more thing about this fight—it took place in spring training. Clearly this man was the ultimate McGraw Giant!

Al Bridwell took the trade hard and briefly refused to report to Boston. That afternoon, he sat gloomily in the stands and watched the Giants do fine without him, beating the Cardinals 4–0 on Hooks Wiltse's two-hitter. Nearly thirty thousand, the biggest crowd yet at the new Polo Grounds, turned out to see Mathewson pitch the final game of the home stand, and he rebounded from his drubbing two days earlier to beat the Cardinals 10–2. Though Matty got rave reviews, the game belonged to Buck Herzog, who made a spectacular return to the New York. The Giants trailed 1–0 when Herzog beat out an infield hit in the fifth inning. He stole second, sliding hard enough to give the shortstop a bloody nose, and scored the tying run, igniting a four-run rally. Later he tripled and scored another run. "He was given the joy mitt on the slightest provocation," noted the *Herald*. Added the *Times*, Herzog "smiled through the nine innings without the grin once leaving his frontispiece." Only on special occasions did Herzog risk hyperextending his frontispiece.

When the Giants left for their second western trip, they sported a 51–33 record, two losses behind the first-place Cubs, who awaited them at the end of the four-city odyssey. With Herzog sparking the romp in the home finale, optimism abounded. Sid Mercer echoed Damon Runyon's earlier comments, writing that "the idea pervades the McGraw camp that this trip is going to be abundant in breaks of the sort they are looking for. They believe they are set for a sprint."

The road trip opened on July 24 with an 8–3 win in Cincinnati. Rube Marquard socked two triples to lead the offense and somehow survived despite allowing nine hits and five walks, hitting a batter, and throwing three wild pitches. Nevertheless, McGraw was steaming that day about losing what he believed might be a more important battle—the Marty O'Toole sweepstakes. McGraw saw O'Toole, a spitball wizard from St. Paul, as the missing piece in his pitching staff, available immediately. Instead, O'Toole signed with the Pittsburgh Pirates. In papers filed in his protest to the league, McGraw claimed that O'Toole was offered to the Giants for $15,000, but when McGraw sent a check, it was used to drive up the price with Pirates owner Barney Dreyfuss. The sale price of $22,500 eclipsed the previous record and more than doubled what McGraw had paid for Rube Marquard three years earlier. McGraw eventually did get O'Toole—late in 1914, in time for the twenty-five-year-old to notch his twenty-seventh and final win in a fizzled major league career that spanned all of one hundred games.

When the Giants hit Cincinnati in July 1911, McGraw didn't know that O'Toole would succumb to what Damon Runyon, citing Marquard as a prime example, identified as "the official jinx which seems to pursue all these high-price marvels." McGraw was mad at Dreyfuss and St. Paul and the whole National League hierarchy, which he knew would support Dreyfuss merely because he had a signed contract and McGraw did not. That frustration accounted for his short fuse when things turned sour in the second Cincinnati game. In the fourth inning the Reds took the lead on a disputed tag play, and McGraw went berserk, earning an immediate three-game suspension.

The disputed run started the Giants toward losing two of the last three games in Cincinnati, squandering the momentum gained from Herzog's return. Add Drucke's demise in the last Cincinnati game and McGraw's own suspension, and the manager had plenty of worries as the Giants reached St. Louis. He should have considered what Damon Runyon and Sid Mercer knew, that the Giants were about to be blessed by extraordinary luck.

ONE QUALITY OF MYTHS is the blurring of truth and legend. Filtered through the eyes of newspaper reporters who embellished freely and contradicted themselves without flinching in the daily battle for readership, the Faust myth defies certainty. About the only thing the observers of the time agreed on was that despite a nondescript past and limited abilities, Charley Faust, the most unlikely candidate, launched a meteoric "career" that brought him mythical status. How it happened, how quickly the facts yielded to legend, has always been a matter of confusion. Consider what should be a simple issue: Faust's initial appearance in St. Louis. You would think his own teammates would remember exactly how Faust came to meet John McGraw in St. Louis on July 28, 1911. Instead, the four surviving versions differ widely, four variations on the creation of the Faust myth.

The best-known version is the Fred Snodgrass account in Lawrence Ritter's pioneering 1966 oral history *The Glory of Their Times*, which introduced Faust to a whole new generation. According to Snodgrass, Faust walked out of the stands at the St. Louis ballpark and approached McGraw on the field, gaining a tryout with a tale of having been assured by a fortune-teller that he would pitch the Giants to the championship. In *Pitching in a Pinch*, ghostwritten after the 1911 season, Christy Mathewson repeated the fortune-teller story but said that Faust first approached McGraw at Planter's Hotel in St. Louis. Only later did he go out to the ballpark and demonstrate just how unqualified he was to pitch for the Giants or anybody else.

A third version is a vivid tale told by Giants outfielder Red Murray in a 1934 interview, an account differing from Snodgrass's in almost every detail. Murray said that he and Art Devlin were in the St. Louis clubhouse when Faust approached them there. Faust insisted that he was a pitcher (there is no mention of a fortune-teller) and produced his own uniform (Murray said the pants didn't even reach down to Faust's knees), so Murray and Devlin sent him out to the field. The Cardinals, not the Giants, were practicing, and Devlin alerted their manager, Roger Bresnahan, to the rube's presence. According to Murray, it was Bresnahan and the Cardinals, not McGraw, who sent Faust stumbling, skidding, and sliding on the first of his trademark dashes around the bases. Only after surviving this ordeal did Faust meet McGraw and declare his intention of pitching the Giants to the title, whereupon McGraw signed him on the spot and put him on the Giants bench.

However much this version conflicts with the others, it remained powerful to Murray. "When the game was over," he told the interviewer, "and the boys went to the showers, what a sight poor Charley

The thirty-year-old FAUST clearly presented himself
to McGraw as a determined young man with a
vision of a glorious future. Within minutes, his Sunday clothes were tattered and filthy, but his mission
to save the Giants was under way. (Collection of
Thomas Busch)

was as he stripped. His body, legs and arms were skinned and bruised
from the base sliding, and he looked like a piece of raw meat. What a
sight he was, and how he must have suffered! When you do not know
how to slide bases and besides, wear no pads, such as ball players wear,
then and only then can you realize what the poor devil went through
sliding bases in St. Louis in mid-summer."

The fourth version belongs to Edwin V. Burkholder, the chief pur-
veyor of misinformation on Faust. Born in Marion in 1895, Burkholder
is buried only a wild pitch away from the Faust plot in the town's ceme-
tery. A real estate salesman, Burkholder peddled a story to *Sport* magazine in 1950, "The Curious Case of Charley Faust." Burkholder's
article was a mixture of misstatements of fact, total fabrications, and an

occasional accuracy lifted from Mathewson's book. The two biggest whoppers came in the first paragraph, thoroughly undermining his credibility. Burkholder quoted McGraw as writing in his last autobiography that "wherever Charley Faust is today, I want him to know that I give him full credit for winning a pennant for me—the National League pennant in 1911." A statement like that carries a lot of weight in a lead paragraph, but in truth McGraw did not even mention Faust in his several autobiographical writings.

Even more damning to Burkholder's credibility was his assertion that "there is some question whether he even played any part of an inning." Considering that Burkholder quoted Faust's postseason comments back in Marion on his New York successes, Faust surely let the hometown folks know that he did indeed play more than one inning. Yet this salient part of the Faust saga eluded Burkholder's memory—or else he didn't believe Faust. On the other hand, Burkholder was willing to report that Faust healed a serious hip injury to Hooks Wiltse merely by touching him. If Burkholder could jazz up his article with this concoction (no such incident was reported in 1911), if he could invent a tribute by McGraw to bolster his opening thesis that Faust was the unanointed MVP of the 1911 Giants, how could he miss Faust's most improbable genuine achievement? How much did Burkholder not know, and when did he not know it?

Burkholder contended that the fortune-teller story was invented by McGraw to generate publicity. On the contrary, said Burkholder, Faust was not only a formidable pitcher but also an "ardent" Giants fan. "Charley was our hero," Burkholder wrote, "the greatest ballplayer we ever knew. . . . To our youthful minds, Christy Mathewson himself had nothing to compare with the galaxy of curves Charley could twist around a batter's head and body. In that bush league, the bravest of the brave usually got weak-kneed when he was on the mound." Burkholder later bolstered this claim with the disclosure that after the 1911 season, Faust returned to Marion and tossed a no-hitter for the Methodists against the Presbyterians in his first start back in the Sunday School League.

This prowess led Faust to boast about the greatness he could no doubt achieve with his beloved Giants. This, Burkholder maintained, encouraged local pranksters to send Faust a fake telegram "signed" by

McGraw, inviting the Marion phenom to join the Giants. The telegram caused such an uproar that the gullible Faust didn't even bother to go home, instead borrowing bus fare to St. Louis, where he presented himself to McGraw at Planter's Hotel the next morning. True to form, Burkholder deviated from the eyewitness accounts by having McGraw dismiss Faust as a pitching prospect right there in the hotel lobby, then give him a uniform and let him pitch batting practice that afternoon.

It is easy enough to picture Charley Faust, a weak-minded thirty-year-old stuck in the middle of Kansas in the middle of a heat wave, racing off to meet his destiny at the instigation of either a fortune-teller or a fake telegram (or both, for that matter). Smarter people than Faust launched screwier pursuits that month. A man named Bobby Leach went over Niagara Falls in an eleven-foot steel barrel (and barely became the second daredevil ever to survive the plunge). In Los Angeles, ex-legend Wyatt Earp was arrested for trying to rig a game of faro. Then there was the bizarre scheme devised by Edward George Bernard to become a St. Louis fireman. Bernard was five feet, five inches tall and needed to be five-foot-seven. As he later explained in court, "I lay in a bathtub filled with warm water for twenty-four hours and then I had myself massaged and stretched until I was two inches longer." Three months after becoming a fireman, he was measured again, found to be five-foot-five, and fired.

Charley Faust let a fortune-teller talk him into thinking he could pitch the New York Giants to the pennant. The difference between Faust and Edward Bernard is that Bernard got to be a fireman until they figured out he couldn't see over the fire wagon's steering wheel, while Faust's insufficiency surfaced immediately and then he nonetheless managed to make that outlandish prophecy come true. Yet even this essential irony—the fulfillment of a prophecy that may not have been made—has become as garbled as the rest of the Faust myth over the years, to the point where several decades later an article in *Baseball Digest* stated that it was John McGraw whose fortune was told.

Somehow, Charley Faust got to St. Louis and wound up on the Giants bench as they shut out the Cardinals two days in a row—and perhaps a third day, as Marquard won his second game of the series on the last day of July. Snodgrass had the Giants leaving St. Louis after the first day Faust arrived, and he also had Faust joining them on the train to Chicago, in direct contrast to the Mathewson story (lifted by Burkholder) of McGraw's tricking Faust into racing back to the hotel for his ticket while the train left the station without him. All three accounts tallied in directing that train toward Chicago, which means that all three accounts were wrong.

The Giants went from St. Louis to Pittsburgh before ending the road trip in Chicago. Faust did not join them, and they paid a stiff price for McGraw's having stranded an undefeated jinx-killer at the St. Louis station. After Mathewson won the opener in Pittsburgh and the second game was rained out, the Giants lost four games in a row, each by a frustrating two runs, while both the Pirates and the Cubs passed them in the standings.

After two losses to the Pirates, the Giants opened a three-game series in Chicago with the traditional matchup of aces Mathewson and Three Finger Brown. Brown began the hostilities by beaning leadoff batter Josh Devore, who was knocked unconscious and left the game. Mathewson was battered by longtime nemesis Joe Tinker, whose key hit had beaten Matty in the 1908 replay that gave the Cubs the pennant. Tinker ripped four hits, drove in four runs, and stole home, a one-man gang as Brown held on to win 8–6.

The losing streak reached four with a tough 3–1 defeat on a day when Doc Crandall and Buck Herzog had their money stolen from their hotel room. The Giants stole nothing at all—no stolen bases for the second straight day—and managed only five hits. They saved their offense for the last game of the road trip, a 16–5 runaway. Chief Meyers drove in five runs, and the Giants stole eight bases. As a gesture of get-away-day goodwill, John McGraw called for consecutive double steals with the Giants already leading 13–4, giving the Cubs something to stew about as they dropped into second place, a half-game behind the surging Pirates and two games ahead of the insulting Giants.

The Giants had split fourteen games on the road trip, leaving McGraw disgusted on the overnight train back to New York. He had long since forgotten about Charley Faust and the St. Louis sweep. Luckily for McGraw and the Giants, Charley Faust had not forgotten about them.

5

The Ice Wagon Cometh

ON AUGUST 11 the Giants began a prolonged home stand that kept them in New York for a full month, except for two days in Philadelphia. For the third time in 1911, an atmosphere of opening-day festivity filled the Polo Grounds, now nearly finished. The second deck was in place, along with the much-ballyhooed asbestos roof and private boxes, the latter prompting Damon Runyon to quip that the resulting restrictions on the press box left it "two sizes smaller than a straw hat." Hot weather held the Friday crowd to ten thousand or so, even though only the bleacher seats remained exposed to the sun all afternoon. When the Giants entered the stadium, many of them were handed horseshoes, perhaps suggesting that they would need extra luck to beat their opponents, the Phillies, winners of nine games out of twelve against the Giants so far in 1911.

The big question on fans' minds that day concerned starting pitcher Christy Mathewson, who had unaccountably lost six of his last nine starts, including an eight-run drubbing in Chicago four days earlier. "To some," wrote Fred Lieb in the *Press*, "it appeared as if Matty went into the box with horseshoes, four-leaf clovers and rabbit's feet concealed on his person." In the *Morning Telegram*, Mathewson's outing got a more historical perspective from Heywood Broun, like Lieb part of the unmatched quartet of 1911 rookie New York reporters that also included Damon Runyon and Grantland Rice. Broun's coverage began, "Every now and then a king is called upon to show down. Christy Mathewson, who has held his title of premier pitcher in the National League by the divine right of the averages, has been compelled to face treason among his subjects this year. More than once the long-drawn cry of 'take him out' has been raised while Mathewson was in the box. The question 'What is the matter with Matty?' has been freely raised and not a few have deserted him for the cause of the French pretender, Marquard the Rube. Yesterday the king stood before 8,000 of his subjects and answered the question 'What is the matter with Matty?' His answer was, 'Nothing at all,' and his argument was clear and convincing."

Mathewson's argument, a 6–0 shutout, highlighted a strong team effort. Josh Devore goosed the Giants offense by leading off the first inning with a single and stealing two bases. The Giants led 4–0 after two innings, allowing Matty to coast. He scattered eleven singles, fanning nine when he needed to, and was helped by three double plays. On this day before his thirty-first birthday, Matty returned to form and, as Damon Runyon put it, "delayed that frequently rumored departure for Hasbeenville."

Midway through his game account, Runyon mentioned something that caught his eye at the ballpark that day. "McGraw introduced his latest volunteer player in the practice before the game," Runyon wrote.

> His name is Faust—Charley Faust—and he comes from Marion, Kansas. Charley is around forty, and is a pitcher and catcher, doing either with equal grace. He had a dream that he was to be a great baseball player, but the dream stipulated that he must play with the Giants and no other club, else the spell was crabbed. So Charley joined on with the Giants at St. Louis, and when McGraw pulled out of there and left him flat he waited around until he acquired enough money to come on to New York. McGraw fell in a fit—presumably from joy—when the smiling features of Charley appeared in the clubhouse door yesterday, but Mac fitted him with a uniform and Charley practiced like a good fellow. "No, I didn't come in a Pullman," he confided to an interviewer. "I can't sleep in the dumb things, anyhow."

This is not our only peek at what the scene must have been like when John McGraw marched into the Polo Grounds clubhouse and found Faust waiting for him. In *Pitching in a Pinch*, Mathewson wrote that Faust "entered the clubhouse with several inches of dust and mud caked on him, for he had come all the way either by side-door special or blind baggage." Hence Runyon's remark about Faust's alleged disdain for Pullman travel. McGraw, however joyless his actual fit, did give Faust a uniform and let him practice, no doubt in deference to his status as an undefeated jinx-killer. Runyon played the item straight, limiting his humor to the subtle sarcasms about McGraw's joy and about Faust pitching or catching "with equal grace," which may have eluded readers who hadn't seen Faust for themselves. All they could tell from Runyon's introduction was that this fellow had a dream, landed on the Giants, smiled a lot, and got to practice with the Giants again at the Polo Grounds.

Runyon, still sizing up Faust himself, postponed overt judgments. Runyon had begun covering baseball in Denver in 1906, but New York was still quite new to him. Earlier in 1911 he made a strong first impression on New Yorkers with a series of articles celebrating the eccentric exploits of Bugs Raymond. Working for William Randolph Hearst's New York *American*, Runyon stayed on the lookout for offbeat characters after Raymond's June exile. Something about Faust captured Runyon's fancy at its most susceptible, before he could know exactly why. He knew about part of their affinity: they were both born in Kansas, Runyon fittingly in Manhattan, seventy miles north of Marion. What he couldn't know yet was that they were born only one day apart, Runyon on October 8, 1880, Faust the next day. Thirty years later, their lives converged again on the edge of Manhattan, New York.

Only one other New York reporter noted Charley Faust's first appearance at the Polo Grounds — Sid Mercer in the *Globe* — another writer who could identify with Faust's humble beginnings. Unlike most writers, but like Faust, James Sidney Mercer was raised on a farm, this one in Paxton, Illinois, about a hundred miles south of Chicago. Also born in 1880, two months before Runyon and Faust, Mercer ran away from home at seventeen, heading for, of all places, Kansas, lured by rumors that wheat harvesters earned $5 a day. He hopped the freights but failed to reach Kansas, got stranded instead in, of all places, St. Louis. There he found a menial newspaper job that grew into a career, landing him in New York by 1905.

It isn't surprising that Mercer, a runaway farmer's son, and Runyon, the son of an itinerant newspaperman, showed the most interest in Charley Faust. More than the other writers, they could appreciate the exceptional nerve it took for Faust to embark on his mission to fulfill the fortune-teller's prophecy. Mercer's account portrayed Faust as a legitimate prospect. He wrote:

> Charley Faust, the all-round performer from Marion, Kan., had a long interview with John T. Brush in deep right field. Charley began talking in the eighth inning, and he was still there when the spectators wended their way across the green. Quite a crowd collected and the Pinks [Pinkerton guards] had to break up the conversation. Faust greatly pleased the crowd by the stuff he had in the warmups. He has a pitching windup that is a bear. His base running is also great. Manager McGraw is deeply impressed with Faust's perseverance and will keep him around for a while. Charley has a lot of new base running stuff, which he will uncork this afternoon before the game. Come early and you will miss nothing. Upon advice of counsel Charley has quit chewing tobacco to improve his wind. They haven't been able to catch him stealing a base yet, and when he gets "right" he will be a wonder.

Only that last comment suggested that there was something "wrong" with Charley Faust. Mercer extolled the crowd-pleasing features of Faust's "all-round" talent; after a single day in New York, Faust was already getting attention from one of the most popular baseball writers in the city. He also got the lowdown on chewing tobacco from the players, the kind of sound, healthful advice that made him trust similar advice down the road.

As for the conversation with John T. Brush, it must have concerned a possible contract for Charley Faust. By the eighth inning, the Giants led 5–0, and Faust no doubt approached the Giants owner with the premise that since he had won three straight games for the Giants in St. Louis and now one more easy win was guaranteed by his mere presence, he ought to get a contract confirming that he was the pitcher destined to lead them to the pennant. Brush watched games from right field, sitting in the back seat of his automobile, confined to a wheelchair by locomotor ataxia, a degenerative disease that ended his life shortly after the 1912 season. Brush, pained and humorless, could dodge Faust's scheme by deferring the contract question to McGraw, but it took the "Pinks" to rescue him from Faust's perseverance once the fans became curious.

JOHN T. BRUSH, the owner of the Giants, was
afflicted with a crippling disease. No doubt he
was laughing on the inside at the antics of
Faust, except when McGraw's mascot pestered
him for a contract. (Transcendental Graphics)

The remarkable feature of the initial articles by Runyon and Mercer is how many of Faust's recurring behavior patterns they pinpointed
right away. His perseverance consisted largely of an ability and willingness to harangue people at great length and with a singleminded disre-
gard for the improbability of success. They also caught his gullibility,
giving up chewing tobacco "to improve his wind" when his wind was
not the problem. The crowd response encouraged his desire to get
everything right so that the fortune would come true. He didn't know
that just a few weeks earlier, eight fortune-tellers were arrested at Rock-
away Beach in New York on fraud charges, and he wouldn't have cared
anyway. All he needed to know was that he was there, the Giants were

winning, the fans loved him, and he was finally where he belonged. As Runyon and Mercer could appreciate, he wasn't in Kansas any more.

Next day, New York readers got an unvarnished portrait of Charley Faust, courtesy of John Wheeler in the *Herald*. In his game coverage, under the subheading "Faust's Bit of Comedy," Wheeler wrote, "There was a capsule of comedy inserted into the preliminary practice that produced laughter enough among the twenty thousand to keep a Broadway comedy in good health for a season. A fortune teller told a product of the soil in Marion, Kan., recently that if he would join a regular club he would be a great ball player."

> "I'm tired of playing with the Marion Marauders," murmured Faust (that's his name), as he scanned the standing of the clubs in a week-old Kansas City Star one day. "The New York nine looks pretty near the top, and I've heard it's a good town."
>
> That's why 20,000 saw a long, angular person in a New York suit among the players. He looks as much at home in a baseball uniform as Mammoth Minnie, the champion fat woman of the Indiana State Fair, would in a cavalry charge. His every move is a picture. He runs like an ice wagon and slides as if he had stepped off a moving trolley car backward. He wears the old Kansas smile that went out of style in this town with side whiskers and affects the brick hair cut—shaved up to his hatline. Besides he is a charity worker, for he draws no salary. That's what a fortune teller in Marion, Kan., did for New York. He is here uninvited and says that, like the postage stamp, he is going to stick to one thing until he gets there. He plays ball as if he were a mass of mucilage.

Through figurative exaggeration, Wheeler made Faust an object of ridicule above and beyond the laughter of the Polo Grounds crowd. The concoction about Faust choosing the Giants made him sound dim and vaguely bored. Why would Faust choose a team from so far away when there were two teams in St. Louis? Four hundred miles wasn't far enough away from Marion? If Faust wanted an example that a Marion "product of the soil" could be a major leaguer, he might have followed the path of William "Tex" Jones, a first baseman from Marion who had a nine-game trial with the Chicago White Sox earlier in 1911 and might have been back in Marion in time to join the marauding city team which began a one-week road trip against towns like Twin City and Cottonwood Falls the same day that Faust was stranded in St. Louis. Would a man sporting an old Kansas smile peruse a newspaper and decide on New York? Or would a man who gave up chewing tobacco in a day be persuaded by a fortune-teller to seek the Giants?

August 13 marked the first appearance of Charley Faust in the New York *Times*, where Harry Cross wrote, "There was plenty of amusement for the early arrivals when 'Rube' Faust, a long lank person from St. Louis, started to cut up capers in the field. Faust has a hallucination that he is a ball player and is sticking to the Giants in the hope of landing a job. Just to let Faust show how good he was the Phillies let him get to the bat while they were warming up. He stole first, stole second, stole third, and scored while the Phillies were getting over a fit of laughter. 'Rube' says he is the only ball player who ever stole first. He did it while the pitcher was over at the bench getting a drink of water." No doubt. In addition to giving him the traditional "Rube" nickname (Rube Marquard was the exception to the rule, tagged with the monicker not because he was a goofball hick but because his pitching reminded people of Rube Waddell, a true goofball and the best early left-handed pitcher), the *Times* added this item in its Notes section: "The Giants seem to be pursued by persons with strange notions; first it was 'Bugs' Raymond, and now it's 'Looney' Faust." Another nickname came from Damon Runyon. "Prior to the opening of hostilities," Runyon wrote, "the big crowd was entertained by 'Hay Foot' Faust, McGraw's latest acquisition, under the personal humorous direction of McGraw himself. Faust is the Kansan who dreamed he was to become a great ball player with the Giants and who came all the way from the Sunflower State to attach himself to the club. Mr. Faust has already attained fame. It took the crowd about two minutes to get him in all his various angles. He pitched a little, caught a little, and ran a few bases, assisted by members of both the Phillies and Giants, while the crowd lay back and took in the show with loud screams of admiration and delight. Mr. Faust is a success as a provoker of laughter if nothing more."

"Mr. Faust has already attained fame." Two whirlwind days in New York and he was famous, "a success as a provoker of laughter." Charley Faust as laughingstock was the common thread of these early accounts. Notice that the Phillies went along with the charade of letting Faust show off his baseball skills, just as the Cardinals had gotten with the program in St. Louis. What truly made spectators howl at Faust's capers was the sincerity of his efforts to perform like a real player. In those days, spectators spent several hours in the ballpark, most of it before the game started, so everyone worked to provide steady entertainment. Even John McGraw, milking the crowd's acclaim, took part in Faust's early exhibitions.

All this and a ballgame, too, which unfortunately saw the return of the Red Ames hoodoo. Ames dueled with George Chalmers, a young right-hander with an exaggerated windmill windup. Chalmers held the Giants to four hits and struck out ten, while Ames's customary jinxed no-hitter lasted until the sixth inning. The game was scoreless in the eighth when Fred Merkle bobbled a ground ball for an error. One out later, a bunt single was compounded by a wild Buck Herzog throw, moving the lead runner to third base. A long fly ball scored the run that beat Ames. Doc Crandall allowed a ninth-inning run to make the final 2–0, leaving the large crowd deflated after Faust's riotous pregame show.

Sid Mercer's observations on that game did not appear the next day because his paper, the New York *Globe and Commercial Advertiser*, did not publish on Sunday. In Monday's edition he wrote that "Charley Faust, who would be leading the National League in stolen bases if he was a National League player and could get his practice stunts on the records, has been assigned to lookout duty. He will warm up to-day from 2 o'clock until the end of the second game. Charley steamed up on Saturday and would have stepped in at any moment to relieve Ames if his orders had read that way." Mercer almost made Faust sound like a legitimate double threat.

The *Herald* pinpointed the timing of Faust's Saturday warmup efforts. "After three men had fallen before Ames in the seventh—zing, zing, zing—McGraw sent Faust out to warm up in great trepidation." Damon Runyon noted that Arlie Latham helped Faust get loose, and Latham was just the man for the job. Walter Arlington Latham was the Giants' resident clown since becoming major league baseball's first full-time coach several years earlier. As a star third baseman in St. Louis in the 1880s, Latham emerged as the funniest man in baseball, and McGraw employed him as a part-time base coach and general agitator. The August 13 *Herald* also noted that "Arlie Latham is not jumping into the air and cracking his heels together when the Giants do stunts nowadays. He made a misstep while in Pittsburg on the recent trip and sprained his back."

Monday brought a doubleheader with the Phillies, one game the makeup of the one postponed by the April 14 fire. This prospect drew twenty-three thousand fans to the Polo Grounds, a massive Monday turnout rewarded by a pair of thrilling victories. John Wheeler wrote: "There comes a tide in the affairs of a ball club which if taken at its flood may lead on to a pennant, but if the tide goes out it probably means the baseball tomb and low, soft music. The double header yesterday was such a time in the schedule of the Giants."

The opener matched Rube Marquard against the great Philadelphia rookie, Grover Cleveland Alexander, who already had twenty-one wins to lead the majors. Both pitched masterfully, and Marquard led 2–0 until the Phillies tied it in the eighth inning on a bonehead play. With two outs and two strikes, catcher Chief Meyers tried to pick a runner off third base, and his wild throw allowed the tying runs to score. Aside from that, Marquard remained unscathed, and the two young stars dueled on into extra innings until the Giants won in the twelfth on Josh Devore's RBI hit. In a dozen innings, Marquard fanned thirteen and yielded only seven hits, strong enough to outlast Alexander, who held the Giants to six hits.

With Charley Faust continuing his lookout duty, Hooks Wiltse faced Giants nemesis Earl Moore in the nightcap. Because of the extra innings, everyone knew that darkness would claim this game before it went the distance. It was dark enough in the top of the fifth inning that Beals Becker couldn't spot a long fly ball, which went for a two-run home run to tie the game 4–4. In their fifth the Giants went ahead on a brilliant bunt single by Fred Merkle with two outs and two runners on. "It was as dark as the inside of a tar barrel" (said the *Times*) in the top of the sixth inning, and the Phillies knew this might be their last chance to tie the game. Wiltse got the first two Phillies, but catcher Tubby Spencer doubled, and Clarence Lehr pinch-ran for him. When Tom Madden smacked a single to center, Fred Snodgrass charged the ball while Lehr rounded third base. Lehr, who scored only two runs in his major league career, narrowly missed a third. He met Snodgrass's throw at the plate in a swirl of dust that erupted out of the darkness in front of umpire Mal Eason. Eason called Lehr out and in the same breath declared the game called on account of darkness. The Giants, sudden 5–4 winners, got to watch another team go berserk for a change. The Phillies mobbed Eason as thousands of joyous Giants fans stormed the field. Believe it or not, John McGraw came to the rescue, stepping between Eason and the Phillies and leading him safely off the field. That's how lucky the Giants got as soon as Charley Faust joined them. Even the umpires seemed to be on their side.

Details of the sweep filled the morning papers; only Sid Mercer commented on Faust. There is good reason why Mercer contributed the majority of known references to the man he later dubbed "the Human Blaster." The major New York newspapers were the morning papers, including the *Times*, Wheeler's *Herald*, and Runyon's *American*. Mercer's *Globe* hit the streets in mid-afternoon. By then, Giants fans already knew what happened yesterday and were on the verge of today's game. That freed Mercer to write almost anything he wanted. He hit the high points of yesterday's game, then moved on to commentary, profiles, historical perspectives, league business, trade rumors, miscellaneous notes, and extraneous oddities. Charley Faust began as a star of the last category but moved quickly up Mercer's ladder. At first, Mercer had the time and the room to keep Faust in print, so he did. Before long he couldn't help himself.

After the Monday sweep, he told his readers, "Here is some positive information about the pitching selections for the final Philadelphia game to-day. McGraw may train his Big Six gun on the enemy if he doesn't think it wise to start Otey Crandall or Plaintiff Drucke. If the Giants have the Phillies 15 to 0 with two out in the last inning and two strikes and three balls on a weak hitting pitcher, Charley Faust will go in to stop the rally." This was no idle exaggeration. McGraw had worked his pitchers hard all summer; except for two outings by Drucke, McGraw had used only his core of five pitchers since the start of July. They also had a doubleheader scheduled on Thursday. The fans were well aware of the pitching shortage, and here came Faust, ready to pitch. Faust, three days into his Polo Grounds adventure, couldn't fool the fans at the ballpark, but relatively few New Yorkers had seen him in action. Mercer felt a civic obligation to inform the reading public of the precise remoteness of Faust's chances of pitching in a real game.

The pitching staff got a break when Tuesday's finale with the Phillies was rained out. There were no days off, however, in Faust's crusade. Mercer again: "While the clouds burst over the Harlem yard yesterday the Giants were talking over their chances in the clubhouse. Charley Faust is getting to be a pessimist. Manager McGraw has informed him that a peculiar handicap may prevent him from appearing with the Giants. So far none of the visiting teams have been able to catch Charley stealing a base and a general complaint has been filed against him. He is too fast for the league, and his speed may bar him out." The Faust puzzle abounds with pieces like this, which make you wonder whether he ever popped a hamstring from constant leg-pulling. His gullibility caught everyone's fancy; in McGraw's case, his only defense against Faust's persistent pleas was to concoct reasons why he couldn't give Faust his richly deserved chance. To Faust, each excuse presented one more obstacle which he would simply have to overcome.

Each day presented a new opportunity for Charley Faust to fight for his due. In his notes section the next day, Mercer had this item: "Charley went downtown yesterday looking for his license to sign a New York contract, but couldn't locate the baseball commissioner." Modern readers can empathize with his plight, but this was nine years before Judge Landis became the first to hold that job. Too bad we don't know which player (or reporter) instigated this impossible mission. Baseball did have a governing three-man National Commission in 1911, headquartered in Cincinnati, with which Faust did become acquainted, but not until much later.

August 16 marked the opener of a five-game series with the Cincinnati Reds, Christy Mathewson's perennial patsies. He celebrated their arrival by beating them for the twenty-second time in a row. This one was a gem, a one-hitter to the ninth inning, when an unearned run made the final score 6–1. In his twentieth win of the season, Matty threw only ninety-two pitches, acclaimed as the new efficiency record. The Giants supported him with a six-run fourth inning sparked by a trio of hit-and-run plays, including triples by Fred Snodgrass and Chief Meyers. This outburst caught the attention of Red Ames, whose last pitching line, also against the Phillies, equaled Mathewson's but who lost 2–0. Mercer described Ames's reaction:

About half-past seven innings Leon Kalamity felt that he would not be needed any more, and so he sauntered to the clubhouse with Charley Faust, the applause provoking kid. He was dressed when the other Giants emerged. . . . "Boys," spake Leon K. Ames, "I wish to congratulate you on your expert support of expert pitching. It was great stuff. But . . . I would slip you a warning now concerning myself. . . . I am scheduled to heave one game of tomorrow's double-header. Now, my heart is apt to go pitty-pat if any great excitement bursts forth in my immediate vicinity, so I ask you all not to do anything like you did to-day. If you scored six runs behind me in one inning I'm afraid I just couldn't stand it. I love to pitch where the score is naught-naught, and I'm afraid that six runs would make me careless."

Somebody, Ames or Mercer, was joking, but the Giants got some kind of message. In the Thursday doubleheader, they pounded out twenty-five runs, scoring in all but four times at bat. Ten of those runs supported a no-doubt startled yet grateful Red Ames, who got his secret wish as the Giants gave him a safe 9–2 lead after five innings. In the second game, six first-inning runs allowed the unassuming Indiana cornshucker Otis Crandall to coast into the sunset until the game yielded mercifully to darkness in the eighth inning with the Giants ahead 15–2. This sweep lifted the Giants back into second place for the first time in two weeks, only one game behind the Cubs, due to follow the Reds into New York.

Everyone on the Giants had a big day, including Charley Faust, who got another load of publicity. The *Times* had a fine account of his performance. "Dick Hennessey and Rube Faust furnished so much fun between the two games that the crowd almost started a petition to have them perform instead of Cincinnati. Dick Hennessey is the Giants' batboy. Rube Faust isn't a boy. Dick is 10 years old, and covered first base in the practice with Merkle's glove. Manager McGraw covered second and Larry McLean was behind the bat. Red-hot grounders and throws with lots of steam were peppered at little Dick and he ate them up. The Reds envied him. Faust was warming-up Rube Marquard, and one of the shoots slipped through his hands and caught him in the eye. Down he went, and when revived went out and circled the bases on a bunt." That last image is Faust in a nutshell, a superb physical comedian in spite of himself, flattened one moment, up and away on another mad dash the next.

The between-games display made the lead paragraph in Heywood Broun's coverage in the *Morning Telegraph*, though Broun's first comment on Charley Faust was a succinct judgment. "The double bill at the Polo Grounds yesterday was certainly a bargain," Broun wrote. "For one admission the fan was able to see twenty-nine separate and distinct players in action, forty-seven hits and thirty-one runs. In the olio— and the term is pertinent, for both the first and second games were burlesques—Rube Faust, the hopeless case from St. Louis, made his thrilling dash around the bases, and Dick Hennessy, the schoolboy marvel, showed how first should be played."

The Charley Faust show also made Damon Runyon's lead. In fact, Runyon devoted the first third of his game coverage to Faust, but with the off-the-wall flamboyance that was already making his reporting style famous in New York. Runyon, who could write any kind of story but leaned toward features and odd sidelights, included play-by-play details in most of his game accounts, but his leads and recurring themes got more eccentric as the summer of 1911 went on. His Hearst editors loved Runyon's flights of fancy because they pulled in readers. He devoted half of one famous 1911 account to debating whether Fred Merkle or Roger Bresnahan was the best player to come out of Toledo. Another day, it was Josh Devore versus Three Finger Brown for the bragging rights of Terre Haute, Indiana. On August 18 he made Charley Faust the subject of one of his tangents, a long tangent to start his readers' day.

> "I don't know very much about this baseballing business," observed the slender young lady in the pink dress and ochre-tinted hat who had occupied a seat behind one of the steel pillars. "I don't know much about it, as I say, but I do think that was a splendid little entertainment they gave before and between the games. That Harry Sparrow is just killing."
>
> "That wasn't Harry Sparrow," denied her escort. "That was Charley Faust."
>
> "Well, I don't care," said the lady. "They play a lot alike, and I thought it was the best part of the programme. The rest was too serious." You can't please everybody.

There were some present who alleged that the Reds were endeavoring to steal Charley Faust's stuff. Charley was the very life of the party, starring in a vaudeville sketch which John J. McGraw arranged, with considerable forethought, for the intermission. It was well perhaps that he did so, because outside of that the bill was rather monotonous.

Mr. Faust, as may be remembered, is the first citizen of Marion, Kan.—a dreamer of dreams, and a player, after a fashion, of baseball. Moreover, he is the only warm-up entertainer in the world, discovered and copyrighted by John J. McGraw. Mr. Faust did a little batting yesterday, also a little base running; ditto a little sliding, which Mr. Faust does entirely upon one or the other of his ears. He was removed from the scene of the struggle by McGraw only because he was endangering the velvet surface of the sward.

Leave it to Runyon to provide a doll's-eye view of Faust and to prefer the comic relief to the Giants' scoring twenty-five runs. Harry Sparrow was a socialite who dabbled at baseball and occasionally worked out with the Giants, a dashing figure much admired by ladies in attendance. Runyon pursued the ironies of confusing Sparrow with Faust the next day in this note: "Charley Faust put on a brief performance for the audience prior to the storm, although McGraw had some difficulty in getting that incensed athlete to put on a uniform after Faust learned that a young lady had taken him for Harry Sparrow. McGraw compromised with his Kansas recruit by benching Sparrow for the day, and then Charles went forth and did things." It almost makes you believe it could have happened that way.

That day's game was rained out, leading to a Saturday double-header, the Giants' third twin bill in six days—all with a five-man pitching staff! Saturday afternoon's *Globe* carried this front-line reportage by Sid Mercer: "Charley Faust prepared for today's double header by arising at 7 o'clock this morning and partaking of a light breakfast, consisting of one cantaloupe, a planked steak with French fried potatoes, several slabs of toast, and much coffee. He holds the gastronomic belt at the Hotel Braddock, where most of the unattached Giants have their beans and beds." Mercer, it turned out, met with Charley Faust for more than breakfast. Monday morning, he published a column about their remarkable Saturday mission:

Charley Faust, the Kansas Zephyr, has declared himself in for whatever is coming to the Giants next fall. If he accomplishes all the tasks that are set forth in the contract that he signed last Saturday he will deserve one of the prize automobiles that are to be awarded to the best all around performers. Charley met the license commission downtown Saturday morning and was presented with a document of fearful and wonderful clauses. An ordinary athlete would have quailed before the conditions, but not Charley. He says he can pass the examination with flying colors, and now considers himself a full-fledged Giant, although the contract has not been countersigned by Manager McGraw.

The clause that Charley likes best is the one specifying that he shall inhale a planked steak with appropriate trimmings for breakfast each morning so as to give him strength to stay on the warming pan all afternoon. He says that sort of morning practice is not new to him.

When Charley spilled his name on the contract he was informed that the signatures of Capt. Larry Doyle and Manager McGraw would be required before it was binding. Forthwith he hurried to the Hotel Braddock, where Doyle is confined to his bed, and Larry added his signature, but Charley was loath to approach McGraw after Saturday's games, which sorely ruffled the temper of the Giant chieftain. When Faust put his John Hancock on the contract he paused a moment while Dick Taylor photographed him holding the pen, and then wrote in firm hand "Charles V. Faust."

"What does the 'V' stand for?" inquired Commissioner Billy Long. Charles drew himself up and tossed on a mantle of dignity. "Victory," he declared, "is my middle name."

What a strange scene that must have been, hardly the signing of the Declaration of Independence despite Mercer's Hancock line. Doyle was sidelined by back spasms and didn't go to the Polo Grounds for the Saturday doubleheader, so Faust took his quest to Doyle. They were joined by a team photographer, officials of a License Commission with no jurisdiction, and Mercer, who may have orchestrated the whole thing. The mock ceremony aimed to pacify a balky Faust, who insisted on getting a contract so he could launch his major league career.

McGraw's signature provided a gaping loophole in the fake contract Faust signed.

However bogus, Mercer's saga of the contract quest indicates the progress made by the "Kansas Zephyr" in his first whirlwind week in New York. This item led off Mercer's daily column (followed by an item about Harry Sparrow, no longer the prime pregame comic relief), and Mercer quickly assured his readers of Faust's intention to remain with the Giants. His confidence increasing daily, Faust eagerly committed himself to the contract's rigorous terms. The planked steak clause was essential for keeping him strong enough to meet his weighty new obligations. In truth, nobody put in a longer day at the ballpark than Faust did. After performing his assorted baseball stunts for a couple of hours before the game, he spent most of each game warming up beyond the outfield, eternally preparing for the moment when he would be called on to pitch the Giants to another win on their march to the pennant. Clearly this routine worked, for the Giants won seven of nine games in his first week in New York, leaving them only one game behind the Cubs heading into their Monday showdown. No wonder he claimed Victory as his middle name.

Only the second game of the Saturday doubleheader "ruffled the temper" of Manager John McGraw, though the whole afternoon tried his patience. The Giants entered the day with five straight complete-game victories, but that streak ended quickly when Rube Marquard couldn't make it through the first inning of the day. Marquard faced seven Cincinnati batters: walk, triple, single, line-drive double play, walk, single, and one more walk to load the bases. McGraw quickly brought in Hooks Wiltse, who got out of the jam and went six more solid innings. The Giants grabbed a 5–4 lead in the fourth inning, and that's where the score stayed. Wiltse left after seven innings, and McGraw brought in Christy Mathewson, scheduled to start the second game. He stifled the final six Reds hitters to save the tense win, the Giants' sixth in a row.

The nightcap brought the unthinkable—the Reds beat Mathewson for the first time in more than three years, ending his streak against them at twenty-two victories. Outfielder Mike Mitchell did most of the damage, hitting for the cycle and scoring three times. Matty departed after five innings, trailing 6–2, leaving a record Polo Grounds crowd of around thirty-five thousand stunned. The score stood at 7–2 when the Giants got their first two men on base in the bottom of the ninth, but Chief Meyers was called out on strikes. Meyers argued the call with umpire Cy Rigler, pitching a fit over the outside corner. Arlie Latham, coaching third, joined the beef, as did McGraw, and pretty soon all three Giants earned ejections. The Giants got two runs, but the rally fell short, and McGraw was in no mood to discuss the finer points of Charley Faust's contract.

The problem was that Faust's singlemindedness left no room for patience; he could not help pressuring McGraw to sign the contract. McGraw refused, of course, with an unexpected result, as Mercer reported in his next column:

> Charley Faust's desertion on the eve of an important set of games is considered rank disloyalty. Charley blew the job yesterday, and says that he will join the Brooklyn team. He thinks the Dodgers need help more than the Giants. Faust's grievance was the delay over his contract. He signed one, but Manager McGraw said his team was stocked right up to the limit and the only way for Charley to stick along was as a free agent. "It's now or never with me," declared Faust. "I have tried out and made good. If I am ever going to amount to anything I must sign a contract so I can get in the game. I have read in the papers that the crucial moment is at hand—a lot of crucial moments—and they are my favorite kind of moments. You need me in this Chicago series or you don't need me at all. If I don't sign to-day I leave the team flat on its back, that's all." There was nothing doing, so Charley turned in his uniform, and if he can't get a job in Brooklyn is going back to Kansas.

Impatient, Faust couldn't help bluffing, but a threat to defect to Brooklyn (or return to Kansas) would not change McGraw's mind. We don't know how far he got in Brooklyn, but it's certain that had he stayed there, he would have faced a scarcity of those crucial moments he favored. The Dodgers had a solid grip on seventh place, twenty-five games behind the Giants, making it doubtful that even Faust could do much for them. McGraw tried to mollify him by letting him remain with the team as a "free agent" (a status accorded the likes of Harry Sparrow), but Faust knew that he should be more than that. His bold assertion that the Giants would need him against Chicago or not at all was a deft bit of left-handed prophecy.

More than twenty thousand fans turned out for the Monday opener of the Cubs series, and with Charley Faust absent they had to wait for the game itself to witness baseball buffoonery. In the fourth inning, McGraw got ejected for the second game in a row for arguing a called third strike (with the bases loaded). This time he sent Larry Doyle (still benched by back spasms) out to take his coaching spot at third base. Doyle said the magic words as he passed plate umpire Bill Klem, who instantly banished Doyle back to the bench. McGraw's next coaching choice was Arlie Latham, baseball's first buffoon. Latham's ensuing stunt was not intentional, though. The Giants still had the bases loaded with two outs when Chief Meyers singled to center. One run scored and Fred Merkle rounded third base with the tying run. Latham got the notion that Merkle would be thrown out, but Merkle was going too fast to apply the brakes. Foolishly, Latham threw himself in front of Merkle, who was five inches taller and forty pounds heavier. They collided. Latham got some bruised ribs and rattled teeth, while Merkle was tagged out near where he fell, ending the rally (and numbering Latham's days as a base coach).

Yet the Giants rebounded from Latham's blunder to win this key game and get within percentage points of the Cubs. Rube Marquard saved them, working into extra innings for the second time in a week and limiting the Cubs to six hits in ten innings. The Giants won with two outs in the tenth inning and Beals Becker on third, when Art Fletcher bounced a single off Joe Tinker's glove. The Giants moved into a virtual three-way tie for first place with the Cubs and the Pirates, who suffered a blow that week when perennial batting champion Honus Wagner severely sprained an ankle that would cause him to miss twenty games.

In the middle game of the series, the Giants pitted Red Ames against Cubs ace Three Finger Brown. Ames wasn't sharp and got the hook after walking the first two batters in the fifth inning. Doc Crandall let those runners score, giving Brown a 5–2 lead. The Giants fought back, led by Josh Devore, who amazed the crowd with five first-pitch singles off Brown (prompting the Damon Runyon column about bragging rights in Terre Haute, where both Brown and Devore wintered).

Devore's fourth hit ignited an eighth-inning rally that tied the game 5–5. Crandall held the Cubs scoreless after the fifth inning, and in the bottom of the ninth, Brown walked Chief Meyers leading off. Red Murray ran for him and went to second on a sacrifice bunt by Crandall. Devore nailed another single, sending Murray to third, and Murray scored on a hit by Larry Doyle, back in the lineup after missing three games. The two late rallies thrilled the twenty thousand fans at the Polo Grounds, who saw their Giants move into first place for the first time since July 13.

"We take back everything we said about Charley Faust being a disloyal subject," wrote Sid Mercer the next day. "His pout was short-lived, and he was back on job yesterday running the bases in his own inimitable style and warming up like an oven before the game. In preliminary batting practice the Cubs missed everything Charley pitched, and he says that he will surely shut them out if McGraw permits him to pitch to-day. Charley is still a free agent, but will stick because he would be conscience-stricken if he deserted in the thick of the hottest fight of the year." That last comment was echoed in the *Herald*, which noted that "All is not lost. 'Charley' Faust has rejoined the Giants and warmed up yesterday. He said that he hadn't the heart to jump the club at such a critical time." Of course Charley Faust wouldn't desert the Giants. As the *Herald* added one day later, "Charles Faust is no 'simp.' When the Giants gained first place he reported again."

Mercer's comment about batting practice was the most significant item of the day. This was the first mention of Faust's pitching batting practice to the opposing team. Earlier, the Phillies let him bat and run the bases against them, but getting to the mound meant much more to Faust. After all, he was a pitcher, so any chance to pitch to a living, breathing batter was a major event to him. He didn't care that it was batting practice, and he probably didn't notice that the Cubs missed his pitches on purpose. The amazing thing was that the Cubs, visiting New York for a crucial series, would allow anyone wearing a Giants uniform to strike them out, albeit as part of a pregame, crowd-pleasing charade. Even the hated Cubs succumbed to Faust's endearing enthusiasm, shilling for the sham pitcher. Their failure to hit the ball only increased Faust's confidence in his claim that he would pitch the Giants to the pennant.

The Cubs took the final game 6–2, beating Hooks Wiltse to regain first place. "The preliminaries were better than the main bout," commented the *Herald*. "Four fights in the grandstand kept early comers on edge." The main bout turned early when the Cubs scored three times in the first inning. Lew Richie held the Giants down with help from catcher Jimmy Archer, who picked two Giants off and allowed no stolen bases. In fact, the Giants didn't steal a single base in the whole series, the first time that happened in 1911.

An August 24 doubleheader (their fourth in eleven days) began a four-game series with the Pittsburgh Pirates. More than thirty thousand fans endured intermittent rain to catch a pair of swift pitching duels. Three hours sufficed, thanks to a paltry total of seven runs and twenty hits for the afternoon. The opener went to the Pirates, 3–1, as Babe Adams outdid Christy Mathewson. The nightcap belonged to Rube Marquard. He tossed a two-hitter, both hits in the fifth inning, and struck out eleven while walking none, the best start of his young career. The Giants managed only four hits but scratched out a pair of runs, all that Marquard needed.

With action on the field scarce, the fans diverted themselves by scanning the sky. They hoped for a view of that month's biggest celebrity, aviator Harry N. Atwood. Unknown two months earlier, Atwood typified the meteoric celebrity accorded to adventurers. Motorized flight, still in its infancy, provided a steady source of amazement to the public, with weekly news of fresh records (distance, speed, duration, altitude, or some combination) and fresh deaths (crashes killing one or two fliers at a time). Indeed, 1911 began with the New Year's Eve deaths of record-setters John Moisant and Arch Hoxsey, whose records expired almost as quickly. That did not slow the pursuit of greater feats, even while nearly one hundred aviators perished during the year.

The public loved the notion of daring explorers who might suddenly appear right above you. The mere sight of something in the sky energized people. On August 20 a runaway hot-air balloon drifted over from New Jersey, and a reported crowd of ten thousand chased it across Manhattan until it descended near Times Square.

Atwood, a Bostonian, entered the public's eye in July, when he won the New York *Times* Trophy by flying from Boston to Washington,

D.C., there greeted by President Taft. His next exploit was to challenge the world distance record of 1,155 miles, set earlier in the year in Europe. On August 14 Atwood took off from St. Louis, heading for New York via Chicago, Cleveland, and Buffalo. He hoped to make the 1,265-mile trip in ten days, though the usual combination of mechanical problems and spotty weather extended him two extra days. In Cleveland, 150,000 spectators lined the shore of Lake Erie to cheer him on, and crowds dotted the landscape of every town Atwood passed over en route.

By August 24 Atwood and his biplane were wowing citizens along the Hudson River, and he was expected to land in New York City that afternoon. At the Polo Grounds, word of Atwood's approach spread like fire around the stands early in the second game, and the game nearly stopped as everyone looked up. Even John T. Brush struggled out of his car to see Atwood. It was a false alarm, with Atwood nowhere in sight; in a typical mishap, the engine had fallen out of Atwood's plane near Nyack, twenty-five miles from the city, forcing an emergency landing and a final delay for repairs. Atwood set his record on August 25 instead, simultaneously thrilling and disappointing thousands. He thrilled the spectators who lined Riverside Drive and other streets and watched his approach, but a huge throng who paid to get into the Sheepshead Bay track, the expected stopping point, came up empty when more mechanical problems forced a landing at Governors Island.

In 1911 only one industry was equipped to exploit instant fame: vaudeville. The *Times* reported that "vaudeville managers got after Atwood as soon as he reached the Knickerbocker Hotel Friday. One of them offered him a big salary for a ten weeks' engagement." Atwood had netted only $6,000 from his trip, and this would enable him to double or triple that sum without risking more than his pride. "It would mean enough money for me to finance my trip across the continent without outside backing," said Atwood, very tempted. William Randolph Hearst had offered $50,000 to the first aviator to fly across the continent, the biggest aviation prize yet. Atwood wound up passing on both undertakings. Instead, the Hearst Prize went to Calbraith P. Rodgers, who didn't even have time to spend the money (or accept a pending vaudeville offer) before a crash in California killed him early in 1912. Such was the fragility of fame.

That week, the *Herald* introduced a daily baseball feature that became known as the Frame of Fame, a boxed-off paragraph on the star of the day. Fred Snodgrass got the first boost for driving in three runs in the second Cubs game, and Rube Marquard earned it for his two-hitter against the Pirates, with the assurance that "if Marquard continues to be the hero of each game in which he appears his cabinet will glow as often in this paragraph of uplift." The *Morning Telegraph's* Heywood Broun wrote that "Mr. Marquard afforded his brother member of the Association of High Prices, Mr. O'Toole, an object lesson. Meantime, Charley Faust was kept warmed up in the outfield to spur the Reuben onward." Marquard, relaxed with his safety net in place, took a no-hitter and eight strikeouts to the fifth inning.

Charley Faust had more on his mind that day than backing up Marquard. Sensing his fame growing daily, he tried to figure out how to cash in on it. A playing contract still his main goal, he again approached the team owner. The *Times* reported that "Rube Faust had a long talk with President John T. Brush yesterday. There seems to be some slight difference of $10,000 in the terms of Rube's contract." That's a delicious item, considering that Christy Mathewson's salary in 1911 was only $9,000. If the *Times* was accurate, it's fair to estimate that Faust asked for $10,000 and Brush countered by offering him nothing.

The August 25 game proved one of the strangest of the year. It probably should not have been played, for an overnight downpour left the field muddy and dark clouds threatened a further deluge, but the alternative was yet another doubleheader the next day. So, in front of only a few thousand diehard fans, they played a sloppy game with a wild finish. How drenched was the field? It was too wet for Charley Faust. As Sid Mercer put it, "Charley Faust says he will take no foolhardy chances on the base canals to-day, as his rubber uniform has not arrived. After one header in the second base morass yesterday the Kansas athlete arose with gobs of affectionate mud clinging to various parts of him. And besides, he can't swim." How dark was it? Midway through the game, John T. Brush had his auto's headlights turned on so he could see balls hit to the outfield. How sloppy was the game? Larry Doyle committed three or four errors (depending on which paper you read), and Red Ames walked four batters and hit another in less than three innings pitched.

Luckily for Ames, Doc Crandall rescued him, setting down Bill McKechnie with the bases loaded to end the third inning with the Giants trailing only 1–0. Crandall's sacrifice fly tied the game, and the combatants sloshed along at 1–1 until the eighth inning. That's when it got weird. The Pirates took the lead thanks to Doyle, who booted a leadoff grounder and let another ball skid through his legs with two outs to send the runner home. Leading 2–1, Pirates pitcher Elmer Steele walked Buck Herzog on four pitches and threw two straight balls to Art Fletcher. For some reason, Arlie Latham (coaching at third base again, with McGraw at first base) chose that moment to get rambunctious. The *Herald's* John Wheeler provided the richest account of the bizarre scene that followed:

> Latham began reciting some of his own lines, making [plate umpire] Henry O'Day the hero of the monologue. Henry did not care for the publicity, and turned toward Latham to put him off the field just as Steele wound up and unravelled one that McKechnie on first base almost caught. Of course it did not count, as O'Day was not looking. Henry then walked toward third base and induced Latham to leave. "Arlie" paused to make some reply, no doubt charged with his frostbitten wit. . . . The game was held up and Steele had the much needed chance to rest and to steady his nerves. McGraw rushed over from the first base coaching box. "Get off the field," he shouted at Latham in the voice which he does not use at afternoon teas. Latham ran for the club house. This is the first time in the history of the game, according to the records, that O'Day and McGraw have agreed on anything. Steele . . . pitched another ball, which would have been the fourth if Latham had not sidetracked the attention of O'Day.

Instead, Fletcher popped out, and it almost cost the Giants the game. Almost. With two outs, Doc Crandall singled, and he and Herzog both scored when Josh Devore blasted a triple. Crandall preserved the lead in the ninth, and the Giants had overcome the Pirates, Doyle and Latham to record a 3–2 win that put them into first place again.

On Saturday, August 26, the finale of the Pirates series drew a crowd of twenty-five thousand despite early rain and dark skies that hampered visibility. They came to see Christy Mathewson pitch but remembered the pregame hijinks just as much, thanks to one of Charley Faust's most celebrated performances. Four accounts exist, including the first mention of Faust by Fred Lieb in the New York *Press:* "Before the game the gathering throng was treated to a variety of entertainment. The Catholic Protectory Band did a musical turn in front of the grand stand and Charley Faust, the pride of Marion, Kan., who yearns to be a Giant, slid around the bases, collecting much mud, applause, and many laughs. The comedy ended with Faust leading the band, wielding the baton as he would a baseball bat, while Rube Marquard and Josh Devore marched across the field with extended chests, keeping brisk step to a lively march." The *Times* carried a more perfunctory note: "The boys' brass band from the Catholic Protectory played ragtime, and everybody seemed quite happy, even if it did look as if the rain would spoil the day's fun. Rube Faust showed more of his versatility by leading the band. He did that just about as well as he plays ball." We would expect no less.

For once, Damon Runyon did not feel compelled to embellish: "Charley Faust was on hand and all the members of the warm-up team, under the management of Harry Sparrow, furnished their customary entertainment for the early comers. Rube Marquard, in a red sweater, marched in alone and unattended to the tune of 'Alexander's Ragtime Band,' and received an ovation which caused him to doff his little cap in astonishment, but not chagrin. Charley Faust took the baton from the band leader and conducted the youngsters through the mazes of a dreamy waltz to the vast amusement of the crowd. Charles explained afterward that he used to play with the Sunflower State Cornet Band when he was home in Marion, Kan."

Even combined, these accounts paled next to the *Herald's*, the best coverage yet of Charley Faust. Fittingly, the only sour note in John Wheeler's comic description was Faust's contract lament. Under the subheading "Faust Features Again," Wheeler went to town.

> "Charley" Faust, the famous favorite of Marion, Kan., kneed his way into the calcium glow before the game. First he did splendidly—ran around the bases.
>
> "What you need to time that guy," pointed out an observer, "is a calendar and not a watch."
>
> Then the "bug" stepped up in front of the band, seized a piece of music and led with the grace of Gatti-Casazza. The

CATHOLIC PROTECTORY BAND members show their sound training by ignoring the directorial efforts of Charley Faust, trumpeted by John Wheeler as the former leader of the Silver Cornet Band of Marion, Kansas. (New York *Herald*)

chauffeur of the French horn thought it was so funny that his face slipped and he got off on another tune altogether, and had to be recalled by the cornetist.

"Sure," said Faust, "I've had experience. I used to lead the Silver Cornet Band back in Marion when Hiawatha was first popular. But I want you to make my grievances known in the press, the powerful press. Here I've been with this club for two weeks now and have brought them up into first place and I haven't any contract yet. It's going too far."

McGraw wants to take Faust on the next trip with the club. It is an old superstition among ball players that when a "bug" joins a club it will win a championship, and the players fully believe Faust is a good omen.

There was more. In the Notes section, Wheeler mentioned Faust twice, though one was a summary of the above. "Everything was merry at the start except the moisture. Before the curtain rose fully twenty-five thousand were spread across the timbers. Charley Faust played Sousa with the Catholic Protectory Band and the noise was torn off in chunks." The other item mocked Faust's reputation with double-edged humor. "'Who's the most valuable man on the Giant team to-day?' asked one fan of another. 'Faust,' was the reply, 'because they won't let him play.'"

Best of all, the *Herald* published a photo of Charley Faust leading the band, the only "action" shot of Faust in print. Faust appears in profile, loosely lumped into his Giants uniform, a smallish cap perched atop his large head. The conductor's baton, gripped waist-high, seems a useless prop as Faust gazes past his long nose at a dozen seated youngsters whose eyes are clearly focused on their music sheets. Not one of them is looking at their "leader," unlike the rapt fans in the front rows and several players standing by the dugout. Faust had no more influence on creating the music (Sousa, a waltz, ragtime, or whatever) than he had on creating baseball wins, yet there he stands, frozen in time, a farcical figure devoted to his task.

After this performance, the Giants thrashed the Pirates 6–2, aided by six errors and four stolen bases. Christy Mathewson picked up his twenty-first win but got as much notice for stealing a base, as did Chief Meyers. Suddenly the Giants had a game-and-a-half lead on the second-place Cubs, while the Wagner-less Pirates had faded four games back.

John McGraw made the *Herald's* Frame of Fame for his general leadership and for forcing his running game on a league worn down by the long summer. He had maneuvered his five-man pitching staff wonderfully, so that when the Cardinals came to town on Monday, August 28, he had his two left-handed starters ready to stifle them as they had in St. Louis during Charley Faust's debut weekend exactly one month earlier.

The Giants scored only a pair of second-inning runs in the opener, but the Cardinals were never in the game. Rube Marquard, the hottest pitcher in baseball, followed his two-hitter against the Pirates with a one-hitter this time. The lone blemish was a solid single by Rube Ellis leading off the seventh inning, and Marquard fanned nine to take over the league lead in strikeouts and raise his record to an eye-opening 18–5. The only threat came in the ninth inning, when two errors and a walk loaded the bases, but Marquard got Pee-Wee Hauser for the final out.

The Tuesday game should not have been played. Another rainy night turned the field into a swamp, and the wet, dark day limited the crowd to no more than a thousand amphibians. Why play the game? John McGraw didn't want to squander a shot at another easy win over the hapless Cardinals. Or so he thought. Hooks Wiltse was unable to follow Marquard's act this time, and the visitors led 4–1 in the sixth inning before McGraw got his wish. The Cardinals ace, Bob Harmon, lost the strike zone, according to plate umpire Jim Johnstone. As Harmon struggled to his ninth walk of the game, Johnstone cleared the Cardinals bench for criticizing a strike zone they could hardly see, ejecting fourteen players. The Giants took advantage of a dozen walks to come from behind and win 7–5.

Despite the travesty and the skimpy crowd, playing that game turned into a blessing when the last two games of the series were postponed by rain. Because it was the Cardinals' last visit to New York in 1911, the games were rescheduled for the final New York invasion of St. Louis in mid-September. Another rainout would have meant three straight doubleheaders in the heart of the long road trip. Only McGraw's greed for winning spared them.

Charley Faust received only one mention in the press during this series, a brief note in the *Herald*. "There is a rumor that 'Tony' Faust has been gunning for 'Arlie' Latham's job. The well known coach was again among the missing. Gone, but not forgotten." Latham's absence stemmed from a three-game suspension for his run-in with Hank O'Day in the Pittsburgh series, but there is no evidence that John McGraw ever let Faust coach the bases. The strange thing was the moniker Tony. Why Tony Faust? It was probably a reference to a St. Louis restaurateur who had landed on the front page of the New York *Times* three months earlier. A son-in-law of famed brewer Adolphus Busch, Tony Faust suffered a nervous collapse in New York en route to Europe. According to the *Times*, the next day "Mr. Faust had so far recovered from Tuesday's attack as to attend a ball game [the Giants hosting the Cubs], but the excitement and exertion at the ball grounds brought on a relapse and yesterday he was sent to a sanitarium." Was the *Herald* suggesting that the excitement and exertion of Charley Faust's quest to be a Giant might lead him to a sanitarium?

In the short run, Faust's efforts landed him in vaudeville. Witness this extraordinary feature by Sid Mercer in the August 31 *Globe*:

> Charley Faust had business down town yesterday and didn't show at the ball yard. Charley is going into vaudeville—for one week only. He will not sign for a longer engagement because he feels that he will be needed on the western trip of the Giants.
>
> Willie Hammerstein heard about Faust and is going to pay him more for one week than he could make working all season in the Kansas harvest field. Charley is crazy like a fox. He has had a lot of press agents working for him here, though he didn't know it, and his accomplishments are well known to thousands of the fans.
>
> Faust started rehearsals for his act yesterday. Owing to the limitations of the stage, the Kansas Zephyr cannot pull all of his Polo Ground stuff, but he is working on a new "wind up" which would make a contortionist curl up with envy. With a big sheet and a colored spotlight this wind up will resemble a fire dance.
>
> Finishing the act, Charley will slide across the stage on his gastronomic department to a make-believe base. He has a new slide which he calls the "fall-apart." His act ought to go well.
>
> "I learned it all out of a book," Faust informed McGraw, "not only how to run bases but the pitching motions that I use."
>
> "It must have been a blank book," replied the manager.

Wow! Less than three weeks after arriving in New York, Faust had enough of a following to cash in, even though a vaudeville deal couldn't quite make up for the continuing lack of a playing contract with the Giants. Chief among Faust's "press agents" was Sid Mercer, who probably collected some kind of fee for "discovering" Faust and, for all we know, wrote the act himself. Certainly Faust, whose show-biz career to date extended only as far as wielding that conductor's baton a few days earlier, would have had no idea how to piece together an "act." Instinctively he might come up with a "fall-apart" slide, but not a whole act. Still, the fact that someone would pay him to learn and perform an act indicates that he was no idiot, not the retarded incompetent some observers have believed him to be.

Amazingly, in this wondrous time when vaudeville was king and spawned the same frenzied competition as every subsequent form of entertainment, Charley Faust was precisely the kind of attraction sought by Willie Hammerstein, the ultimate vaudeville huckster. Son of the first Oscar Hammerstein, the opera impresario, and father of Oscar Hammerstein II, the Broadway songwriter, Willie was a Barnum-like entrepreneur who would do anything to get people into his theater. No act was too outrageous for Willie, who proclaimed that "vaudeville is one damn thing after another." His most notorious booking was "Sober Sue," who offered a $1,000 prize to anyone who could make her laugh. Nobody could. The best comics tried, and their antics drew big crowds for months. Eventually word got around that Sober Sue's facial muscles were paralyzed. She had been laughing the whole time—at the people who paid to see her.

Willie Hammerstein ran the Victoria Theatre of Varieties, which sat on "The Corner" of Broadway and 42nd Street. Widely regarded as the acme of vaudeville theaters and the nuttiest place in town, the Victoria was the hub of the city in 1911. Decades before Ed Sullivan, Hammerstein satisfied the public's eternal appetite for glimpsing the newest celebrities in the flesh. He would book them for a week or two, though the exposure was quite often humbling. He reached his all-time low in this regard in 1911, when he booked Lillian Graham and Ethel Conrad. In June the pair shot a hotel owner named W. E. D. Stokes during a dispute over the newly married Stokes's attempt to retrieve compromising letters he had sent to Graham. Each girl initially claimed to have pulled the trigger, which should have tipped off Hammerstein that they might have trouble learning their act. The story splashed across front pages for weeks, while the public took sides on whether or not Stokes deserved it. Stokes recovered; the girls got out on bail, and by December they were playing the Victoria. True to form, Willie billed them as "The Shooting Stars." But they couldn't remember their lines and had a disastrous run.

Despite the Hammerstein hype, Charley Faust did not perform at the Victoria that first week of September. A seventeen-act extravaganza was set to open the Victoria's fall season, so Faust, like many novice troopers, played one of the smaller houses for seasoning. He wound up at the Manhattan Theatre, owned and managed by Billy Gane, a big Giants fan. The Manhattan Theatre was originally the Manhattan Opera House, built by Oscar Hammerstein. Financial troubles in 1909–10 forced Hammerstein to sell it, and it became a vaudeville house. One of the smaller vaudeville venues, it had 1,100 seats and a top price of twenty-five cents. We do not know whether Willie Hammerstein and Billy Gane had a working arrangement or whether Gane jumped in when Hammerstein hesitated. Undoubtedly the Manhattan suited Charley Faust better than the mammoth Victoria, at least for his inaugural booking.

Sid Mercer concluded his announcement of Charley Faust's detour to vaudeville with a curious addition to Faust's original fortune-teller saga. "After the world's series," Mercer claimed, "Charley is going to take his divvy and hike to 'Frisco. The same fortune teller who sicked Faust on to McGraw by telling him that he must join the Giants induced Charley to cough up another half dollar, for which he smoked a pill and saw a girl who is waiting for Faust. Her name is Lulu, and she lives in 'Frisco. Charley has never been in that city, and he doesn't know her last name, but minor details like that doesn't [sic] bother him. He found the Giants, and he is going to find Lulu."

What do we make of this piece of the puzzle? Sid Mercer did not as a rule make things up, and he already had a major scoop with the vaudeville news. Yet only one other writer mentioned the possibility of a Lulu, and not until weeks later. If Faust had mentioned Lulu before, someone would have trumpeted it. Of course, if Faust had mentioned Lulu right away, it would have made him seem twice as daydreamy and hopeless and possibly made people leery of giving him any chance at all. In the context of Mercer's whole article, however, it can be seen as the logical progression of Faust's expectations as he expressed them to his biggest booster. By this time, Faust sensed his indispensable place on the Giants, allowing himself only a brief self-indulgence in vaudeville before rejoining the team for their final western trip. He also knew he'd be there for the World Series, now that he'd led them into first place. The vaudeville offer was recognition enough of his talents to let his confidence soar, so he dared to share with Mercer the second part of the fortune-teller's prophecy. When Mercer predicted that Faust would find Lulu, how could anyone doubt him?

While Charley Faust remained in New York to rehearse, the Giants made a two-day trip to Philadelphia to play three games, one a makeup of an April rainout. His present absence only made his future presence more vital, according to the papers. Sid Mercer, discussing the upcoming road trip, wrote that "At the same time McGraw will have five games on his hands in St. Louis, but he will muster a strong array of pitchers. Every twirler now with the team—even Charley Faust—will make the trip." In the *American*, Damon Runyon explained why: "Charley Faust, of Marion, Kan., who is now being prepared for a vaudeville performance, will have a regular job with the Giants for the balance of the season. Charles will probably be taken on the final swing around the ring by McGraw, who has the proper appreciation of an attraction. Charles was kept warming up in the outfield during a recent game when Marquard was shutting out his opponents with a pair of hits, and after the game he approached the manager with a broad smile: 'Well, I certainly did my share,' quoth Charles, mopping his brow."

The Giants spent the first two days of September avenging their disastrous Fourth of July trip to Philadelphia. They swept the series, winning three nailbiters. In the opener of Friday's doubleheader, Christy Mathewson outlasted Giant-killer Earl Moore 3–2 in eleven innings. Matty got his twenty-second win thanks to a two-out, game-winning double by Josh Devore.

The nightcap brought another scintillating performance by Rube Marquard, who pitched his second consecutive one-hit shutout. This game was scoreless to the eighth inning, when the Giants got a pair of cheap runs for their new ace. Only one man reached base against Marquard, a two-out single by first baseman Fred Luderus in the fifth inning. For the third straight start, Marquard made two runs look like a dozen as he completed what was arguably the most overpowering three-start sequence in pitching history. In twenty-seven innings, he allowed a paltry four hits and one run, walking just three and striking out thirty. If this last start was any indication, he could even pitch great ball without Charley Faust backing him up in the outfield.

John McGraw unleashed another hot pitcher for the Saturday game. Doc Crandall hadn't started in two weeks but had picked up three wins in relief since then. This game looked easy for a while, especially when Crandall's two-run home run gave the Giants a 7–2 lead in the sixth inning. But Crandall faltered in the eighth, allowing three runs, and got in trouble again in the ninth. Who came to the rescue of the Giants' chief rescuer? The untouchable Rube Marquard, relieving for the first time since July 4. Marquard entered with one out and two runners on, and a walk plus a Larry Doyle error cut the lead to 7–6 and left the bases loaded. Nobody could hit Rube, though, and he retired Fred Beck and Fred Luderus to save the game and complete the sweep that left the Giants three and a half games ahead of the second-place Cubs.

"Comedian Faust Ill," read a subheadline in Damon Runyon's coverage of that Saturday game. "McGraw did not bring all of his vaudeville show on this trip, Charley Faust, the noted Kansan, being ill in New York. Little Dick Hennessy, the sixteen-year-old mascot of the Giants, was brought along from the Polo Grounds, however, and gave an exhibition of first base play that almost made up for the absence of Faust." What a concept: "almost made up for the absence of Faust." Long before Charley Faust first set foot in the Polo Grounds, Dick Hennessy had wowed crowds with his legitimate fielding prowess; now Faust's inept displays upstaged him. His stock rose again in Faust's absence, and days later Runyon reported that "'Spud' Hennessy, the Giants' mascot, is one proud young man just now. McGraw is going to take him on the final trip arrayed in a miniature Giant uniform. . . . He has reveled in the possession of a Giant cap all season, but now he is to have a real uniform throughout."

On Monday, the Giants rode an eight-game winning streak back to the Polo Grounds for a Labor Day doubleheader against the Boston Rustlers. The morning opener satisfied the crowd of ten thousand, who saw the Giants steal six bases and give Red Ames a big early lead that helped him coast to a 6–4 win. The afternoon game drew more than thirty thousand fans anticipating another gem by Rube Marquard. If anything, Marquard was stronger than ever. Through seven innings, he had a 5–0 lead, a two-hitter, and a dozen strikeouts. Facing a Boston team with an atrocious 32–91 record, Marquard looked like a sure bet to extend the winning streak to ten games.

Instead, Marquard's joyride ended with a jolt in the eighth inning. Two hits and a walk loaded the bases with nobody out, and a pair of errors by Art Fletcher opened the floodgates. Five runs scored, and suddenly the game was tied. Marquard got through the ninth inning safely, tying his National League season high of fourteen strikeouts, but he ran out of gas in the tenth. With one out, five straight Rustlers banged hits off a clearly weary hurler. For some reason, John McGraw left Marquard in to take this second pounding in three innings, even though Christy Mathewson was well-rested and the Giants had the luxury of two off days to follow. The fans went into shock as the lowly Rustlers took an 8–5 lead to the bottom of the tenth. At that, the Giants almost pulled the game out, rallying for two runs and leaving the bases loaded as Chief Meyers was robbed of a hit on a screaming line drive to end the game.

Charley Faust missed this shocking loss, and from Marquard's swift demise you might almost think that sometime in the eighth inning Marquard surveyed the outfield and noticed the absence of his grinning shadow who had faithfully warmed up during earlier gems. It's as if Rube thought, "Gee, it's too bad Charley ain't here to see this one," and lost his focus on reality. How else can you account for a pitcher's allowing six hits over thirty-four innings and a dozen hits in the next three? What about McGraw's paralysis? Without their good-luck charm on hand, the Giants and their leader were powerless against a belated assault by a last-place team.

We don't know how the news of Marquard's collapse affected Charley Faust on his first day in vaudeville. No Faust news appeared until Wednesday's disquieting note from Sid Mercer. "Charley Faust has been forced to temporarily cancel his baseball and vaudeville engagements. Muscular rheumatism or something like that prevents him from exercising his talents. Charley has asked for waivers on his ailment." Considering how much rehearsal must have gone into perfecting his "fall-apart" slide on a wooden stage, he should have had a couple of broken bones by this point. Not that such minor details would stifle a man of his talents for long.

Sid Mercer got a quick refresher course in Kansas determination. On Thursday, his notes column began

> Charley Faust wishes to correct the statement in yesterday's *Globe* that he is not working. Although feeling "porely" Faust is doing a stunt at a Broadway vaudeville temple. The Kansas Zephyr says it is easy money, but vaudeville can never rival baseball in his affections. "I'll quit any time McGraw gives the word," says Charley; "there is more money in this theatrical game, but I don't want to be an actor. I am keeping in good condition doing my famous windup and slides, but I expect to go west with the Giants next

week. McGraw needs all us good pitchers." Faust embellishes his act by throwing Matty's fadeaway and Marquard's drop. It takes an expert to distinguish the difference between them. Faust says there is a difference, but he refuses to point it out.

Faust's act received no reviews, which was probably just as well, judging from Mercer's comment. Only the theater-oriented *Morning Telegraph* carried a notice, headlined "Faust Is In Vaudeville":

> Baseball fans are given an opportunity to look over a recruit from the West that is billed in bold type in front of Gane's Manhattan Theatre, where he is playing the latter part of this week as "McGraw's Dark Horse" and "The Coming Sensation of the World's Series." Inside he is discovered to be the fellow who dreamed he should be a Giant and proceeded to clown at the Polo Grounds. Charles Victor Faust is his name and he plays the game, not for mercenary purposes, but for the love and glory that is attached to the sport. At the Manhattan he shows the different poses of celebrated pitchers, and the positions of famous sluggers at the plate, and illustrates sliding to bases.

So what if nobody could tell the difference between Charley Faust's imitations of Mathewson and Marquard? He recognized this vaudeville fling as a brief interlude before returning to his mission of leading the Giants to the pennant. Marquard's Monday collapse may not have bothered him very much. During the two off days he could enjoy his vaudeville romp with a clear conscience, but what happened Thursday truly distressed him. Brooklyn came to town, a team the Giants had beaten twelve games out of thirteen in 1911, and Christy Mathewson couldn't beat the seventh-place Superbas.

Matty pitched well enough to win, but he got little support after the first inning, when Red Murray and Fred Merkle drove in runs. It stayed 2–0 until the sixth inning, when Brooklyn's pitcher, Cy Barger, struck out leading off and the Giants treated him like Charley Faust. Chief Meyers dropped the ball, and his throw down to first was muffed by Merkle. Barger eventually made his way around to score, cutting Matty's lead in half. Another error in the seventh inning cost Matty two more runs. Art Fletcher dropped Matty's throw at second base on a sacrifice bunt attempt, and Brooklyn cashed in the mistake with two outs and the bases loaded on a two-run single by shortstop Bert Tooley.

The Giants tied it 3–3 in the eighth inning but gave the game away in the ninth. Matty walked Tooley on a three-two pitch with two outs, and Jake Daubert crashed a high drive to right-center field. Fred Snodgrass reached the ball after a long run, then dropped it as Tooley raced around from first base with the winning run. The Giants, who managed only four hits off Barger all day, got a leadoff single in the bottom of the ninth but couldn't score.

This brutal loss made two in a row for the Giants without Charley Faust. In Chicago the Cubs swept a doubleheader from Cincinnati to move within a game. This sudden threat to the pennant expectations of the Giants affected Faust deeply, causing him more anguish than his halfhearted mid-August defection. At some point, he told Billy Gane that he intended to rejoin the Giants on Friday, that the Giants needed him more than vaudeville did, especially with Rube Marquard due to pitch. However much this notion made Gane's head spin, he had "McGraw's Dark Horse" under contract for two more days and was not about to turn him loose. The Manhattan Theatre and the Polo Grounds were both on Eighth Avenue, a mere one hundred twenty-five blocks apart. Charley Faust had four to six performances a day at the Manhattan, but between shows Gane could give him a peek at his precious Giants.

Before September 8 Heywood Broun, the Harvard-bred rookie reporter at the *Morning Telegraph*, had scarcely paid attention to Charley Faust. While Sid Mercer and Damon Runyon looked for excuses to drag Faust into their daily coverage, Broun mentioned Faust only twice during the August home stand. On August 18 he called Faust "the hopeless case from St. Louis." Nine days later he gave this scant coverage to Faust's most trumpeted stunt to date: "The Catholic Protectory sent a band and Rube Faust was induced to lead it, which he did with much aplomb." Broun hardly seemed a candidate for Faust's burgeoning fan club—until September 8, when the New England skeptic witnessed Faust's good-luck jinxing at its finest. Broun focused his game coverage on endorsing Faust's powers:

> The real reason of the Giants' success, however, lay not in the staunch arm of Marquard, nor the ready bat of Fred Merkle, but in the presence of Charlie Faust. McGraw's dark horse has been absent for the past few days, and it is absolutely certain that the

defeats at the hands of Boston and Brooklyn would hardly have happened if he had been within call. Billy Gane, the manager of the Manhattan Theatre, took his phenom to the game yesterday and the Giants promptly drove Rucker out of the box. The time for the next show at the Manhattan was approaching, but Gane found that the call of art was drowned by the call of the ball field. Marquard was going great guns, but Faust was anxious to warm up in order to be ready in case an unexpected break should come. Gane at last persuaded him to leave the fortunes of war in the hands of Marquard and McGraw, and no sooner had he left the field than the tide of battle turned. The Giants made not another run or hit, and Brooklyn, in a hard finish, came very near victory. In future McGraw plans to rig up an emergency call from the bench to the stage of the Manhattan. Whether it was really on account of the departure of Faust or some other cause, Marquard was in grave danger in the seventh . . .

Marquard took his usual two-hit shutout to the seventh inning, leading 3–0. Three straight hits with one out plated two runs, but Fred Snodgrass made a great catch to squelch the threat. In the eighth, Marquard got out of another jam without help from Faust, Mathewson, or McGraw, and he sailed through the final inning to nail down the 3–2 win, his nineteenth of the season. With only one game remaining on the home stand, there was no urgent need for McGraw to invent the pager so that he could summon Faust from the vaudeville stage when needed.

Charley Faust finished out his whirlwind week in vaudeville on Saturday, September 9, while the Giants struggled again with Brooklyn. Outhit 15–5, the Giants felt lucky to escape with a 4–4 tie in a game called by darkness after nine innings. The Giants got three first-inning runs for Doc Crandall but had to come back in the bottom of the ninth to tie the game in rapidly fading light. Fred Merkle entered the *Herald's* Frame of Fame for the second straight day by tripling in two runs in the first inning and scoring the tying run in the ninth.

So ended the long home stand, with Faust's comings and goings influencing the team's success as never before. Fred Snodgrass, in the inaccurately truthful interview he gave to Lawrence Ritter when he was nearly eighty years old, recalled that week clearly. Faust, said Snodgrass, "was such a drawing card at this point that a theatrical firm gave him a contract on Broadway in one of those six-a-day shows, starting in the afternoon and running through the evening, and he got four hundred dollars a week for it. He dressed in a baseball uniform and imitated Ty Cobb, Christy Mathewson, and Honus Wagner. In a very ridiculous way, of course, but seriously as far as Charlie was concerned. And the fans loved it and went to see Charlie on the stage. He was gone four days, and we lost four ball games!"

Except for placing this event in 1913 (and giving Faust credit for being with the Giants two full years, rather than three weeks, before becoming "such a drawing card"), Snodgrass had the right idea. In the space of four games, the Giants lost two and tied one, and Heywood Broun linked Faust's brief attendance directly to their lone win during his absence. Carrying an eight-game winning streak into a week of play against the two worst teams in the league, the Giants should have continued winning with or without Faust. Their failures in his absence only convinced Faust doubly that they weren't going anywhere—literally or figuratively—without him.

In the month since he had ridden the rails to New York to save the Giants, Charley Faust and the team had come a long way. The Giants moved from third place to first thanks to a 19–6–1 record. At least two of those losses occurred with Faust not in uniform, and most of the wins were gained while he warmed up to pitch, solemnly devoted to his obligation to pitch them to the pennant. Once a stranger and a buffoon, he was now a stalwart counted on to contribute to the team's success. Even his clowning had been rewarded, thanks to his unsolicited press agents. The ice wagon not only had cometh; he had conquered New York, too.

How would the road treat Charley Faust and his New York marauders? When they took a train to Boston on September 10, their next scheduled home game was on October 6. In between lay twenty-three games, an odyssey reaching every city in the league. How would Charley survive the trip? And how would the league survive Charley?

6

Victory on Tour

A Kansas Cyclone

"What are the people shouting for?" said Rooter-on-Parade.
"It's Charley Faust! It's Charley Faust!" the Centerfielder said.
"What makes you look so pale, so pale?" said Rooter-on-Parade.
"I fear he's going to get my job," the Centerfielder said.
"For this lad from Hector, Kansas, is the finest of the fine,
When it comes to stealing bases, he's a Jimmy Valentine.
And if Charley gets a try-out, it's the minor leagues for mine—
He'll be copping out my job tomorrow mornin'."
"You seem to be afraid of him," said Rooter-on-Parade.
"You bet I am, you bet I am," the Centerfielder said.
"Why don't they give the boy a chance?" said Rooter-on-Parade.
"I hope they don't! I hope they don't!" the Centerfielder said.
"For he's like a streak of lightning, though he's now a trifle fat.
He can do a hundred yards in forty-seven minutes flat.
He's a whirlwind on the bases and a wizard with the bat:
He'll be copping out my job tomorrow mornin'."

     L. C. Davis, St. Louis *Post-Dispatch*, September 21, 1911

IN *My Thirty Years in Baseball*, published in 1923, John McGraw reminisced fondly about causing mayhem on road trips like the one late in the 1911 season. Aggressive anyway, McGraw and his Giants regarded having rocks thrown at them in the streets as a small price to pay for excitement at the ballpark. In most National League cities, they received the same sort of welcome that Attila and his Huns got on their tour of Europe. And McGraw loved it! "Nothing ever gave our players more delight," he wrote,

> than to go back at fans and players who had started to give them a razz. I never tried to discourage them in this, either. A team that will fight back on an enemy diamond and before an enemy crowd is pretty well able to take care of itself. The players gain confidence in themselves by maintaining this cocky spirit. Fans always resent the fighting back of a visiting ball club and that usually leads to trouble. . . . While on the road we had hot arguments of this kind daily. Often the fans got so enraged that they would follow our carriages and hurl epithets—and other things—at us. All of this tended to make us a great drawing card on the road. Fans could rest assured that when the Giants arrived there would be action of some kind at the park. . . . It's much better to be knocked and roasted than to be unnoticed.

McGraw basked in this universal vilification, intoxicated by the aura of menace and villainy which surrounded the Giants as they invaded each new city. Once, egged on by John T. Brush, McGraw wired ahead to Cincinnati to request police protection even though it wasn't needed. Mission accomplished. "The public couldn't understand what it was all about, but for fear something might happen and they would miss it, they filled the park."

Picture a baseball team managed by Earl Weaver, with an infield of four Billy Martins, three Pete Roses in the outfield, Thurman Munson catching, and Greg Maddux pitching two or three times a week to anchor the pitching staff. Add Jimmy Durante coaching third base and a Forrest Gump–like aspiring pitcher turned mascot, and you have the September 1911 edition of John McGraw's road show.

Despite this defiant attitude, McGraw knew quite well that more things could go wrong more quickly on the road. Being attacked by irate fans was the least of it. There were the train wrecks, the pedestrian perils, and all those aviators falling out of the sky. The Giants missed a fatal train wreck outside of Pittsburgh by only a few days, the third wreck by that particular train in two months. Even safe train rides made road trips seem longer, usually overnight treks that gave the players haphazard, uneasy rest before the next day's game. This road trip ended brutally, with games in different cities four days in a row, more like a barnstorming tour than a league schedule.

Venturing forth into the unknown to soar in the public limelight, the Giants had it easier than hopefuls in other fields. Aviators had an especially tough time during the twenty-five days it took the Giants to make their National League circuit. Harry Atwood, the toast of New York when he flew in the last week of August, ran afoul on the ground on September 13. He got a ticket for speeding, fined $5 for driving 28 mph down Fifth Avenue. His luck did not change back in the air; two weeks later, his plane collided with another in midair near Canton, Ohio. Though he wasn't hurt, his plane was out of commission, removing any thoughts of pursuing that $50,000 prize offered by William Randolph Hearst for a transcontinental crossing.

Chasing that prize proved no bargain. The day the Giants began their trip, two aviators, one on each coast, launched futile attempts. In California, Robert Fuller left San Francisco but wrecked crossing the Sierras, then had his plane's parts scavenged by souvenir-hunters. In New York, James Ward took off from Governors Island (where Atwood had landed), headed in the general direction of the Pacific Ocean. He spent the first day zigzagging across New Jersey, totally lost, and touched down that night in Paterson, eighteen miles from where he started. Two days later, he wrecked his biplane, escaped injury, and took off again. Mechanical woes ended his trip by the end of the week before he got past upstate New York, leaving him temporarily stranded along with fellow hopeful Calbraith Rodgers, who eventually collected Hearst's money.

Amateur and amateurish aviators caught the public's fleeting attention only by dying. On September 25 an unlicensed "pilot" climbed into a plane on Long Island and got it into the air. His first flight lasted four minutes, until he plunged to his death. Had some fortune-teller convinced him that he was destined to break the aviation records?

In the realm of lamebrained schemes, Charley Faust was lucky to be steered toward baseball, where even ignorance and rank incompetence probably would not get him killed. No amount of conning or razzing by teammates and fans could make Charley do what aviator

Frank Miller of Toledo did at a county fair near Dayton. Forced by engine trouble to miss one day of exhibitions and to abort his final flight, Miller found himself jeered by a crowd that gathered after the fair ended. The spectators called him a coward for not flying again, and Miller took their challenge personally. Angered, he had his biplane brought from the hangar, climbed in, and showed those folks by circling the race track from two hundred feet in the air. Then his engine failed and sputtered, the gasoline tank exploded, and Frank Miller burned to death in midair, giving thousands of spectators that final thrilling moment they had demanded.

The meteoric rise and fall of Cromwell Dixon was sadder still. Dixon, already renowned as a balloonist, turned his daredevil ambitions to airplanes, getting his aviator's license August 31. Within weeks, he gained fame as one of the first to fly over the Rockies. On October 2, near Spokane, his plane caught a cross-current and plunged one hundred feet to the ground, killing him. Cromwell Dixon was nineteen years old.

During those twenty-five days, disaster loomed everywhere you looked and as far away as you could see. Terrible fires ravaged parts of Rio de Janeiro and Antwerp, while an eruption of Mount Etna left thousands of Sicilians homeless. All across Europe, political tensions and threats of war mounted. Germany, France, and England argued over Morocco, and on September 30 Italy attacked Tripoli, precipitating a war with Turkey that Italy won in two weeks, before the Austrians could make good their threat to intervene. In Kiev, Pyotr Stolypin, the repressive premier, was assassinated, moving Russia one step closer to revolution. The world was a mess, and the Giants, without taking the time to realize it, were lucky to have nothing worse to dodge than vegetables, fastballs, and an occasional brick.

Charley Faust and the Giants found danger and obstacles aplenty on their trip, but first they were blessed with the best gift the schedule-makers could give them: four games in Boston. Fattening up on the 33–93 Rustlers could provide the momentum John McGraw needed to make his troops storm the western cities. If they blew the Boston series, the trip might be a nightmare. For this trip, McGraw banned poker playing and other such diversions, threatening heavy fines for anyone caught devoting himself to any game other than baseball. McGraw sealed his devotion to the cause with a pledge to avoid getting ejected and thereby deprive the team of his leadership.

Rain postponed the Monday opener in Boston, forcing yet another doubleheader for the Giants on September 12. Since August 14 they had played six twin bills, sweeping three and splitting three, including Rube Marquard's Labor Day collapse against the Rustlers. McGraw announced that Marquard and Mathewson would pitch on Tuesday and waited impatiently to see it happen. All the writers dispatched notes columns, including items about themselves. "There are now thirty-two in the party," reported Damon Runyon, "including Charles Victory Faust, little 'Spud' Hennessey, the club mascot; Eddie Brannick, assistant secretary, and the newspaper men. The latter will be augmented by a delegation of half a dozen more at Pittsburg, making the largest corps of baseball writers that has ever followed the club on a circuit trip." Part of that record corps was Runyon himself, making his first road trip with the Giants after spending the season covering whichever New York team was at home.

Sid Mercer struck a familiar note. "Charley Faust eyes the Rustlers with suspicion, and even Mascot Dick Hennessey is nervous. Faust says that the time has come when McGraw must begin to lean on him." The *Times* had this scoop: "Charley Faust is expounding a theory about a new curve, which he threatens to spring on the 'Hub' tomorrow." Tomorrow brought this note: "Rube Faust pleaded with McGraw to pitch the first game. Marquard wishes McGraw had let him."

For the second time in eight days, Rube Marquard blew a big lead. Leading 5–1 in the seventh inning, Marquard weakened and got ripped for six hits and five runs. The Giants bailed him out with a four-run eighth inning, and Doc Crandall pitched the last two innings to preserve Marquard's twentieth win of the season. Fred Merkle got a leg up on making the Frame of Fame with a two-run triple that broke a 6–6 tie, then left no doubt by homering twice in the nightcap.

Sid Mercer reported bad news: Marquard's arm had gone lame during that five-run collapse. "In yesterday's game he had to work hard to get the proper breaks on his delivery and when he felt a sudden shooting pain he knew it was time to quit." In 1911 pitchers were supposed to finish what they started, so Marquard didn't mention anything until he had taken his pounding like a man. "Marquard's arm is tape-bound to-day," Mercer added, "but he thinks he will be able to go in against Pittsburgh on Saturday. His opinion is that a ligament or a muscle has been wrenched." No big deal. Heck, Fred Snodgrass had been playing for a week with a broken rib (also treated with tape) and refused to take time off. Rube would find out next start whether he could still pitch.

The September 12 nightcap provided a slice of baseball history, with Christy Mathewson matched up against the already immortal Cy Young, forty-four years old and hanging on in the final month of his career. Eleven thousand fans, the biggest crowd at the South End Grounds all season, anticipated a duel to remember if Young pitched as he had recently. Young began well by fanning Josh Devore, who was born the year Young's career began, but he surrendered long home runs to Larry Doyle and Fred Merkle later in the inning. The life quickly fizzled out of the Cy-Matty brew, and Young walked off the mound late in the third inning, trailing 8–0. Blessed with a safe lead, John McGraw gave Mathewson the rest of the day off. Doc Crandall pitched the last seven innings of the 11–2 drubbing, adding a home run of his own. The Giants, whose forty-one home runs on the season ranked fourth in the league, used up four of them and added six stolen bases, one by Mathewson, in humiliating Cy Young. On day one of the trip, McGraw was taking no prisoners.

Mathewson and Marquard sweeping Boston surprised nobody, so skeptical fans looked to the Wednesday game for omens of Giants success on this make-or-break trip. Not many of them looked from seats in the ballpark, for cold winds held attendance to roughly one thousand. The skeptics observed from the press box and from their living rooms back in New York, waiting for news of whether Red Ames's celebrated jinx had joined him in Boston. Ames had been left out of the pitching party most of the summer, scraping along on a 7–9 record while Matty, Rube, and Doc piled up win after win. Unable to start more than once a week, Ames had failed to complete four of his last six starts. His fate in Boston might well mirror the team's prospects.

Ames always preferred cold weather, and his arm came alive on that frigid Boston afternoon. The Rustlers got a second-inning run on a two-base error and two outs, but they didn't get a hit off Ames until the sixth inning, repeating the all-too-familiar pattern of doomed Ames efforts. Leading 3–1, Ames had to wonder whether the jinx's hammer would fall again, but the Rustlers continued to hit his curves and drops right at fielders. Though he did not strike out a batter all day, he completed a solid 4–1 win despite a pair of ninth-inning hits that made McGraw briefly anxious. The unexpected gem landed Ames in the Window of Fame for the first time, a timely arrival, with Rube Marquard nursing a sore arm.

"Ames Unloads Jinx," read the *American's* headline, and Damon Runyon made sure to point out that "this being the thirteenth day of the month, Ames's performance is all the more impressive." In truth, Red Ames gave an even more impressive performance that evening, when he graced Sid Mercer with the quote of the year:

> I'm glad Faust is going to stick because he certainly has brought good luck to us all. You remember that he showed up in New York when we returned from the second western trip. We won sixteen out of twenty games. Then Charley left us flat and went into vaudeville for a week. What happened to us? We had a terrible time with Boston and Brooklyn. Faust came up for the morning game on Labor Day and we won. He wasn't there in the afternoon and we lost. He was not on the job when we lost to Brooklyn, but on the following day he showed and we beat Brooklyn. Last Saturday he stayed away and the best we got was a draw. He's been on the job here every day and we haven't lost a game. You can say for me that I think he is a great man for the team even [if] he never gets a chance to pitch.

What an amazing testimonial from the acknowledged expert on hoodoos, the man usually portrayed as brooding over inevitable bad luck. The man whose nickname was Kalamity spewed out Faust's day-by-day jinxing achievements with the fervor of a man keeping close track of every variable. Who could take the other side after Kalamity endorsed the man whose middle name was increasingly given as Victory? If only Ames could develop similar confidence in his own good fortune.

Mercer's report continued, "It is amusing to note how the athletes have warmed up to Faust since they have come to regard him as a talisman. They play pool with him, take him to the theatres, introduce him to everybody, and sympathize deeply with him when he complains of his failure to get in a real game. As for Faust, well, they couldn't lose him if they tried. He is the Human Blaster."

This is one of the few references to how Faust passed his time away from the ballpark. During his month in New York, he had spent almost two weeks involved in rehearsing and performing his vaudeville act. He probably made that one-day excursion to Brooklyn, but otherwise his postgame life is a missing section of the puzzle. Though he roomed at the Hotel Braddock with a number of other players, they probably ignored him in the early days, living their own lives and seeing no reason to drag this rube around with them. The gregarious Faust may have drawn some attention by hanging around the lobby, or he may have explored New York City on his own. It is easy enough to visualize him wandering the streets of New York with the dazed, vaguely over-whelmed expression seen on some Manhattan pedestrians to this day. Perhaps Sid Mercer acted as his tour guide. Or perhaps he ventured forth once and retreated to the safety of his hotel room for the rest of his New York stay.

We know much more about Charley Faust's doings on the road, enough for a clear picture of his social place on the team and what it meant to him. Two days into the trip, Mercer chuckled at the players adopting Charley and shepherding him around Boston, trying to protect their full-blown talisman while humoring his incessant insistence on pitching in a real game. Regarding that thorny issue, Mercer included another note that same day in which John McGraw showed the way in simultaneously humoring and gulling the Human Blaster. "Charley Faust has secured a promise from McGraw at last. He approached the manager last night and said, 'Mac, I want to work and I wish you would set a day for me to go in.' 'All right,' replied McGraw briskly. 'You work Friday.' When Charley hunted a schedule to see what team he would face, he discovered the team would be on the road Friday, and the best work that he will do is with the knife and fork in the dining car." The players understood why it might take a few games of pool or a good show to calm Charley down after such a steep rise and fall of his pipe-dream hopes of pitching for real.

On September 14 the Boston *Globe* published a large team photo of what it labeled the "National League's One Best Bet for Pennant Honors, As Things Shape Up At This Stage." The photo shows twenty-three uniformed members of the New York Giants. John McGraw sits cross-legged front and center. On his left, Buck Herzog has one arm draped over the shoulder of a beaming Dick Hennessey, listed as mascot. Arlie Latham sits two spots to McGraw's right, clowning with Larry Doyle, behind him in the second row. Looming over McGraw's left shoulder is Louis Drucke, sidelined since July and wearing a body cast which insured that he would not soon shed the nickname "Plaintiff." Drucke's cast is even with the injured hip of Hooks Wiltse, the injury supposedly healed by Charley Faust's laying on of hands, if you believe Edwin Burkholder's claim. Wiltse stands in the middle of the top row, ten players wide, proud Giants standing tall. The big five pitchers are there, Mathewson and Marquard side by side and grinning. At the far right, Fred Snodgrass faces the camera head-on, arms folded, looking a little like a DiMaggio. Next to him stands Charley Faust. His arms are folded, too, in imitation of his neighbors, head tilted toward the team. To his right, Chief Meyers leans much farther toward the team as if telling them Charley's latest pitching scheme. The Giants look loose, leading the league and going nowhere without Charley. This was the only Giants team photo in which he appeared, proudly displaying the NY stitched into the left sleeve of his uniform, a New York Giant in equal standing with the more well-known members of the team.

The teams played a wild finale that afternoon. Hooke Wiltse struggled on the mound but helped himself by driving in four runs on a pair of singles. Wiltse faded in the eighth inning, and this time McGraw got an aching pitcher out of there. Christy Mathewson got two key outs to hold the 7–4 lead, setting the stage for a ninth-inning scoring frenzy. The Giants scored six runs in a final 1911 salute to Boston hospitality. Josh Devore stole second base twice in the inning, and Mathewson cleared the bases with a three-run double, earning the bonus points needed to land him in the Frame of Fame on a day when the *Herald* declared, "It is as hard to pick a hero out of the game to-day as it is to identify a single egg when five or six are served scrambled." McGraw excused Matty with a 13–4 lead, and Doc Crandall delayed their triumphant march to the train station by getting pummeled for seven hits and five runs in the bottom of the ninth, fraying McGraw's nerves one more time before getting the final out.

The Cubs lost a doubleheader that afternoon in Pittsburgh, leaving the Giants four games ahead of them (and six over the Pirates) as they thanked the Rustlers and headed west. The reporters had to telegraph their game accounts in before the train left, so they didn't have much space for Charley Faust. He garnered four brief mentions, including his first ever in the New York *Sun*, which belatedly joined the bandwagon. "Charles Faust, whose antics at the Polo Grounds have afforded spectators much comedy, has been such a success as a mascot that the Giants will probably take him around the entire trip." Arriving late, the *Sun* did not realize that Charley Faust was more than a mere mascot. He was a force. He was the Human Blaster, sent to make the Giants immune to the vagaries of chance. He was invincible, as Sid Mercer pointed out that day. "Charley Faust is still the leader in the mascot race. Faust is batting 1.000, as the Giants haven't lost since he deserted vaudeville and returned to them."

In the *Herald*, John Wheeler sounded an odd note which became a recurring theme over the next two weeks. "McGraw says that if he has the pennant won when he gets to Chicago he will work 'Charley' Faust in one of the games. 'I'd give a hundred to be able to do it,' laughed McGraw. 'I'd sign him just to put him in.'" That sentiment said more about how McGraw felt about the Cubs than how he felt about Faust. Nothing would give McGraw a greater charge than marching into Chicago with the pennant clinched, except maybe getting to rub it in by letting Faust pitch. McGraw couldn't help laughing at the prospect, keeping in mind that the Giants would have to win virtually every game to make it happen.

Faust also got a passing mention in a rare note of buoyancy in the *Times*. "The whole Giant cavalcade, with outriders, postillions, Dick Hennessy, Arlie Latham, Rube Faust, and a carload of confidence, steamed out of here to-night for Pittsburgh to call on Buccaneer Fred Clarke." If that makes McGraw and company sound like Robin Hood and his Merry Men, consider two similar reports from the following day, after the cavalcade arrived in Pittsburgh. John Wheeler's item appeared in the morning:

> "Charley" Faust helped the gemmed Giants to while away the time on the road by repeating his vaudeville act many times. "Jack" Murray acted as impresario, rehearsing Faust and putting filigree work on the borders of the act which did not appear with the original. Some one loaded four or five railroad spikes and a

few pounds of pig iron into Mr. Faust's dress suit case to-day when he carelessly left his back turned, and he carried them all the way out to the hotel in it.

"This feels awful heavy," he declared to "Larry" Doyle, as he picked up the bag.

"That's because you've been layin' around in the train all day and haven't been working," explained Larry.

Moral—Never turn your back.

Faithful to the cause, Faust went to sleep with his arm in the hammock in his berth last night and with blankets wrapped tightly around it, while his body was exposed, and he shivered. He says that he must take care of that arm. He predicts that the Giants will win the pennant by five games and so superstitious have the players become that they believe it. They say that he can always call the turn on a hit while on the bench during a game. If he should quit the club now it would never win the pennant. The players believe in him absolutely.

Sid Mercer's obsession with Charley Faust's misadventures ripened during this trip. Even without a Sunday edition, the *Globe* published no fewer than thirty-four Faust items gleaned by Mercer, an eager sponge among Faust aficionados. When the Giants hit Pittsburgh, he filed four reports on Faust. Among them was one of those passing scenes which couldn't be comprehended fully unless you saw it happen. "George Stallings [managing Buffalo in the International League] met McGraw in Buffalo yesterday noon, the train stopping there a half hour. Stallings told McGraw that he had a great youngster in Shortstop Groh, whose career in Buffalo was cut short by an attack of typhoid fever. McGraw offered to loan Charley Faust to Stallings for the remainder of the season, but his players objected to losing their mascot, and Charley himself declared that he would pitch for no team other than the 'Junts.'"

Mercer was right about the prospect, Henry Groh; "Heinie" joined the Giants in 1912, was traded to the Reds in 1913, spent eight productive seasons there, and found himself reclaimed by McGraw for a few more good years. What about McGraw offering Faust to Stallings? Was the offer made in private and then passed along to Faust and the team, or was it a boisterous charade in front of the whole team just to get a rise out of Faust? The train stopped in Buffalo, where McGraw talked shop with one of the few baseball men more superstitious than he was. Stallings managed the New York Highlanders late into the 1910 season and resurfaced in 1913 in Boston, where he led the "Miracle Braves" of 1914 to the pennant, dethroning McGraw's Giants. The best indicator of the seriousness of McGraw's offer was the players' reaction. A few players had objected when McGraw tried to run Faust off shortly after he arrived in New York. Their objections in Buffalo reminded McGraw that, all joking aside, they wanted Faust around. No wonder. Faust was more fun than a poker game. They could pull a dozen pranks on him at once and he would go for every single one. They could tinker with his act and get him to say or do anything they told him to. Balanced against the frenzy of the ballgames—they stole fourteen bases in three days in Boston—it relaxed them to sit back and let Faust entertain them. With his presence, they had another five-game winning streak going. You bet they objected.

Mercer's next Faust update renewed the threat to Chicago. "The Giants are sore over the slurs cast on them and upon McGraw, and the games at Chicago will surely be scrappy. If the pennant is won when the Giants reach Chicago it is McGraw's intention to pitch Charley Faust in one of the games, play third base himself, and put Arlie Latham on second. The chances are, however, that the race will still be close at that stage, and so Faust may not have his ambition gratified." Note that Mercer did not say "McGraw may not have his ambition gratified." He saw it from Faust's point of view. McGraw's "intention" was a joke; Faust's ambition was genuine and his efforts so determined that Mercer stepped up his steady campaign of publicity on Faust's behalf.

One Faust routine that Mercer missed was the prognostication mentioned by John Wheeler. The next issue of the *Sporting News* (published in St. Louis) wrung an extended space-filler out of "C. Victory Faust as Prophet." The article under this heading, penned by former New York *American* columnist W. J. McBeth, detailed Charley's astounding powers:

> If there had been any doubts as to the finish of the National League race—and the big doings to follow—Charles Victory Faust has removed them. Let it be recalled that it was on the word of a soothsayer that Charles Victory first identified himself with

Camp McGraw. It was but to be expected, therefore, that when doubts shook the hearts of Gotham as to the outcome of the pennant struggle, that Charles Victory should again appeal to the oracle. He communed with the occult and returned with the answer: the Giants are to win the pennant by five full games. So sayeth Charles Victory, and there isn't a man in town who doubts him.

Charles Victory, by the way, will get most of the credit—after Marquard. This peculiar character has worked wonders as a mascotter in McGraw's camp. It is a strange superstition that has overcome the Giants, but they believe his presence spells luck. Furthermore, Connie Mack, who also believes in "haunts," has stated publicly that Faust will bring the Giants enough luck to win. If there isn't magic or black art twined around this somber Kansan, he has the delphic oracle beaten to a whisper.

Giant athletes state that on the bench Faust calls the turn on nearly every man, predicting base hits or runs with rarely a miss. Upon looking back into the records again they find that he has been on the bench 28 days, and that in that time they have won 26 games. The days they lost he was absent or not in uniform.

In a game against Brooklyn he left early, when the Giants were 3 to 0. Then Brooklyn tied it up. They have never lost a game with him on the bench, save the first battle against Pittsburg on August 14, when he arrived late. Then they won the second.

There's no hoss stuff about this Faust business. The Giants have taken his presence as a winning hunch, and even as business-like as John McGraw is, the Giant chief says that he would rather lose any one man on the club. Faust not only predicts that the Giants will win the pennant by five games, but that Marquard and Mathewson will beat the Athletics four games out of seven.

That etched Faust's reputation in stone; the *Sporting News* was "the Bible of baseball." The Faust myth took on another dimension; having sprung full-blown from an oracle, Charley had, as if by osmosis, developed supernatural powers of his own. Common sense could argue only so long against that tall stack of victories in Faust's column.

All the Giants had to do was keep winning, and they did, sweeping three games to knock the Pirates out of the race. The Saturday opener drew twenty thousand fans eager to see Marty O'Toole, the Pirates'

$22,500 phenom, pitch against the team that had tried so hard to sign him. O'Toole had launched his career with a 3–0 start and would face the man he was supposed to equal, Rube Marquard, "the $11,000 Beauty" (formerly "Lemon"). Marquard, despite a lingering sore arm that limited him to four strikeouts, outpitched O'Toole and beat him 6–2. McGraw removed Marquard quickly when he weakened in the eighth inning, getting Mathewson in there in plenty of time to squelch the Pirates. Matty, showcasing the relentless drive of the Giants on this road trip, stole his third base in four games in the ninth inning, starting a double steal with Beals Becker that brought home one last insurance run.

Charley Faust also had a banner day in Pittsburgh before giving the Giants their turn at romping on the field. Damon Runyon noted that "Charles Victory Faust, the official jinx for all opposing clubs, appeared in the box with a large medal upon his breast and striking out Hans Wagner with the high 'up-in' ball, while little Dick Hennessy performed at first base." Runyon also reported that "'Red' Ames is now wearing a startling red necktie as a good luck emblem, and he declares that he will continue wearing it until he loses again. The necktie comes from his home in Warren, Ohio." We don't know where Faust's medal came from or whether it was presented to him anonymously, in private, or in a home-plate ceremony reminiscent of his debut weekend in St. Louis, when Steve Evans presented him with that enchanting trick watch. Faust, like Ames, knew a good-luck symbol when he saw one, and that medal adorned his uniform for the rest of the season.

The *Times*, for a change, contained a fuller description of Faust's antics than Damon Runyon managed. Skeptical, but fuller. "Before the game Charley Faust, the eccentric and mysterious individual who seems to have brought the Giants a great deal of luck, tried out his pitching arm against the mighty Wagner. Once, twice, and thrice the Teuton swung at the ball and collided with nothing but air. After this colossal feat Faust walked to the bench amid a storm of applause." Sid Mercer had to wait until Monday to trumpet Faust's feat. "No story of a day in McGraw's camp would be complete without a few lines on C. Victor Faust. Faust made a great hit on his first appearance at Forbes Field. He struck out Hans Wagner in batting practice, the mighty Dutchman failing to get as much as a foul."

FAUST proudly displayed his prized possession, the medal presented to him in Pittsburgh. He liked it much better than the tribute he received his first weekend in St. Louis, a trick watch that shattered in his hands. (Brace Photo)

Think about that for a moment. Honus Wagner, advancing rapidly on his seventh National League batting title, consented to take part in this pregame stunt to make Charley Faust look like a real pitcher. Wagner, rather simple and good-natured himself, could not deny this hard-working clown. How could it hurt anybody to wave at three pitches and pretend that Faust had performed the unheard-of feat of throwing three straight pitches past the best hitter in the league? Well, it may have hurt both of them. In the three-game series, Wagner scratched out a lone single and failed to score as his team was held to five runs.

As for Faust, the only person in the ballpark who thought Wagner was trying to hit the ball, this represented one more exhibit in his case for being a real pitcher, one more crystal-clear proof of his undeniable talents. Why else would the crowd have given him that ovation as he strode proudly to the bench? They weren't cheering that medal. So his delusion grew.

Monday's game featured an even more relentless attack by the Giants. They stole eight bases, three each by Fred Snodgrass and Larry Doyle. Three times they stole home, twice on double steals, twice by Doyle. Christy Mathewson started a four-run second inning with a single and held the Pirates hitless until the fifth. It added up to a convincing 7–2 win, Matty's twenty-fourth. According to the *Herald*, after the Giants' early flurry, "the pastime had by this time become more or less disintegrated, and most of the crowd stopped watching the game and gave attention to 'Charley' Faust warming up. That was lots more interesting." Look at it through the Pittsburgh fans' eyes. Having spent the past decade watching Mathewson mow down their Pirates, they found themselves gratefully distracted by this novelty character, delighted by this buffoon who continued to warm up as if Mathewson might need his help.

Sid Mercer contributed the bulk of the Faust hype from Pittsburgh, expanding on earlier themes. After making the no-longer-bold prediction of a Giants pennant, Mercer pretended to hedge. "Of course if Matty and Marquard fall into some of the flooded streams around Pittsburgh and the throwing arm of Chief Meyers drops off and McGraw suddenly decides to quit baseball there would be a large hole shot in the dope, but none of these things is likely to happen. Even if they did, isn't

Charley Faust still with the team?" The next day, he wrote that "Charley Faust doesn't believe the Giants are going to lose any more games. He is the most popular man in camp because he is regarded as the best jinx destroyer the team ever had." In Pittsburgh the Giants extended their latest winning streak to eight games. They had also had a six-game and a nine-game streak in the five weeks since Faust donned a Giants uniform for good. The mounting evidence overwhelmed casual and caustic observers alike.

Charley Faust could not be stopped; he could only be detained, sidetracked by his secondary role as the chief butt of practical jokes. Sid Mercer delivered one beauty to his readers on September 18: "Charley thinks the Hotel Schenley piazzas are great places to loaf. This morning he planted himself in a big chair and started to digest a Pittsburgh sporting page. Some joker quietly touched a match to the paper and a moment later there was a commotion on the veranda. Charley's big hands turned in an alarm when the blaze began to scorch them. He blew at the flames, then doubled up the paper, squeezed it between his mighty paws, and the fire struck out." They had to go for the hands; given his running style, a hotfoot couldn't have made him move that fast.

After the second win in Pittsburgh, which put the Giants five games in front of the Cubs, Mercer got the lowdown from John McGraw. "McGraw is so sure that the Cub special will be completely wrecked by Saturday night that he is grooming Charley Faust to pitch one of the Chicago games. Faust will sign a New York contract so as to be eligible to pitch and the ambition of his life will be gratified when he faces the Cubs. He may not survive the fusilade of balls hit back at him but he is willing to take a chance. He fanned Hans Wagner in practice again yesterday and thinks he is the invincible kid." Wagner should have been cited for contributing to the delinquency of a minor intellect, or to the delusion of a farmer. Imagine making that poor fellow think he was as invincible on the mound as he was on the sideline. Throw McGraw's impulse to humiliate the Cubs into the picture, allowing a sane observer like Mercer to believe that Charley would pitch in Chicago, and it's no surprise that Charley felt his destiny calling. His invincibility blossomed with the realization that he was truly going to be a major leaguer.

On Tuesday the Giants completed their second sweep of the trip, playing more invincible ball. They stole four bases and gave Red Ames an early 3–0 lead. Ames, inspired by his lucky tie, carried the shutout to the ninth inning, then got the final out with the tying runs on base to give the Giants their eleventh straight road win.

On the train to St. Louis, the younger Giants, exuberant at the prospect of getting their hands on some World Series money, began speculating on how much their share might be. Christy Mathewson, still scarred by the 1908 debacle, told them, "You fellows had better soft pedal your conversation for a few days. I've seen many good things go wrong in the ninth inning." According to Sid Mercer, "Youth is irrepressible. Matty's [speech] was received with noisy expressions of contempt."

Mercer's afternoon report brought New Yorkers their first Giants news from St. Louis. Naturally he featured two Faust stories. First the fans read that "Charley Faust completed his first round of the National League course when the Giants registered at the Planters Hotel to-day. It was here that Charley first attached himself to the New York team. . . . After four days of doing without apple pie, Faust says it's great to stop at a regular hotel." There was no apple pie in Faust's original contract or regimen. If he missed it in Pittsburgh, the mania must have appeared in Boston, where apple pie helped him lead the Giants to four straight wins. In St. Louis he renewed his new superstition, not suspecting how big a role it would play in the road trip.

Mercer's second Faust story struck an unexpected chord—criticism. Of all people, Mercer seemed the least likely to knock his favorite subject. But hunger for a story did not motivate Mercer as strongly as devotion to the truth; in 1917 his integrity forced a bitter showdown with McGraw that ruptured their long association and caused Mercer to abandon the Giants beat. Thus, as the Giants reached St. Louis, Mercer saw fit to add some cautionary notes:

> Suppose you were a rough, unpolished chip of the diamond, that you were placed in a setting of scintillating gems, that the operation trimmed off the rough edges and improved you so much that you attracted no attention at all, and that all you got out of the refining process was a reputation as a high class phoney, wouldn't it make you sore on the theory of evolution? Well, that may be the

experience of one C. Victor Faust. The Kansas zephyr still retains his reputation as a jinx destroyer, but he is acting so much like a regular ball player these days that he isn't near as interesting on the field as he used to be. Charley has copied the latest styles of sprinting and sliding until his daily shows have lost much of their comedy, and if the Giants cinch the pennant soon his job as a mascot will be gone. However, he will be good for a winter in vaudeville over the National League circuit.

In short, Mercer accused Faust of becoming competent! It's hard to tell who Mercer thought was most threatened by this development—Faust, the fans, or himself.

Two days later a real threat to Faust emerged. The *Times* reported that "Charley Faust got a black hand letter from Chicago to-day. He is accused of being a 'jinx' for the other teams in the league, and if he doesn't hurry back to Marion, Kan., the letter says, something is going to happen to him. Faust is now considered the official 'jinx' for the other teams, and Manager McGraw wouldn't release him for money." Black Hand letters were nothing to joke about; the Black Hand meant crime organized with ruthless efficiency, using extortion, bombings, kidnappings, and assorted threats to prey upon small businessmen and anyone else who had something they wanted. As alleged in this rumor, they wanted Charley Faust's jinxing power and couldn't have it, leaving the alternative of persuading Faust to desist.

Sid Mercer's daily Faust update mentioned the threat, but not prominently. "This is Charley Faust's day to pitch, according to the soothsayers, but Charley is under the weather, and Matty will probably hook up with Laudermilk. Faust ate too much apple pie yesterday and warmed up so often during the two games that he was all in last night. He says it made him sick to see the Giants lose a game. It was the first time he had seen them defeated since August 24. The boys are watching Charley closely as they have a tip that he would be kidnapped here by agents of the Chicago club."

There is always the possibility that the whole thing was a setup by John McGraw. When he pulled the police-protection trick to hype that series in Cincinnati, he relied on the writers to spread the falsehood. Anticipating a hostile reception in Chicago as the Cubs made their last stand of 1911 against the avenging Giants, McGraw might well have planted the Black Hand rumor so that the publicity would buy them protection when it was needed. No doubt these two reports made the threat sound legitimate to the fans back in New York, who always welcomed a fresh excuse to scorn Chicago and its villainous Cubs.

The Giants were in St. Louis when the letter supposedly arrived from Chicago, but they were too neck-deep in doubleheaders to dwell on vague threats. They played two games the day they arrived, and naturally McGraw tapped Rube Marquard for the opener. The Cardinals still couldn't touch Marquard, sore arm or no, and he pitched a four-hitter for his third shutout in four starts against them, winning 4–0. The Giants executed McGraw's old Baltimore offense perfectly, using four stolen bases and three sacrifice bunts. The first run scored on a double steal, and Marquard singled in the last run. That made eight straight wins on the trip.

Doc Crandall started the second game, making his first appearance since bombing in Boston. He left in the sixth inning of a 2–2 game with two runners on and two outs. Christy Mathewson relieved and promptly allowed the only extra-base hit of Jim Clark's career, a two-run triple. For the first time on the trip, the Giants trailed later than the second inning. It started to rain; ominous clouds darkened the sky. Facing a crisis for the first time in ten days, the Giants turned threats to their advantage. How? With luck, of course. With two outs in the seventh inning, Cardinals pitcher Gene Woodburn (lifetime record: 2–9) uncorked an extremely wild pitch that allowed both Josh Devore and Larry Doyle to score, tying the game 4–4. As the eighth inning started, the *Times* said, "rain and thunder filled the air and it grew so dark that the fans yelled for Umpire Rigler to stop the game. Not yet a while." Woodburn rotted in the rain, walking Red Murray and hitting Fred Merkle and Buck Herzog to load the bases. Singles by Chief Meyers and Devore handed the Giants a 7–4 lead, but the worsening storm threatened to drench the field before the inning could be completed. That would make the score revert to a 4–4 tie. There ensued a brief travesty of the kind that afflicted games occasionally until the loophole was closed a couple of decades ago. The Giants tried to speed through the last few outs (Meyers deliberately ran into an out to end their half of the eighth), while the Cardinals stalled, hoping Cy Rigler would decide he had heard enough of the thunder and the pounding rain and the fans screaming at him to call the game. Rigler stubbornly made the Cardinals keep moving, and the serious downpour held off long enough for the Giants to record the three outs they needed to stretch their winning streak to ten games.

They played two more the next day, but it didn't seem to matter any more to the Giants, who ran wild again. They stole seven bases in each game, giving them fifty steals already with a dozen games left on the trip. McGraw later wrote, "The players got the notion that they could steal on anybody, and that belief was so strong that they went out and did it. On one trip West we arrived in Chicago with a club in rags and tatters—had to telegraph for new uniforms—nearly every man on the club had slid the seat out of his pants. We had patched and patched until the principal feature of our pants was safety pins." Maybe the Giants figured that stealing fourteen bases in one day would hasten the arrival of fresh uniforms. Damon Runyon wrote that "the seven speed marvels have slid right out of their garments, so essential to the preservation of a sense of modesty. . . . Josh Devore will have to use mascot Dick Hennessey's apparel very shortly unless John T. Brush takes pity on the destitute and sends on more knickers with reinforcements." They got new uniforms—for the World Series.

The Giants needed every one of those stolen bases and a clutch relief job by Christy Mathewson to win the opener 3–2. Hooks Wiltse took a 3–1 lead to the bottom of the ninth, gave up a run and put the tying run at second with one out. Mathewson mowed down two Cardinals to give Wiltse the win, extending the streak to eleven. Watching it all unfold, Charley Faust spent more and more time thinking about what it would be like to pitch in Chicago.

Several unusual factors combined in the second game to cause the unthinkable: the Giants lost a game. The biggest difference was that, for the first time since July 27—since the day before John McGraw met Charley Faust—someone pitched for the Giants who wasn't called Matty, Rube, Red, Doc, or Hooks.

What a juggling job McGraw had done, nursing five pitchers through a late-summer stretch of forty-six games, including nine doubleheaders. Mathewson pitched in eighteen of the games, Marquard and Crandall sixteen apiece; buoyed by the presence of the greatest nonpitcher in history, the Giants won thirty-four of those games to move seven games ahead of the second-place Cubs. The back-to-back doubleheaders finally forced McGraw to try someone else. Of the big five, everyone but Matty had started in the last forty-eight hours, and Matty had just relieved in two straight games after starting three days ago. That left Louis Drucke and his body cast, Charley Faust and his low-velocity windmill delivery, and Bert Maxwell, the untried youngster from Birmingham who joined the Giants early in the trip. McGraw went with Maxwell, and he almost got away with it. He stayed with Maxwell after the Cardinals scored five early runs, and the Giants nearly caught up. Two runs in the ninth inning brought them within a run, but they lost 8–7.

This aberrant occurrence—a loss—could be chalked up to McGraw having to rely on an overmatched pitcher, but another strange factor may have had more to do with the outcome than the dozen hits surrendered by Maxwell. Why didn't Charley Faust do his job? Would you believe that he was kidnapped? That's right, but not by the Black Hand, despite the reports of a threatening letter. This scoop belonged to John Wheeler, who disclosed it through Christy Mathewson in Matty's book published that winter. "One contest that we dropped in St. Louis was when some of the newspaper correspondents on the trip kidnapped Faust and sat him on the St. Louis bench." Who knows whose bright idea that was, or even if it happened like that. It's hardly kidnapping if they left Charley in plain sight, where any time during the game he could have moseyed on over to the Giants dugout to resume his jinxing duties. Did someone challenge Charley to test whether his jinxing powers would work from the opposition's dugout? Was he conned into believing that hiding on the St. Louis bench would prevent the Black Hand from kidnapping him from the bench where he was supposed to be? Did the Cardinals team have anything to do with it? The St. Louis writers? One of them, S. Carlisle Martin, interviewed Charley at length during the series, so perhaps a between-games meeting turned into a gamelong conversation, Martin getting the inside story while they sat like innocent bystanders on the Cardinals bench.

A more diabolical speculation: could Charley have boycotted Bert Maxwell? With all the regular arms used up and the team winning every game, Charley had to believe that his chance would arrive any day. He pestered McGraw every day, warmed up every day to be ready, so when McGraw snubbed him in favor of this kid who hadn't even joined the Giants until after Charley brought them up into first place, Charley might have taken it personally. If Maxwell was that good, he must not need any help from Charley Faust. So Charley watched the game from the Cardinals bench. Did he predict hits for the Cardinals? Did they appreciate him? We can only guess. All we know is that without him, Maxwell lost, ending the winning streak at eleven games. The single-game finale on Friday, September 22, must have seemed like a holiday to the two teams, who struggled through a nerve-racking ten-inning thriller. The Giants faced a major obstacle, the by-product of their success. The New York *Tribune* reported that "the base stealing campaign of New York was temporarily halted, and not a pilfered bag was recorded by the team during the fray. The fallaway slide has proved so disastrous on the team's uniforms that McGraw refused to run the risk of having anyone arrested for indecent exposure." Red Ames pitched in trouble all day, giving up eight hits and walking four, yet he took a shutout to the eighth inning. He led 3–1 in the bottom of the ninth but loaded the bases with one out on two singles and walk.

Enter Rube Marquard, with nearly two days of rest. Marquard struck out Otto McIver, but Ed Konetchy, the Cardinals' best hitter, stroked a two-run single that tied the game and sent it to extra innings, just what the teams needed. The Giants got an unearned run in the tenth. With two outs, Chief Meyers was safe on an error and managed to score on a Josh Devore double, inspiring Damon Runyon to lead off his coverage with this verse:

> Listen, my children, while a bard perspires
> Over the daylight gallop of big Chief Meyers,
> Who rode from first on a two-base blow
> With the winning run as the scorebooks show.
> I reckon you'll say, as soon as you hear,
> That it beats the record of Paul Revere.

Marquard had a chance now to pick up his twenty-third win. Instead, he found more trouble. A leadoff walk preceded a bloop hit, and the runners were bunted over. Marquard walked Jack Bliss to load the bases, creating the same situation he failed in the inning before. His overworked arm didn't feel that great, and he wondered how he could get out of this jam.

He needn't have worried. Sid Mercer picked up the story right there:

A hit here would have lost the game for the Giants. Out in centrefield Matty and Charley Faust were warming up together. "Charley," said Matty, "you better hike to the bench. You know you were not there the other day when we almost lost in the ninth inning." Faust looked at Matty a moment, and just then Marquard passed Bliss and filled the bases, with one out. Without another word the "Kansas Cyclone" tore out across the green and sped madly toward the grand stand.

He cut across left field like Casey Jones going down hill and a moment later steamed into the coop puffing, but bringing much good cheer. "I'm here, boys," he panted. "Now, Rube, go get 'em." Those Giants seated on the bench, and McGraw was among them, hailed the coming of the Kansas rube with cries of joy and relief. They praised Matty for turning in the alarm. "We can't lose now," yelled Beals Becker, "look, here comes Charley." And Charley just chased that jinx right out of the ball yard. Clarke, a substitute batsman, sent a short fly to Devore and nobody on the bases stirred. Miller Huggins . . . got a count of three and two and as Rube swung his arm the three runners got in motion with wild yells to disconcert the Rube.

If the Rube had not been game and if Faust had not been there choking the jinx to death this paean of joy would never have been written. . . . Huggins had to swing and Herzog ferried the ball to Merkle for the third out. Then the Giants decamped a triumphal procession with Faust proudly marching in the lead.

The version in Mathewson's book differs slightly. "Marquard, in the box, was apparently going up in the air. Only one was out. Faust was warming up far in the suburbs when, under orders from McGraw, I ran out and sent him to the bench, for that was the place from which his charm seemed to be the most potent. 'Charley' came loping to the bench as fast as his long legs would transport him and St. Louis didn't score and we won the game. It was as nice a piece of pinch mascoting as I ever saw."

Rube Marquard raised his eyepopping record to 23–6, yet Charley Faust picked up most of the credit. Through sheer hustle and leadership, he got Marquard through the crisis. After missing a game, he gave the most convincing demonstration yet of his uncanny ability to guarantee victory for the Giants, ending their one-game losing streak. Whether it was McGraw's idea or Mathewson's, the ploy of making the Cardinals wait while the ice wagon lurched across the field to encourage Marquard worked. Somehow, the Giants prevailed again, winning the series four games to one.

ON SEPTEMBER 24, two days after the Giants left town, S. Carlisle Martin's feature article on Charley Faust appeared in the St. Louis *Post-Dispatch*. A lengthy, comprehensive history of Faust's legend, it ran five columns wide, covering more than half the front page of the Sunday sports section. Around 1980 it was found by Thomas Busch, a Kansas historian doing the first original research on Faust. Busch dubbed Martin's article the Rosetta Stone of Faust's career. Martin relied heavily on quotes by Faust, statements which give a more accurate picture of Faust than those in the New York papers. Unlike the New York reporters, who twisted any subject's words into their own peculiar vernacular, Martin reproduced Faust's statements with his pronounced German accent, starting with his middle name, "Wictor."

Charlie Faust Has "Come Back" So Often McGraw Has Decided to Let Him Remain

WORDS AND PICTURES BY S. CARLISLE MARTIN

Dodged, Side-Stepped, Left Behind, the Marion (Kan.) Comedian Still Bobs Up to Tell the Giants How to Play the National Game.

"WELL, I helped New York win the pennant, and now I'm going to Frisco to find Lulu. The lady fortune teller told me both would come to pass, so maybe I'll get married this winter."

To yours truly the gentleman spoke quietly, but firmly, in his Marion (Kansas) drawl. Charlie also spoke with great feeling. Charlie— well, you know Charlie, don't you?

Charlie "Wictor" Faust? Wictor, he told me, was spelled with a "Wee" (V), like Sam Weller spelled his surname. But I forgot to tell you who Charlie is and why.

Of course, fellow fans, you have doubtless observed the grotesque vaudeville stunts that were pulled by Mr. Faust daily as he cavorted on the diamond here with the New York Giants, giving correct, life-like impersonations of Christy Mathewson, Ty Cobb, Honus Wagner, and other great stars of the diamond, and doubtless you have laughed heartily. Everyone does who has seen the gentleman sliding bases.

But aside from being the greatest clown in baseball (and, by the way, our hero takes himself seriously), Charles "Wictor" has a "purpose" in life; or, rather, two or three purposes. To become a great ballplayer, to marry Lulu, and to stop only at hotels that furnish apple pie are three things from which Charlie will not be sidetracked.

But, to begin in the front of this story:

FORTUNE TELLER TIPPED CHARLIE TO HIS TALENT

About six months ago, away out in the corn belt of Kansas, a young man was busily engaged in tilling the soil, or killing potato bugs, I don't remember which. At any rate, he was in association with others in agricultural pursuits.

Now, whether Charlie was called from the plow, a la Cincinnatus, or not, the "dope" sayeth little. At any rate, he was "called"—and called good and plenty. Dropping the plow handle and giving the old gray hoss a kick on the shins, Charley hied himself straight for Wichita and a fortune teller. And, believe me, Chas. is husky for that clairvoyant stuff. Firmly convinced is he of her prophecy that he would join the Giants and would help win the pennant for McGraw must, as he puts it, "come to pass."

At first Manager J. McGraw enjoyed the joke immensely, when Charlie presented himself here in St. Louis, armed with his fortune-telling credentials, and he smilingly consigned him to the wardrobe-keeper of the Giants, who rigged out our six-foot-two-inch recruit in a costume that would have cramped Willie Keeler when he was a boy.

And everybody laughed. It was great sport, and the boys from the "Great White Way" fell for the fun in bunches. All sorts of tricks were played on Charles, such as telling him to lay his arm in the sleeper hammock at night, that that was the way Christy Mathewson and other great pitchers did; or little things like filling his grip with pig iron and telling him, as he staggered under it, that it wasn't heavy, but that his arm was weakened from riding in a Pullman all day. To see him carry the load to the depot kept the boys in good humor all the trip.

On the ball field they've had their fun, too, for Charlie has pitched to all the stars of the National League, and never a one from Honus Wagner down has ever been able to connect with his rare assortment of twisters. When he himself hits the ball and starts around the bases, somehow no one can hold the throw, and when he gets about midway between second and third they all yell "slide, Charlie, slide," and Charlie slides, believe me, or rolls, 45 feet to third. But the third baseman never seems to hold the ball.

When Charlie pulls the squeeze play, the throw home to catch him is always wild.

Great sport, and the boys have long since forgotten "Bugs" Raymond.

MR. FAUST HAS IT ON THE "COME-BACK" CAT

But after awhile, McGraw tried to shake Charlie. When the players gathered at Union Station to depart for Chicago, Charley came running up to McGraw and asked for his contract and railroad ticket.

"Oh, didn't you get them?" said Mack. "Why I left them at the hotel for you."

That was 10 minutes before train time and Charlie hiked back to the hotel and as the train pulled out Mack and the boys had a good laugh.

But in Boston, when they went up to register at the hotel, who was there to bid them welcome? Why, Charlie Faust, of course!

Because Charlie is the "come-back kid." After trying the shaking business two or three times, Mc-Graw gave it up and now the New York club pays for Charlie's "eats," and they do say that he can smother a planked steak in three bites—in fact, can go the whole route from soup to nuts without showing the least fatigue.

The club also pays his railroad fare and other incidental expenses.

So far, Charlie has not signed a genuine contract from McGraw, although he has signed a great many others with fancy red seals, etc., furnished by his brother ballplayers. But we are of the impression that he will not have to sign one. In fact, we think it would be hard to pull Charlie loose from the Giants at the present writing.

Why? Because Charlie has the hoodoo sign on the other members. He is the mascot. He has their goat strong, and they are now as superstitious as he is, and dislike to play when Faust is not on the bench. The reason, plainly, is that, with one exception, here in St. Louis, they have never lost a game while Charlie was on the bench.

And then Dame Rumor has it that McGraw has a weakness for comedians, as it tends to keep the club in good humor.

Thus doth Charlie tarry with the "Gi'nts."

But maybe Charlie is not cognizant of the side show stuff he is pulling—and then again, maybe he is. He's as big a mystery as our friend George Kimmel.

"Did you ever play in the minors, Charlie?" I asked.

"No."

"Then where did you learn to play ball?"

"Oh, I played a liddle in Wichita, and then, besides, I bought a couple of books."

"Books?" I chirped.

"Yes; Spalding's Guide and Reach's books, too."

S. CARLISLE MARTIN's caricatures captured Faust's eccentricities, not to mention the German accent no other writer mentioned in these pre–World War I times. Picture Faust plodding around the bases on those feet and you can understand why he became the main attraction of the pregame show.

HE'S BATTING .300 NOW IN THE TIPPING CLASS

With the above answer Charlie slipped me the smile which you see depicted in the drawing above.

"How do you find it in the big League?"

"Oh! Id taigs more hade work," said Charlie, as he passed that smile around again.

"Then you have absolute confidence in the fortune teller, have you, Charlie?"

"Yes." And after a pause and some more smile. "It must come to pass."

"How about finding Lulu? What's her last name?"

"I don't know, bud I'll find her and may be ve'll ged married dis vinter."

All the while Charlie is there with that awful semi-toothless smile.

"Tell me—how did you help McGraw win the pennant? You were not in a game?"

"No, but I did my work on the bench. I've god my own signals." More smile—I mean from Charlie.

"They tell me you have been in vaudeville, Charlie?"

"Yes. One veek at Hammerstein's and mebby two or dree more dis fall. Bud I'd rather play ball for McGraw."

And say, brother fans, it is claimed that his vaudeville stunt is a scream and that he is the only real successor to the Cherry Sisters. Everything from dodging vegetables, giving imitations of great ballplayers, sliding bases, and finally being yanked off the stage with numerous hooks, takes place.

"They tell me you come from a family of ballplayers, Charles," I resumed.

"Vell, not egsactly. But I've god a brudder who can pitch. I've caught him and he's got more breaks dan Wiltse or Mathewson, I t'ink."

But Charlie is learning himself, and who knows but some day he may make good. He is watching the other members of the team and catching on and now tips everybody who does him a service.

The other day McGraw saw him give a nickel to the hat girl in a hotel and slyly remarked: "Charlie, you're getting along all right. Here you are tipping the waiters, and there is Drucke, who has been in the majors three years, and nobody ever saw him give up a nickel to anyone. You've only been with us three months and you're batting .300 already. You'll do, Charlie."

MARTIN COVERED ALL the Faust essentials and then some—the fortune, Lulu, vaudeville, apple pie, pig iron, Honus Wagner, fake contracts, base running, and George Kimmel. George who? On September 18 a convict who had served time under the aliases J. W. Hosmer, J. W. White, and W. A. Watson was released from a New York state prison. He had recently identified himself as George Kimmel, a banker who had disappeared (in Kansas) in 1898 and was long presumed dead. Visited in prison by Kimmel's mother and sister, he insisted he was Kimmel even after they called him a faker. Upon his release, he was greeted by an old Kimmel friend and taken to Kimmel's hometown of Niles, Michigan. En route, he explained that he was mugged in 1898 on a business trip (to St. Louis) and lost his memory for several years, then drifted to New York and began accumulating aliases and jail terms. His last stretch was five years—for forgery.

George Kimmel arrived in Niles on September 19 and was greeted fondly by dozens of old friends and a couple of cousins. But Mrs. Stella Kimmel remained skeptical and refused to let this alleged son in her house. Stories appeared about an insurance policy which would not be paid if George Kimmel still breathed. A two-day standoff ensued until the big showdown took place. To the great surprise of the citizens of Niles, who threw parties to celebrate George Kimmel's miraculous return after thirteen years of oblivion, he failed Mrs. Kimmel's test. He made mistakes about objects in her home which George Kimmel should have known easily, and she didn't buy his amnesia story either. She sent the impostor packing, whoever he was, back to oblivion.

That was the mystery alluded to by S. Carlisle Martin in his assessment of Charley Faust. A man says that he is this or that, makes some bold claim he cannot plainly prove. Dozens of people surround him and accept him for what he says he is. Only one person doubts him— unfortunately, the only person whose opinion matters. So his claim is denied and he is ruined. But what of the dozens of people who believed in him? What did their acceptance of him reveal about them? Wasn't he real to them? Or did he merely fool them? Could he have fooled them, or anyone, forever?

The same day that Stella Kimmel flunked her "son," Charley Faust aced his quiz from S. Carlisle Martin and even passed muster with John McGraw on the matter of tipping. Charley's indisputable record as a good-luck charm gave credence to the rest of the fortune-teller's work, so Martin made much of the Lulu angle. "Some day he may make good," Martin conceded at the end of his remarkable Faustfest. Already famous as "the greatest clown in baseball," Charley had genetics, books, the examples of Mathewson and Marquard, and concerned teammates to help him "make good" as a major league pitcher. If only he could convince John McGraw.

As long as the article was, S. Carlisle Martin's seven superb illustrations took up just as much space, splashed across the top half of the page. Two views of Charley Faust's pitching motion were done from photographs taken for the *Post-Dispatch* but not published. One showed Charley leaning way back, left foot thrust forward, labeled "Correct

Position for Beginning the Fade-away (Faust got this from a baseball guide book)." In the other, mammoth arms extended way over Charley's head, the top of the windmill windup, helping to highlight the medal he received in Pittsburgh and wore proudly on his chest. Martin called this "Starting the Spiral Dip (from a well-known correspondence school course)." In these and two other illustrations, Charley's feet were twice as large as his head.

One drawing, a group portrait, was simply captioned "Since Charlie Joined the 'Joints." The nine figures sported Giants caps and flashed goofy grins. Some of the faces resembled some of the Giants, but the grins all looked like Charley. The full semitoothless Faust smile appeared in two of Martin's illustrations. One, "Charlie 'Wictor' Faust," was a portrait of Charley wearing a tie, jacket, and hat, his wide smile a trio of white rectangles in a dark cavern. His face looked much goofier in the small caricature of his hatless head in one corner of the collage. Captioned "Dat was good apple pie," this was Faust at point-blank range: unruly hair plastered to a small flattened skull, weak eyes squinting nearly shut, big ears, a long narrow nose, and that gaptooth grin above a sagging chin. It was not a pretty picture.

Below that visage, Martin placed an enormous, elongated Charley Faust sitting in a hotel lobby telling Martin "Yaas, it must be. She saad it would come to pass." Martin's caption: "The Marion, Kansas Recruit Is a Firm Believer in Clairvoyance."

Martin summed up Faust's talents in the final illustration, called "Snapshot of Charlie Winning the Pennant on the Bench." Charley, all feet and crossed legs, sat on a bench, leaning back, arms folded, left hand reaching up to stroke his chin. The balloon above his head simply said "Thinks." That's all it took, folks. Charley sat on the bench, pondered what must "come to pass," and willed it to happen.

CHARLEY FAUST'S "pinch-mascotting" stunt helped the Giants to their eleventh win in eleven days on the road. Leading the Cubs by seven games with eighteen to play, their reward was another chance to monkey with Charley, his pitching arm, and his vaudeville act on the overnight train ride to Cincinnati. Hooks Wiltse and Louis Drucke detoured to Youngstown, Ohio, to visit "Bonesetter" Reese, an orthopedic physician noted for treating athletes, the Frank Jobe of his time. Wiltse started only two more games in 1911. Neither Reese nor Charley could fix his hip.

You have to wonder what John McGraw thought about at the St. Louis train station that day. Eight weeks earlier, he had conned Charley Faust into running back to the hotel so that the train could leave without him. Now here he stood, the Little Napoleon, having led his team through so many winning streaks that he could finally concede to the press and the fans back home that the Giants had sewed up the pennant. And what did he have to show for it? A telegram from his boss, John T. Brush, back in New York, a telegram that reached McGraw just before the train departed, a telegram with a starkly simple message of encouragement: "May good luck and Charley Faust stay with you." Amazing. No "nice job, John" or "keep up the good work." Just make sure Faust is there.

In Cincinnati, McGraw found himself overshadowed by his team's success and by Faust's growing celebrity. At League Park the Giants were greeted by signs proclaiming them the "next world's champions." Christy Mathewson took care of the day's game, resuming his mastery over the Reds with a 6–2 win. The Cubs lost again, and the Giants moved eight games ahead of them. No big deal. It was business as usual for Faust at the ballpark, judging by this note in the New York *Sun*: "Charles Faust, the peerless mascot, tried his hand in the outfield in practice and was hit squarely on the top of his shapely bean by a fly ball."

There is no record of how John McGraw passed that Saturday evening in Cincinnati, but we know what Charley Faust and the writers did. The *Times* reported that "August Herrmann, who confesses to the ownership of the Reds, and is also the Chairman of the National Baseball Commission, gave a dinner to-night to the troop of New York newspaper reporters who are traveling with the team. Garry is O.K." Garry Herrmann was quite a character. A major cog in the political machine that ran Cincinnati, he became part-owner and president of the Reds in time to help orchestrate peace between the National League and the upstart American League. In 1903 he was chosen to join the two league presidents as the third member of the new National Commission. His

AUGUST HERRMANN was the universally respected
head of baseball's ruling National Commission. He
enjoyed watching Faust perform but wasn't about to be
fooled into declaring Faust a major league ballplayer.
(Transcendental Graphics)

geniality, diplomacy, and dedication made him the right choice, and he
remained the commission's only chairman until yielding to the first
commissioner in 1920.

Herrmann loved throwing lavish parties for fellow owners and
other luminaries; in their absence, he eagerly courted the press with
goodwill gatherings like the one mentioned in the *Times*. Sid Mercer
provided the rest of Saturday's story in the Monday *Globe:*

> Faust attended George Evans's minstrel show. He went on
> between acts and gave his monologue. Then he was introduced to

Garry Herrmann across the street at the Hotel Havlin. On Herrmann's request the jinx disperser repeated his performance. He declined at first, but finally agreed to declaim "For the Good of the Game." Herrmann thanked him in behalf of the National Commission, and as Faust left he was presented with a $25 bouquet of roses that had adorned the festal board. He bowed himself out, went back to the Monroe and presented the roses to a chambermaid. The players induced the chambermaid to give up the flowers and presented them to Charley again at the ball yard yesterday afternoon. If they stay fresh and do not wilt he will receive them again to-day. Great stuff!

Performing his act to kill time on train rides was one thing, but in Cincinnati, Charley Faust gave two command performances in one night. Unfortunately, the text of "For the Good of the Game" escaped publication, so we can only guess at the mental acumen necessary to recite it over and over again. It was also too bad that the Giants couldn't have stuck around St. Louis awhile longer. The day Charley performed in Cincinnati, President William Howard Taft attended the game in St. Louis. Poor President Taft—he cheered the visiting Phillies as they lost to the Cardinals in the bottom of the ninth inning, and he probably didn't get half the postgame show that another rotund Ohioan, Garry Herrmann, did.

Jack Ryder, baseball columnist of the Cincinnati *Enquirer*, gave Charley Faust some publicity after his Cincinnati debut. Ryder, in his extensive Notes of the Game section, mentioned that "Charley Faust, the real mascot of the Giants, is a fan of true-blue character. He gave up a hundred-dollar-a-week job at a vaudeville theater in New York to come West with the Giants and give the new champs the benefit of his beaming presence. They have lost only one game on the trip so far, and Charley is the killer of hoodoos and jinxes." If Charley was the "real" mascot, what of the nominal mascot, the incumbent, Dick Hennessey? Ryder didn't leave him out of the picture: "Dick Hennessey, a clever youngster who is helping Charley Faust win games for the Giants, got a big hand for his work around first base in the preliminary practice. He handles thrown balls a la Fred Merkle."

On Sunday, September 24, a strange thing happened—the Giants lost a game—so startling that it took detective work by the whole corps of New York writers to determine why it had happened. Here are the facts: The Reds, who had beaten Rube Marquard in his traumatic debut way back in 1908, continued to be his nemesis, pounding him for five runs in five innings. The Giants caught up in the sixth inning, tying the game 5–5, but the Reds got a run off Hooks Wiltse in the eighth and hung on to win 6–5. That's what happened, but why?

John Wheeler of the *Herald* came up with a couple of reasons, one small, one large. The small reason was that "Brownie" Burke, the Reds' mascot, took Dick Hennessey to lunch, and "it is thought that there was underhand work and that 'Brownie' got into 'Dick' for some of the Giants' signals, which explains the defeat. . . . 'Brownie' was returned to the Montana Legislature four times as pageboy, so it's easy to surmise that he must be pretty slick, and besides he ain't buying the Giants' mascot lunch for nothing." McGraw's remedy was to prohibit Hennessey from eating with "foreigners" any more.

Wheeler knew that wasn't the reason the Giants lost. Check out the headline over the game coverage: "'Rube,' Rattled by Friends, Loses Game to the Reds." Friends? Yes, between eleven hundred and two thousand of them invaded Cincinnati in two special trains. They came from Indianapolis, where Marquard had won twenty-eight games in 1908 before John McGraw signed him. "The folks back home," wrote Wheeler, "were all up around the hotel this morning to see the 'Rube' and tell him about the events which he has missed while he's been away. At first they were sort of bashful when they saw Richard in all his glad draperies and the diamond ring on his finger which sparkled and glittered in the morning light." That evening in the hotel, after Marquard was roughed up by the Reds, the Indianapolis folks had no trouble calling him "Rube" rather than "Mr. Marquard" as they had that morning.

Their well-wishing presence by itself would have put a little extra pressure on Marquard to come through, but there was more. "News of Engagement of Old Sweetheart Upsets Giants' Great Twirler," read the subheadline. It turned out that one Jennie Coakley, long admired by Marquard, had accepted a marriage proposal, and this news so disturbed Rube that he couldn't concentrate on the Reds. Other reporters mentioned the Indianapolis rooters, but only Wheeler uncovered the scoop of the indomitable Rube rattled by romance.

Wheeler had a few words to say about Charley Faust's role in the defeat, too. "It was the first game that the Giants have lost with Faust on the bench. He said that he didn't have anything to-day because he was up late last night, and anyway, he doesn't believe in playing ball on Sunday. He declared to-night that it would not occur again." Maybe he meant it; this was the Giants' first Sunday game since he had joined them.

Sid Mercer knew more than Wheeler about Faust's comings and goings. His report: "Charley Faust attributes yesterday's defeat to the fact that his repeated requests for slabs of apple pie have been ignored by the waiters at the Hotel Monroe, where the Giants are beaning. He says the jinx is slowly starving. Yesterday's defeat was the first that the Giants have encountered this season with Faust sitting on the bench." Mercer went on about Faust's latest mania. "Jack Murray, who is Faust's manager, has cut down his protégé to one shave and one massage a day. In St. Louis the 'Kansas Cyclone' was blowing himself to two scrapes and two map manicures each day. George Wiltse asked him why. 'Well,' drawled Charley, 'I got one early in the morning, felt fine, then after supper to-night I saw Eddie Brannick go into the barber shop, and I thought I'd go along with him.' It costs Faust just $1.80 a day, including tips, to keep his features tonsorially adjusted."

What was going on? The Giants lost one lousy ballgame, and nobody could say that they simply got beaten. No, it was the mascot giving away signals or Rube distracted by his lost Jennie, or something to do with Faust and apple pie. Two weeks into the road trip, giddy from victory, the writers started flexing their literary muscles. Anybody could write the facts, which mattered less all the time with the pennant suspense vanishing. Blurring fact and fancy was more fun, and nobody knew that more than Damon Runyon.

"'No Pie, No Mascot,' Declares Giant Jinx," read Runyon's headline. The sub-headline: "Failing to Find Favorite Delicacy on Bill of Fare C. Faust Deserts and New York Loses to Cincinnati." There followed an account which showed the esteem for outlandish characters that blossomed in Runyon's later stories of Broadway citizens.

These Monday morning tidings of defeat trace back to the breakfast hour this morning and to the gross carelessness of the proprietor of the hotel where the nearly-next champions of the National League are "beaning." This proprietor, a man with little regard for the epicure or idiosyncracy of genius, ran out of apple pie during the regular Cincinnati rush upon that delicacy Saturday night, and caused the absence from the Giant bench to-day of Charles Victory Faust and the consequent defeat of Reuben Not-So-Victorious Marquard and the almost champions by a score of 6 to 5.

Without his apple pie for breakfast the jinxing power of Charles Victory over the other fellow is wholly nil. He must have that Kansas matutinal bracer, else the charm is lost, and so when Charles spread himself before a table this morning and learned the pieless news he was wellnigh prostrated.

Armed with an appetite for pie, Charles went out upon the highways and byways of the city in quest thereof, but pie foundries are one institution that do not stay open in Cincinnati on Sundays, and before Charley could reconcile himself to "plain sinkers and draw one" and reach the ball yard the Reds had started Reuben on the run.

It was most exasperating and painful, but it only goes to show that a private jinx must be attended to on Sundays as well as week days. This makes the second game the Giants have lost out of fourteen played. . . . The Reuben feels a little bitter toward Faust tonight, for laying off the jinx in favor of pie on a day when the Ohio Frenchman wanted to appear at his best before friends.

Beautiful. Marquard got knocked out because of Charley's absence, just as Bert Maxwell lost the other game on the trip because Charley sat in the wrong dugout. The Giants were playing so well, and Charley killed jinxes so infallibly, that only major breakdowns in both areas made the Giants lose. Yet as Runyon and Mercer pointed out, Charley's jinxing talent was a delicate mechanism that could break down without proper maintenance. You couldn't be too careful, not in a time of falling airplanes, not when even Christy Mathewson could suffer through a couple of bad weeks and start folks wondering whether he was "blowing up" for good.

The Giants knew that the loss was a fluke and did not take it to heart. That evening, Garry Herrmann threw a party for the players, John McGraw, and the writers. Monday morning, they continued a

'No Pie, No Mascot,' Declares Giant Jinx

Failing to Find Favorite Delicacy on Bill of Fare C. Faust Deserts and New York Loses to Cincinnati.

NATIONAL LEAGUE.	AMERICAN LEAGUE.
YESTERDAY'S RESULTS.	**YESTERDAY'S RESULTS.**
CINCINNATI, 9; NEW YORK, 6.	Philadelphia, 5; Cleveland, 5.
Philadelphia, 6; St. Louis, 2.	
Chicago-Boston (rain).	

STANDING OF THE CLUBS.

	W.	L.	P.C.		W.	L.	P.C.
NEW YORK	88	48	.650	St. Louis...	73	60	.549
Chicago....	82	57	.590	Cincinnati.	66	72	.493
Pittsburgh..	82	63	.566	BROOKLYN	54	85	.400
Philadelphia.	76	64	.542	Boston......	36	101	.265

STANDING OF THE CLUBS.

	W.	L.	P.C.		W.	L.	P.C.
Philadelphia	93	45	.679	Chicago. ...	70	69	.500
Detroit ...	84	57	.596	Boston	70	73	.482
Cleveland	74	67	.525	Washington	60	81	.426
NEW YORK	73	69	.514	St. Louis.	40	102	.282

TO-DAY'S GAMES.	**TO-DAY'S GAMES.**
NEW YORK AT CINCINNATI.	CHICAGO AT NEW YORK.
BROOKLYN AT PITTSBURGH.	Detroit at Philadelphia.
Boston at Chicago (2 games)	St. Louis at Boston.
Philadelphia at St. Louis.	Cleveland at Washington.

By Damon Runyon.

CINCINNATI, Ohio, Sept. 24.—These Monday morning tidings of defeat trace back to the breakfast hour this morning and to the gross carelessness of the proprietor of the hotel where the nearly-next champions of the National League are "beaning." This proprietor, a man with little regard for the epicure or idiosyncrasies of genius, ran out of apple pie during the regular Cincinnati rush upon that delicacy Saturday night, and caused the absence from the Giant bench to-day of Charles Victory Faust and the consequent defeat of Reuben Not-So-Victorious Marquard and the almost champions by a score of 9 to 5.

Without his apple pie for breakfast the jinxing power of Charles Victory over the other fellow is wholly nil. He must have that Kansas medicinal braser, else the charm is lost, and so when Charles spread himself before a table this morning and learned the pieless news he was wellnigh prostrated.

Couldn't Find His Pie.

Armed with an appetite for pie, Charles went out upon the highways and byways of the city in quest thereof, but pie foundries are one institution that do not stay open in Cincinnati on Sundays, and before Charley could reconcile himself to "plain sinkers and draw one" and reach the ball yard the Reds had started Reuben on the run.

It was most exasperating and painful, but it only goes to show that a private jinx must be attended to on Sundays as well as week days. This makes the second game the Giants have lost out of fourteen played.

DAMON RUNYON WAS A ROOKIE in New York along with Faust in 1911. Born sixty miles and one day away in Kansas, Runyon quickly latched onto Faust as the kind of character worthy of his finest hyperbole. (Photo: Corbis-Bettmann/UPI)

spending spree, investing bundles of World Series money before they clinched the pennant. Sid Mercer provided the final tally when the team reached Chicago:

> The Giants are making a real flash here. When they emerged from the Lasalle Street station early this morning and piled into taxicabs, passing pedestrians were blinded by the dazzling reflection from vast chunks of "ice"—the same being slang for diamonds—that encircled the fingers of McGraw's hardy toilers. Visions of wealth in the world's series have pulled the rubbers off bankrolls that are about to be greatly fattened, and the diamond merchants of Cincinnati reaped a rich harvest. The Giants left more than $3,000 in Cincinnati in exchange for sparklers. Rube Marquard blew himself to a $600 ring, and Josh Devore has its duplicate. Josh also bought a pendant for his mother. Arthur Devlin gave up $500 for a ring, and an assay of Athletes in the lobby of the Munroe Hotel in Cincinnati last night revealed several other new and scintillating sparklers of various sizes and prices. Some of them were so large that the hotel clerks nearly strangled with envy. When the Giants make their flash at the west side, which they attend as spectators to-day, handsome Harry McIntyre, the diamond king of the Chicago team, is expected to curl right up and turn green. Our boys are certainly rigged out like a lot of prima donnas. Rube Marquard has ordered another wardrobe trunk for new scenery that he will carry next winter.

Marquard was already regarded in New York as a fashion plate, having quickly warmed to the trappings of fame in the big city. This week also brought the announcement that Marquard would perform in a play titled "Way Down East" during the winter. Devore, his roommate, tried to keep up with him as the Giants outdid each other to reap the early rewards of breaking free from the National League pack.

When it came to imitating people in order to fit in, nobody outdid Charley Faust. If they didn't take him to a show or a poolroom, he would follow them into the barber shop. To be a real player, he knew, he had to look like a real player, no matter how many manicures it took. Over the course of the road trip, his "beaming presence" became more and more welcome. Christy Mathewson discussed the trip in *Pitching in a Pinch:*

"Charley," with his monologue and great good humor, kept the players in high spirits throughout the journey, and the feeling prevailed that we couldn't lose with him along. He was advertised all over the circuit, and spectators were going to the ball park to see Faust and Wagner. . . . His one "groove" was massages and manicures. He would go into the barber shop with any member of the team who happened to be getting shaved and take a massage and manicure for the purposes of sociability, as a man takes a drink. He easily was the record holder for the manicure Marathon, hanging up the figures of five in one day in St. Louis. He also liked pie for breakfast, dinner and supper, and a small half before retiring.

Edwin V. Burkholder attempted to wring something superhuman from these eccentricities with a quote from the Kansas Cyclone himself. Compare Burkholder's reproduction of Faust's diction with S. Carlisle Martin's. Wrote Burkholder:

Eating apple pie four times a day isn't anything unusual for a country boy, or for a good many city boys. Charley had an explanation about the massages and the manicures that shows he had as much shrewdness and understanding of human psychology as McGraw often demonstrated. "I always liked to talk to the boys when they were getting a shave," he explained to me. "When a man is getting shaved, he ain't thinking much about anything. I would tell them that if this happened or that happened, they would get a hit that afternoon. They listened and didn't kid me so much. I'd always see that anything I suggested happened. Lots of times I had to get in a barber chair three or four times in a morning so I could talk to a number of the boys. It always worked."

Burkholder did not indicate exactly how Charley made sure "anything I suggested happened." Perhaps he merely had to suggest to Hooks Wiltse that his hip would get better.

The Giants did make an impression with their diamonds during an off day in Chicago, as faithfully chronicled by a rapt Sid Mercer. "The rocks of the Giants were gathered and placed in the hotel safe last night, and the boys will attempt to win by straight tactics to-day. Even little Dick Henessey helped out in the flash of the crown jewels for he picked up a diamond chip so as to be right in style. Charley Faust is thinking of having an eight carat stone set in the gold filling of his front tooth. He could flash it in the batter's eye every time he pitched and that might help him to deceive." Indeed it might. It might also have been Mercer's idea.

The last day in Cincinnati, the *Enquirer's* Jack Ryder threw one important observation of his own into a hearsay history of Faust's career. Ryder summarized Faust's Kansas origins (saying Faust's father owned "500 of the finest acres in the state"), the fortune-teller, his first tryout and triumphs in St. Louis (claiming that the Giants put him in uniform the first day), and his continuing success with the Giants. Ryder concluded, "That Charley's heart is in his work is shown by the fact that he gave up a hundred-dollar-a-week job at a vaudeville theater in New York to come on this Western trip with the team. He is a big, quiet, good-natured fellow, not a bit fresh or forward, a little simple, but not a fool by any means. He thoroughly believes that he is the main cause of the Giants' fast finish in the pennant race. He is 32 years old and has a little money. He will be allowed to pitch a game in Chicago this week and, no matter how hard he is hit, he will be convinced that that game won the flag for the Giants." Good-natured, simple, but not a fool. You couldn't tell Jack Ryder that Charley Faust was an idiot or a lunatic.

The talk about Faust's pitching a game in Chicago, an outlandish proposal first heard back in Boston, continued in earnest in Cincinnati. Ryder summed it up bluntly: "McGraw will show his contempt for the Cubs by putting Charley Faust in to pitch, Wilbert Robinson to catch, while he will go to shortstop himself and send Arlie Latham to third base. The Giant leader has no particular use for the Cub rooters, and he is glad of the chance to show up their team."

Sid Mercer had two notes on the subject. "If the Giants get away with two of those three games Charley Faust will get the opportunity he has pined for. It will be handed to him in the shape of an assignment to pitch Sunday's game, which the Giants hope to rub in on Chicago as a derisive farewell." Talk about the end justifying the means. "The Cubs," Mercer added, "love to humiliate the Giants no less than McGraw dotes on showing up Chance's team at home. No mercy will be shown, and if the Giants can win all four games they will pile up as many runs as they can in each combat and even try to return Charlie Faust a victor, which is some degree of endeavor."

John Wheeler echoed that theme the day the Giants arrived in Chicago: "McGraw is expecting no lead pipe cinch in the series. He is going after the first game hard and said last night that if he won two out of the first three he would pitch Charley Faust on Sunday. 'They have put it up to us hard here two or three times,' said McGraw to-night, 'and if I can just get two games it's Faust on Sunday. How about it, Charley?' 'You bet I'll go in and pitch,' answered the 'bug,' and he is counting on it and reading about new curves in the book from which he learned to pitch. He is the first correspondence school twirler to chisel his way into the big leagues."

A strange perspective on Faust's fame was provided by the New York *Tribune* on September 26. For the first time, Faust's name appeared in a nonbaseball item, in this case the *Tribune's* boxing notes. "Baseball has its Charley Faust, and boxing has its 'Battling' Keefe, the 'middleweight champion of the world.' Keefe made himself famous among the fight 'fans' recently by wandering into the Twentieth Century Athletic Club and demanding a match with Billy Papke." Papke was the real champion, Keefe some guy who wandered in off the street. Charley Faust's success story had inspired an imitator!

The *Sporting News* sounded an envious note in its September 28 edition. "Who wouldn't be a 'nut' like Charles Victory Faust? When he is not feeding on the fat of the land with the Giants he is drawing $100 a week in a vaudeville theater, giving an exhibition of 'sliding' to bases on a Turkish rug. If C. Victory didn't do it in all seriousness, it wouldn't be funny enough to draw the money." Even today, who wouldn't be a nut like Victory Faust? Any current fan of the Cubs or Red Sox or White Sox would give ten weeks of his life to be the jinx-killing mascot leading his favorite team to its first championship in nearly a century.

The Giants won the last game in Cincinnati 2–0, but the toll of their base-running assault became apparent: all three steal attempts failed, and three times a runner stopped at third base instead of trying to score from second on a single, a routine attempt for a Giant. With tattered uniforms held together by safety pins, with Fred Merkle leaving early with a charley horse, the Giants scraped together a couple of runs and won again. McGraw had the whole staff warming up, but Doc Crandall needed no rescuing, spinning a four-hit shutout that sent the Giants to Chicago with a lead of seven and a half games over the Cubs.

The Giants got to Chicago in time to attend the Tuesday double-header between the Cubs and the Boston Rustlers. Stirring the stands with their fervent cheering for the Rustlers, the Giants felt rewarded when the tailenders used three hits by McGraw's old favorite, Mike Donlin, to take the second game 7–5 and gain a split. Because the Cubs had only eleven games remaining, McGraw might well get his wish of clinching the pennant early enough to slap the Cubs in the face with Charley Faust.

First, however, another earlier story resurfaced. Damon Runyon led off his off-day column by embellishing a rumor spread a week earlier in the *Times* and *Globe:*

> Rumors seeped into the Giants camp this morning that a foul plot is on foot among Chicago fans to kidnap Charles Victory Faust, court jester and official jinx of the big town team. The impression has gone the round of the big ring that the presence of C. Vic Faust on the Gotham bench is the cause of the Giants' amazing string of road victories, and the plan, according to the rumor aforesaid, was to lure the Kansas luck bringer to a remote section of the city and tie him up until the Giants leave town.
>
> A Pinkerton guard was promptly placed over Faust, and all strangers approaching him as he stood around the lobby of the Auditorium Hotel to-day were given the elbow by the detectives. The ball players suspect that Connie Mack ribbed up the Chicagoans so as to get rid of the jinx before the world's series opens.
>
> Charles does not grasp the situation in its entirety, but he appreciates that there is something doing somewhere, and is extremely coy.

That alleged plan could easily have worked in Cincinnati, the morning Faust wandered the streets in search of apple pie. There was no reason to think that the threat was real (if it even existed outside the fevered minds of a few writers), but it was fun to pretend to the world that Faust's jinxing power generated such fear that only a kidnapping might slow him down (remember the loss in St. Louis), and more fun to make Faust think he was going to pitch.

Sid Mercer wrote three Faust items that day without mentioning the putative threat to Faust's person. One note was the item about buying a diamond for his tooth. Another concerned a benefit planned for the Giants back in New York, scheduled for October 8: "Charley Faust is rehearsing a special monologue for the occasion." The third item focused on Faust's noted clairvoyance. "C. Victor Faust thinks he is going to like Chicago. He is a target for curious eyes and has been extensively interviewed. Charley says the Giants will win at least three games here and predicts four victories in the first five games of the world's series. The players take Charley serious as a prophet, as he seldom misses calling a turn."

Charley Faust had every reason to like Chicago. Wide-eyed in anticipation of making his pipedream come true, he basked in the attention he received in each new city. The Giants steamrolled the opposition during the games; before and after, it was Faust conquering fresh territory. By day, he mesmerized the masses with his ridiculously earnest attempts to play ball. By night, he entertained the elite with command performances which highlighted his theatrical flair. After performing for Garry Herrmann in Cincinnati, he found increasing demands for his presence. One day into the Chicago stay, Mercer reported that Charley Faust "gave a special performance of his new vaudeville act at the Auditorium Hotel last night. It was a professional performance in reality, as the audience was made up of DeWolf Hopper, Dustin and Bill Farnum, several Chicago sporting editors, and camp followers. The Chicago club is playing Faust up strong. He is placarded all over the West Side Ball Park." Later in the week, Damon Runyon noted that "Charley is called upon to demonstrate his thespian prowess about every night before appreciative gatherings." It must have been quite a sight—Faust declaiming his monologue before the bespectacled and no doubt astonished eyes of DeWolf Hopper, the histrionic orator who habitually cried when he recited the last verse of "Casey at the Bat."

The four-game series (with a day off halfway through) began on Wednesday, September 27. The New York *Times* detailed the team's reception at the opener:

> A crowd of more than 12,000 turned out to see the speed-mad Giants. . . . They also came because the Giants are expected to win the pennant, and also to see Charles Victory Faust, Dick

Hennessey, and all the other circus features of Manager McGraw's spectacular production entitled, "Winning the Baseball Quilt of 1911." Charles Webb Murphy took advantage of the big attraction and had a huge banner waving in front of the park heralding the advent of "The Kansas Cyclone," Faust, in his marvelous exhibition of base running and base sliding. The Chicago gathering was pleased to the point of unrestrained joy at the afternoon's fun, and is still fishing for a straw of hope. There isn't a chance.

Perhaps Murphy, the Cubs' owner, promoted Charley Faust doubly hard as his way of deflecting attention from the Giants' convincing lead over the Cubs, which robbed the series of much of its suspense. "The practice went off nicely," noted the *Herald*, "'Charlie' Faust performing and getting the crowd. More than ten thousand came out to the game."

Charley Faust won the crowd, but the Cubs won the game. Rube Marquard, nursing a sore arm, lasted only two batters into the fourth inning and couldn't strike out anyone. Wildfire Schulte, whose grand slam cost Marquard a June loss in Chicago, killed him again with four hits in the game, his fourth-inning home run chasing Marquard to the bench with a 6–0 deficit. The Giants couldn't touch Lew Richie, and the Cubs won 8–0.

"Charlie Faust saw it all," reported the New York *Tribune*,

saw the irresistible and all-conquering Giants tagged with an 8 to 0 shutout by the rapidly crumbling Cubs in the first game of the last series for the season between the two old rivals when they met here this afternoon. The great jinx was on hand to witness the rapid disposal of Rube Marquard after four innings of doleful work and to watch New York play the poorest offensive game the team has been guilty of in many a day.

After the harrowing details had become history Charlie Faust's veni-vidi-vici attitude gave way to an imposing lachrymal display. Faust has met the jinxes of St. Louis, Pittsburg and Boston in their lairs and sent them down for the full count, but to-night he admitted that he has met his master. After mature deliberation he declared that the mighty Chicago jinx is one of the most impressive creations in the annals of modern baseball. Word has been sent to Kansas for an entirely new set of formulas and incantations for use in coming struggles.

Remarkably, that was the only regular-season Rube Marquard loss ever witnessed by Charley Faust. The July day Charley showed up in St. Louis, Marquard sported a solid 10–4 record. This loss left him a spectacular 23–7, so he was 13–3 over those two months. The first loss came in Pittsburgh before Charley rejoined the Giants in New York, and the second came on Labor Day, the day Marquard blew the 5–0 lead with Charley away in vaudeville. In the apple-pie episode in Cincinnati where Marquard got knocked out early, the loss went to Hooks Wiltse because the Giants tied the game after Charley arrived. It took the Cubs to inflict this solitary scar on Charley's otherwise pristine record of inspiring Marquard to victory, a record that resumed in Marquard's next start.

On September 28, the same day that aviators Atwood and Ely collided in midair in Ohio, Christy Mathewson collided with his nemesis, Joe Tinker, in Chicago. The result was another tough loss for Mathewson, his thirteenth of the season against twenty-five wins. In the third inning, Tinker belted a double over Josh Devore's head, scoring two runners to give the Cubs a 2–1 lead. It took King Cole only ninety minutes to make that lead stand up, limiting the Giants to five hits. For the third straight game, McGraw's troops stole no bases. New York fans had a short party, according to Damon Runyon: "The Giants got off to a flying start this afternoon, to the intense gratification of De Wolf Hopper, Dustin and William Farnum, Treasurer John A. Whalen, and Charley Faust, the rooting representatives of Gotham on the premises. Charley, by the by, is somewhat flustered over the sudden loss of his jinxing power, and fears that some one has put a thought on him." Good news and bad: though sharing equal billing with Hopper and the Farnums, Charley also experienced the precariousness of fame, that swaying of the pedestal the moment he was placed upon it. After bringing them eleven wins in a row, he had to pray it would take more than two losses in Chicago to ruin his reputation. And just when he was on the verge of pitching!

On this occasion, the New York *World* chose to mention the existence of Charley Faust for the first time, as part of a column on how the Giants spent their day off. They spent it spending more of their anticipated World Series money, this time on clothes. Josh Devore bought a tweed suit that made everyone laugh, while Rube Marquard sprung for "a bunch of shirts" and his ninth pair of shoes. This lavishness in the wake of two straight losses bothered Chief Meyers, the stone-faced catcher. "That is the worst hoodoo in the world," Meyers told the *World*. "It's just the same as a man raking in the money before he has shown his hand in poker. It always brings bad luck." Speaking of luck, the article continued, "Charley Faust, who has been the mascot for the Giants on the trip, is not nearly so popular now as he was a week ago. The players told him yesterday that he would have to show them some results before they would really believe that he had caused them to win so many games on the present trip."

Talk about pressure! How would Faust handle this mutiny by his faithful teammates, the same fellows who only two weeks earlier, at the start of the trip, refused to let McGraw shift him to the Buffalo club? The team looked listless and had stopped running and scoring, managing only three runs in their last three games. Matty had given up two runs and lost. The players seemed more interested in clothing than winning. Now Faust was supposed to do something about it, or else all his good work would be nullified. "Faust didn't have a thing as mascot," said the *Herald*. If his jinxing power was truly lost, he had no reason to be there. He rated no special treatment. After all, if a handful of bad outings could make the writers think out loud about whether Rube Marquard's arm was permanently damaged or whether Mathewson was washed up, then Faust had to measure up in his own way. That meant a fresh set of incantations as the Giants prepared to face Three Finger Brown on Saturday.

As it turned out, Red Ames already had the superstition department covered, as detailed by John Wheeler in a brilliant, digressive lead in the Sunday *Herald*:

> This is the story of a necktie of many colors that hurts the eye. It is of that prominent type of tie which is about as soothing to the eye as is a fish horn to the ear when blown directly into it. "Red" Leon Ames, of Warren, Ohio, has been carrying around this necktie ever since he won a certain game of ball for the Giants in Boston.
>
> "I'll wear it till I lose," he said that day, and it is still decorating his manly personality. One almost wishes that when he contemplates launching himself into a winning streak he would be more judicious in the selection of his ties. Ames pitched against the Cubs this afternoon. The tie is still paralyzing the optic nerves

of the other players to-night. You have guessed the answer. The Giants won by the score of 3 to 1. Or did the Necktie?

At first Ames just wore this fetish when he was up and dressed in his regular scenery. Now he puts it on about the neck of his night garment. Wiltse, his room mate, says so. And he wears it under his baseball uniform. Had it on to-day. And the pink tints are getting to take on the tone of a ballet dancer's dress in a burlesque troupe, and the yellow is smoked brown, while the green shades are holding up best of all, and still he wears it. The edges are frayed, but Ames and Luck and that Necktie are as inseparable as faith, hope and charity. Take the necktie away from him and you would grab everything that he has on the ball. Take it away from him! It would be easier to catch a single flea on a collie dog with boxing gloves on, or get Louis Drucke's bank roll away from Louis Drucke. Yes, but this is the tale of a ball game, not a dissertation on neckwear, so read on.

First, award a prize to that dissertation, a convincing case for the long tradition of superstition in baseball. Charley Faust did not materialize out of a vacuum. It took players brainwashed by the superstitious McGraw and conditioned by years of hoodoos to appreciate him fully.

Despite cold, rainy weather, a crowd of twenty thousand watched Red Ames outpitch Three Finger Brown. Larry Doyle's two-run home run in the first inning provided the winning margin, while Buck Herzog drove in the insurance run and made a great diving play to rob Jimmy Sheckard and help Ames nurse the lead. "Manager McGraw," said the *Times*, "was out to win to-day's game at all hazards. During the fray of nine innings he had Matty, Crandall, Wiltse, Marquard, and Charley Faust warming up." McGraw left Ames and his tie alone, and he got the needed win.

It rained all Sunday morning, soaking the field and keeping what would have been a huge crowd down to about fifteen thousand. They saw a rematch of the Wednesday game, with Rube Marquard pitting his sore arm against Lew Richie. Richie continued his mastery over the Giants, extending his scoreless string against them to sixteen innings by blanking them on three hits over the first seven innings. This time Marquard matched Richie, and the game was scoreless when the Cubs got a single and a double with one out in the bottom of the seventh.

Marquard found the strength to make Solly Hofman pop to short, then walked the next man intentionally to load the bases before getting Richie to fly out to end the threat.

The Giants rewarded Marquard's grit by breaking through against Richie in the last two innings. In the eighth, doubles by Fred Merkle and Art Fletcher scored the first run, and Marquard singled in the second. In the ninth, Buck Herzog singled in another run, and Fletcher's two-run double capped the scoring. Marquard won 5–0, his fifth shutout of the season, earning special recognition in the *Herald*. "Coming into his own again, Mr. Richard Marquard is once more presented in the *Herald* crystal of celebrities. There was a time when Mr. Marquard used to be almost a regular tenant of the Window of Fame. But he hasn't been breaking into 'who's it among the ball players' so frequently lately. He stood out in the game to-day like a mole on a bald head. He gave the Cubs six hits and made one himself in a pinch in the eighth inning."

After the game John McGraw accepted congratulations from Cubs manager Frank Chance, and the Giants prepared for the barnstorming finale to the road trip. The Chicago series ended on Sunday, October 1. The Giants had a game scheduled in Pittsburgh on Monday, one in Philadelphia on Tuesday, and another in Brooklyn on Wednesday. They needed exactly three more wins to clinch the pennant; at worst, they figured to clinch back at the Polo Grounds. Still, a succession of overnight stops provided a brutal conclusion to three weeks on the road. Without those last two wins in Chicago, it might have broken them. Instead, they boarded the train for Pittsburgh carrying light hearts. Sid Mercer:

> They sang songs and told stories and had Charley Faust pull his monologue until the Kansas Cyclone lost his muffler and swept the passing countryside with the thunder of his eloquence. Charley sprang some brand new lines that were received with violent applause, and predicted that the Giants would win four games out of the first five from the Athletics. Just for that he was assigned to a lower berth for the first time on the trip and a special hammock was provided for the rusty arm that has been worked up many times in the last three weeks. Faust's great regret is that he

was not allowed to pitch the last Chicago game, but he consoles himself with the thought that he is being kept under cover to slay the Athletics.

That familiar regret was echoed in the *Herald*. "Faust was disappointed because he could not pitch to-day. This was to have been his time if the Giants had taken two of the first three. His name is down on the score card as No. 13 and he made a kick to Murphy about his number."

Mercer adopted a rare derisive tone in another note that day that sounds almost like drunken bragging in the smoking compartment. "Chicago has as much chance, dear brothers, of winning the pennant as Charlie Faust has of pitching a game for the Giants. From that you can form your own conclusions. . . . We say once again, dear brothers, that the Cubs have as much chance of winning the pennant as Charlie Faust has of pitching the first game of the world's championship." Mercer sounded like a man who knew something. He fed one more morsel to Faust's fans. "In response to numerous requests, Charles Victor Faust has consented to deliver his famous monologue at the Broadway Theatre next Sunday night at the big benefit performance. Charles will be much obliged if his admirers send apple pie instead of the customary flowers around to his dressing room."

In Pittsburgh the Giants found a dismal Monday, cold and windy, with an inch of frost and only a few hundred fans in Forbes Field. "The crowd," wrote Damon Runyon, "comes under the head of 'small but representative.' The six or sixteen people in the stand were the small, and Marty O'Toole was the representative. Charley Faust, Wilbur Robinson, Dick Hennessey and Arlie Latham did their best to cheer up the folks, but Pittsburgh is beyond the aid of anything short of 1912." For the sixth game in a row, the Giants—in the midst of their record-setting season—stole no bases. But they didn't need to, thanks to Hooks Wiltse, that old cold-weather horse who had struggled through the torrid summer, that bearer of a lame hip who had pitched only three innings in the last ten days. Wiltse, thriving on this frigid October afternoon, almost pitched a no-hitter, winning 3–0. Officially he pitched a two-hitter, but only Dots Miller's two-out single in the ninth inning got the official scorer out of a tight spot. The scorer was missing in action in the fourth inning when Max Carey grounded a Wiltse pitch sharply to

Buck Herzog's left. It glanced off Herzog and got past Art Fletcher, but the scorer declined to issue a decision, waiting for the Pirates to get a real hit. He sweated it out until Miller's clean single, after which he credited Carey with a hit but said he had been prepared to call it an error if it meant the difference in Wiltse's no-hitter. The *Herald* called it an error anyway and credited Wiltse with a one-hitter.

"The atmosphere inside the park was like that in the first carriage at a funeral," lamented John Wheeler. "Now how can anything be written about that kind of game?" Wheeler's solution was to write about the Giants' clubhouse banter. Wiltse "insisted that he must win a ball game in spite of his aching hip, because his roommate, Ames, was getting chesty. 'If I win to-day I am going to wear this necktie until I lose, too,' he declared, and you should see the tie! It looks like the badge of the volunteer fireman who has received the most votes at the popularity contest of the Hope Hook and Ladder Company, and he may not pitch again this year.

"'You're stealing my stuff!' protested Ames after the game. 'Why don't you try wearing the same socks until you lose? You'd be safe. Your laundry bills wouldn't be reduced any.'"

As the victory tour moved to Philadelphia, Sid Mercer added a John McGraw quip to the Faust legend: "On the train last night some of the players were discussing the value of a good wind-up to a pitcher. McGraw stuck his bean through the curtains to the smoking compartment, got the drift of the conversation and remarked: 'If a pitcher needed nothing but a wind-up I'll back Charley Faust against the world.'" Faust's windup had been excessive from the start, an exaggerated windmill motion, arms rotated wide two or three times before he made his move toward the plate. Many pitchers used a more modest windmill windup, most notably Walter Johnson, Mathewson's equal from the American League. Picture Faust spending every afternoon warming up, going through that motion over and over again, then spending another night on the train with his arm in a hammock at the insistence of his teammates and going out there again the next day to work on his motion. Even McGraw had to give him credit for that.

In Philadelphia the Giants provided unwelcome excitement for Connie Mack, the manager of the Philadelphia Athletics. Mack, joined by a couple of his pitchers, arrived in the fifth inning to scout his

A three-photo sequence of FAUST's exaggerated pitching motion (see following pages) was taken by the St. Louis *Post-Dispatch* and used by S. C. Martin as the basis for his Faust caricatures. Faust said he learned it from a book. (Collection of Thomas Busch)

upcoming World Series opponents. The score was 3–3 when the Giants spotted him, and they delivered a quick message in the sixth inning. Facing Grover Alexander, who won more games than anyone in baseball in 1911, the Giants erupted for nine runs, the latest in a seasonlong succession of big innings. This one began with a Red Murray single. Fred Merkle doubled, and Buck Herzog singled in the tiebreaking run. Art Fletcher doubled in two runs, and Doc Crandall's one-out single made it 7–3 and knocked out Alexander. The explosion continued against Buck Stanley, a 21-year-old lefty whose major league career consisted of four games. He walked Josh Devore, and Larry Doyle singled in Crandall. After a wild pitch, Fred Snodgrass singled home two runs, and Red Murray capped the binge with a triple, scoring the ninth run on an overthrow. If the Giants were worn out from their long odyssey, Connie Mack saw no sign of it. McGraw removed five regulars, Crandall coasted to a 12–3 win, and the Giants were one win away from the pennant.

Fred Lieb, who covered Giants home games for the New York *Press*, joined the team for the Philadelphia game and the last triumphant train ride home. Lieb, who had mentioned Charley Faust only once, a neutral comment back in August when Faust led the band, now took an excited leap onto the bandwagon:

> The humbling of Alexander was just what was needed to fill the cup of joy. Booming along the trail from Philadelphia last evening everybody felt like a village cut-up. There was horse play enough to please a gang of Shawanaga lumberjacks, with the logs all boomed and the stakes unspent. Every one from the Little Napoleon down to Charlie Faust, who during the massacre in Philadelphia worked up a grouch because McGraw did not let him go on the mound, unlimbered and made merry. . . .
> Charlie Faust was called upon to make a speech. He performed the William Jennings Bryan stunt so well that by the time Newark was reached the Kansas Jester had got four speeches out of his system and was almost all in. Between speeches, while Faust was getting his wind for another eulogy for the obsequies at the burial of the White Elephant, the boys buzzed with World's Series talk.

That evening the Giants arrived at Pennsylvania Station in New York, spending a night at home before heading to Brooklyn for the last two games of what Christy Mathewson called "the greatest trip away from home in the history of baseball." In the four days since Charley Faust's jinxing powers were doubted, they had outscored the opposition 23–4 to run their record for the trip to seventeen wins against only four losses. No wonder a big crowd gathered outside the station to cheer the returning heroes. "It was a big party," said the *Times*, "that detrained at the Pennsylvania Station. First there was Manager McGraw and more than a score of players, besides club officials. Not forgetting, of course, Court Jester Latham, Mascot Dick Hennessey, Mascot Charles Victory Faust of Marion, Kan., and Mascot Extraordinary Wilbert Robinson." Robinson, who coached the pitchers during the spring training, had been summoned by McGraw after the two Chicago losses, joining them in time to straighten out Rube Marquard.

Sid Mercer used the occasion to promote Charley Faust's show-business prospects. "Thirty-nine vaudeville agents met Faust at the train last night, but he strode right through their midst. 'I'm ready to sign,' said Charley, as twenty gamins fought for the honor of carrying his grips while he awaited the rumble of a taxicab, 'but I prefer a baseball to a vaudeville contract.' Joe Humphries has tipped off Pat Casey to approach Faust with a large cut of apple pie in one hand and a handful of one-dollar bills in the other. 'Then put in a clause that you will settle for one shave and massage every day and Charley is yours,' advises Joe."

If Mercer made Faust sound like himself, as most New York writers did, Damon Runyon broke new ground in inventive dialogue that day. Leaving his description of the ballgame for the last part of his coverage, he opened with what could have been a vignette from one of his later Broadway stories, with Faust talking like Nathan Detroit. " 'My friends,' said C. Victory Faust, the Official Jinx, on being interviewed at the Pennsylvania Railroad station last evening, shortly after the train bearing the pennant-winning Giants had slipped through the tube, 'My friends, far be it from me to boost myself, but you can very plainly see what is what.'

"A 12 to 3 victory over Philadelphia, which included the scalp of Grover Cleveland Alexander, was among the spoils of war brought home by the big town boys when they landed on the shores of Broadway at 7 o'clock last evening, and blinked their eyes at the familiar lights."

Later, Runyon mentioned that "On the trip over from Philadelphia C. Victory Faust delivered a sort of congratulatory oration to the players, in which he predicted a clean sweep for the Giants in the world's series, but then C. Victory said something like that before the Chicago games started, and therefore he has come to be regarded as a better jinx than prophet."

Faust bucked the odds by predicting easy success against the Athletics. As Sid Mercer put it, "Not even the most optimistic — Charles Victory Faust excepted — has an idea that only five games will be required." The *Times* supported a modified prediction. "Charley Faust predicts a Giant victory in the world series. Yes, you smile, but, just the same, all of Faust's optimistic predictions about the Western invasion have come true."

On the eve of clinching the pennant, the writers still could not define Charley Faust's role on the Giants. Of course he was mainly known for his jinxing. And as their mascot and the star of the pregame practice. Or for his predictions, or else for keeping up their good spirits by being the butt of their jokes. He had made his mark in so many areas in such a short time. He was magical, ubiquitous; he could forecast plays from the bench and still stay warmed up in the outfield. But what was he? Prophet? Jinx? Mascot? Was he merely C. Victory, destined to do nothing but see victories? He was everything but what he wanted to be — a pitcher.

Almost lost in the shuffle of the team's barnstorming victory tour was Charley's continuing quest to pitch. Almost. Sid Mercer wouldn't forget about it. "Those who think that C. Victory Faust is going to be kidded to the limit about pitching a game for the Giants are chewing the wrong dope. C. Victor would have pitched a couple of innings at Philadelphia yesterday, but the Giants couldn't spare the extra time, and besides they did not wish to shovel Charley up and take him home in pieces. McGraw would have pitched Faust in Chicago if he had not needed every game there, and he now thinks that the greatest mascot the game ever produced will work in one of the Brooklyn games. Might not be a bad idea to pit Faust against the Dodgers on Columbus Day. They might discover him."

That sounded pretty convincing, but first there was the matter of the clinching game. That took place next day in Brooklyn before fewer than ten thousand fans. The Giants survived a wild ninth inning; in the top half, Red Murray hit into a triple play, while the bottom featured a near-fight in the middle of the field between Larry Doyle and Chief Meyers following a botched rundown play. Christy Mathewson ignored the mayhem to grab his twenty-sixth victory of the long season, winning 2–0. That made three shutouts by the Giants in four days, all in different cities!

Summing up this spectacular stretch drive, John McGraw said, "I may have managed ball clubs which I thought were better machines than the present one, but none of which I am more proud. Taking every point into consideration, we have just concluded the greatest trip I have ever known. I have been connected with nothing like it. Here was a young team, a team that had been in and out through the greater part of the year, game enough to rally quickly in the face of defeat and make its winning fight on the road. I have never driven a ball club harder."

McGraw and his Giants had earned the right to relax a little before facing the Athletics in the World Series, scheduled to begin on Friday, October 13. "That date," claimed Sid Mercer with a straight face, "suits McGraw's men. They are not superstitious." Nothing could bother them now. Eight games remained in the Giants schedule, eight lame-duck games in which the regulars would work only hard enough to stay comfortable, eight games that wouldn't matter to anybody.

Except to Charley Faust.

7
The Frame of Fame

WITH THE NATIONAL LEAGUE pennant locked up, the Giants and their fans turned their attention to the Philadelphia Athletics and the World Series. The remaining games seemed an afterthought, especially an October 12 doubleheader that John T. Brush had let Charles Ebbets of Brooklyn talk him into playing in order to milk a big gate in New York on Columbus Day. That gratuitous gesture now loomed as eighteen innings of baseball to be played on the eve of the World Series. The Athletics had no games after October 7, proving that you don't need a computer to screw up a schedule.

Still, the Giants had to play the games, so Charley Faust knew it was only a matter of time before he pitched. Robbed of his ballyhooed shot at pitching a game in Chicago, denied the chance to help finish off the pennant in Philadelphia, he couldn't imagine any more obstacles preventing him from pitching. No doubt he continued to challenge John McGraw to invent new obstacles. Why, for instance, didn't McGraw let him pitch the next game in Brooklyn after they clinched? The big five pitchers needed and got the day off, but instead of using Faust, McGraw chose to give the start to Bert Maxwell, who pitched a complete game to earn one of the four wins in his major league career.

Maybe McGraw told Faust that he'd use him back at the Polo Grounds, where the Giants fans could see him. Maybe he promised him, or maybe he continued to stonewall him. On Friday, October 6, the Giants and Phillies played a doubleheader at the Polo Grounds, and still Faust did not pitch. Larry Doyle, Red Murray, and Buck Herzog played both games, while Red Ames and Doc Crandall both pitched complete games. According to the *Herald*, "For a time in the first game it looked as if the [Ames] necktie, which is as lucky as Charley Faust, would have to go, but it hung on, for the Giants came through and won in the seventh and eighth innings." Trailing 3–1 in the seventh, the Giants won 10–5, exploding for six runs in the eighth. "It was in this inning," said the *Tribune*, "that Ames created a stir in the grandstand by making his second hit of the game. He had already caused quite a commotion by singling in the seventh and bringing home one run, and when he duplicated this performance in the eighth and scored two runners, the 'fans' were ready for most anything to happen, and freely predicted that the next thing to occur would be Charlie Faust pitching a no-hit game."

What did Charley Faust do that day? The same thing he did every other day. He continued to warm up and to bring the Giants luck. This sweep extended the latest Giants winning streak to eight, all of them complete games. Since Faust joined the Giants on August 11, they had played .800 ball, winning forty of fifty games. At least half the losses came when he was not there or otherwise not accountable for the team's fate. "Did 'Charley' Faust win the championship for the Giants?" asked Christy Mathewson in the book he and John Wheeler wrote that winter. "He did a great deal toward giving the players confidence. With him on the bench, they thought they couldn't lose, and they couldn't. It has long been a superstition among ball players that when a 'bug' joins a club, it will win a championship, and the Giants believed it when 'Charley' arrived."

Yet McGraw would not let Faust pitch one of those games against the Phillies, a puzzling piece of the puzzle. Why didn't he announce in advance that Faust was going to pitch? It would have brought fans out to the ballpark to see otherwise meaningless games. He had seen Faust publicized on the road, had seen the huge crowds he helped generate. Surely McGraw and John T. Brush were motivated by greed much of the time, following the same credo as Willie Hammerstein, the vaudeville huckster, who preached that "the best seats, for producers, are those with asses in them." Everything in their characters pointed toward attracting a big crowd; why did they choose this time to resist the temptation? Logically, they must have regarded putting Faust in a real game as a travesty. At best, if he escaped with his life and some dignity, it would still be a farce, because all he could do was lob the ball toward the plate. At worst, he'd walk everybody, or give up ten or twenty hits in a row until somebody smacked a line drive off his head and put him out of his misery. Either way, they must have considered it unthinkable. After all, John McGraw grew up with Ned Hanlon and the old Orioles, who devoted every ounce of their being to winning. You didn't put some clown out on the mound, not if the game counted—except as a symbolic gesture to rub the Cubs' faces in the dirt. So Faust continued to wait.

"The baseball public," reported the *Times*, "didn't fall over itself flocking to see the bargain bill. . . . Less than 2,500 were there to approve of the Giants' action. It threatened to rain and cut the double header down to one game, but no such luck." The fans were interested only in tickets to the World Series, scheduled to begin in New York after Brush won a coin toss earlier in the week to determine the home-field advantage. The opener was also moved back one day, from Friday the 13th to Saturday, October 14. Mail-order requests for tickets stacked up quickly, the demand so exceeding the supply that the eventual distribution of tickets caused a winterlong scandal.

Apathy greeted the game on October 7, along with a cold, biting wind and a muddy field. "Manager McGraw," said the *Times*, "went after the game with the same enthusiasm that a man might rush to seat himself in the electric chair." Instead of luring a big crowd to "Charley Faust Day" at the Polo Grounds, McGraw's team played before the smallest Saturday crowd of the season. The rest of New York decided that if they were going to watch a baseball game in football weather, they'd wait another week until the Athletics came to town instead of rushing to the Polo Grounds to see the 41–107 Boston Rustlers. You can't blame them, nor can you help wondering how many thousands would have showed up if McGraw had spread the word (officially or otherwise) that they would get to see Charley Faust pitch in a real game.

Unfortunately, we don't even know whether McGraw planned all along to use Faust if he got the chance. As the timing worked out, it seemed like an afterthought. Rube Marquard started, a tuneup outing two days before his (and Faust's birthday). Marquard went five comfortable innings in his last work before the World Series, leaving tied 2–2. What a perfect spot this would have been for Faust, a chance to be the winning pitcher if he could somehow retire the Braves and get some run support. But no. McGraw resurrected Louie Drucke, who hadn't pitched since July 27, the day before McGraw and Faust met. This move proved that McGraw didn't care about the game, and Drucke promptly gave up two runs. The Giants, with only three regulars playing, stalled against Lefty Tyler, who nursed the 4–2 lead through eight innings.

Then history happened, an event celebrated by the *Herald*, which announced "Faust's Face Fixed in Frame of Fame." Next to Faust's profile, fans read:

> The three most persistent things—Tennyson's "Brook," the rent collector and Charles Victory Faust of Marion, Kan. If he should ever decide that he was going to be President the janitor of the White House might just as well wind the clocks, let the cat out, dust off the furniture, beat the rugs, put new paper on the closet shelves and buy a door mat with "Welcome" worked on it. C. Victory announced not so long ago that he would pitch for the Giants, and every one laughed long and loud. Listen. You can hear the echo of the smile yet. He pitched for them yesterday. This morning he is in the Window of Fame. Anyone who can get away with anything like that deserves to be made immortal.

Below the Frame of Fame, John Wheeler provided the fullest account of Faust's great adventure:

> Charles Victory Faust, of Marion, Kan., better known as the man who has made the Giants famous, has come into his own at last and fulfilled the predictions of the fortune teller who sent him to McGraw. While he was busy in the outfield yesterday afternoon taking apart a grasshopper to look for the spring that made it jump, and intermittently warming up, as he has been doing for many days, McGraw beckoned to him. It was the last inning of the last game with Boston, and the Giants were behind a matter of two runs. No time could be more propitious for Faust's entry into the great American game as a big leaguer. He was there in the pinch, the jam for which he has been waiting. Opportunity did not have to knock twice. "Charley" has sensitive ears. It only tapped, and Faust forced his way into the box from the outfield.
> "My moment has come," said Faust, as he stepped on the rubber.

C. Victory Faust Makes His Debut with Giants

In Pinch Against Boston in Ninth, with New York Only Two Runs Behind, Jinx Jams Into Game—Contest Is Lost, 5-2.

National League Results.

Boston, 5; New York, 2.
Pittsburg, 5; Chicago, 0.
Other games—rain.

Standing in National League.

	W.	L.	P.C.		W.	L.	P.C.
New York	98	51	.658	St. Louis.	73	73	.500
Chicago...	90	61	.596	Cincinnati	68	81	.456
Pittsburg.	85	67	.559	Brooklyn..	61	85	.418
Phil'phia.	79	71	.527	Boston....	42	107	.282

National League Games To-Day.

Pittsburg at Chicago.
St. Louis at Cincinnati.

Charles Victory Faust, of Marion, Kan., better known as the man who has made the Giants famous, has come into his own at last and fulfilled the predictions of the fortune teller who sent him to McGraw. While he was busy in the outfield yesterday afternoon taking apart a grasshopper to look for the spring that made it jump, and intermittently warming up, as he has been doing for many days, McGraw beckoned to him. It was the last inning of the last game with Boston, and the Giants were behind a matter of two runs. No time could be more propitious for Faust's entry into the great American game as a big leaguer. He was there in the pinch, the jam for which he has been waiting. Opportunity did not have to knock twice. "Charley" has sensitive ears. It only tapped, and Faust forced his way into the box from the outfield.

"My moment has come," said Faust, as he stepped on the rubber.

At this point the game was delayed by an agent of Faust, who rushed out on the field and demanded that McGraw desist.

"This bug has been a thorn in my side for months," protested McGraw, "and

"CHARLEY" FAUST

The three most persistent things—Tennyson's "Brook," the rent collector and Charles Victory Faust, of Marion, Kan. If he should ever decide that he was going to be President the janitor of the White House might just as well wind the clocks, let the cat out, dust off the furniture, beat the rugs, put new paper on the closet shelves and buy a door mat with "Welcome" worked on it. C. Victory announced not so long ago that he would pitch for the Giants, and every one laughed long and loud. Listen. You can hear the echo of the smile yet. He pitched for them yesterday. This morning he is in the Window of Fame. Any one who can get away with anything like that deserves to be made immortal.

THE FRAME OF FAME. Ironically, Faust's day of triumph came during one of the few Giants losses he witnessed. The New York *Herald*'s John Wheeler was ready to concede the White House to Faust but settled for conferring immortality upon him.

At this point the game was delayed by an agent of Faust, who rushed out on the field and demanded that McGraw desist.

"This bug has been a thorn in my side for months," protested McGraw, "and lately he has been a young cactus. He's got to pitch in spite of your protests."

At last the agent reluctantly consented, and Faust was permitted to go on. The thousand spectators exchanged congratulations at being present when the faithful Faust at last got into the box. "I'm glad we stayed," was the refrain, and they cut loose with a cheer.

Faust reached for his cap, his exquisitely manicured nails glistening just as if he were appearing in vaudeville, and brushed a little dirt out of the pitching box with it. His hair was perfectly cut and his face as smooth and shiny as a ballroom floor. Then he wound up like a worm that has been cut in three pieces and uncoiled.

"Strike!" commented Mr. Finneran. Most of Charley's face disappeared behind the grin.

"It's a bad pinch, Charley," warned McGraw.

"Look out for his fast one," coached Latham, tipping Rariden at the bat.

"Great day for Charley's speed," said Hartley, catching, pointing to the overhanging clouds, and then Faust produced another one out of his tangled self that could be timed by a watch without a split second hand. Rariden must have felt like a commuter waiting for a train on the Erie as he lingered for the ball to come up to the plate.

"Ball!" said Finneran.

Faust wanted to take it up with the umpire. Then he kicked to McGraw. "I want Meyers to catch me," he protested. "I'm afraid this youngster can't hold my in-up."

Charley announces the signals himself down by the side of his leg, and he gave Hartley his hold hand on the next one, which is his "in-up." Mr. Finneran concluded that this did not meet the requirements of a strike. Rariden hit the next ball over Burns' head. If he had been playing deep he could have caught it. Rariden went along to second, and would have died there had not Devlin dropped the throw. Tyler bunted, and Faust threw him out at first, Rariden going to third. Sweeney sent a long fly to Burns on

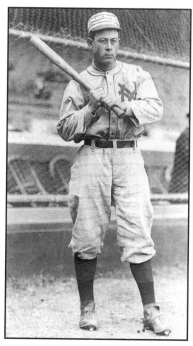

A TALE OF TWO CATCHERS. GROVER HARTLEY, left, had appeared in only a handful of games when he became Victory Faust's catcher. Despite this dubious honor, he had a long career as a catcher and coach, making his final appearance at age forty-five. BILL RARIDEN, right, was the first batter Faust ever faced. He smashed a long double and later applied the tag that ended Faust's romp around the bases. This prodigious feat persuaded McGraw to trade for Rariden and make him the regular catcher on his 1917 N.L. champions. (National Baseball Hall of Fame Library & Archive, Cooperstown, N.Y.)

which Rariden scored. Donlin nearly broke his back reaching for one of the slow balls and walloped a weak one to Fletcher. That is all they did to Faust.

It didn't look as if Charley would have a chance to go to bat in the ninth, as Burns, the first man up, flied out, and so did Paulette. Nevertheless, Charley, the optimist, picked out his stick and got ready. Herzog doubled and Fletcher was hit. Hartley came to the plate. It was Charley's turn next. Hartley lifted a simple fly to Sweeney. That made three outs, but what are three outs to Faust? He strode to the plate, and the Boston team fell for him, as every one does. He swung his bat as if he was a peg man driving stakes for a circus and rolled an easy one to the pitcher. Then he made the trip around the bases by easy stages, some of the distance travelling on his tonneau and the rest of the way on his feet. One has as broad a beam as the other. The crowd was on the field, and he slid over the feet of several spectators and across the plate.

"Gee!" wept the agent, "if McGraw had only tipped me I would have had a moving picture of that." Some days some people don't have any luck.

"Mac," said Faust in the club house later, flushed by his efforts. "Mac, I want to pitch the first game against the Athletics."

"You are released," said McGraw, "for letting Boston score when I put you in there in a pinch. I thought you told me you were right."

"I'll show them. I'll actually show them in the world's series," declared Faust.

"You'll show me first."

EVERY NEW YORK NEWSPAPER (except Sid Mercer's Sundayless *Globe*) covered Faust's debut, with varying slants and conflicting details, but only Wheeler included all the key elements: what Faust did before he got in the game, what happened when he took the mound, what he did on the mound, what happened in the bottom of the ninth, and how everyone else responded. The elements form a portrait of Faust that closely resembles the Faust who first declared his intentions to John McGraw the day they met in St. Louis. Despite vaudeville, the hype, the command performances, and ten long weeks of anticipation, Faust was very much himself at the moment of his dream's fruition. A closer look at how Wheeler treated these elements will allow the rest of the accounts to speak for themselves.

1. *Warming up.* On this frigid day, Faust spent the whole day warming up, not sparing himself even though he had already brought the Giants the pennant. He remained intent on fulfilling the entire prophecy (only the conquest of Lulu remained after this), and that meant hard work. Determination—like the rent collector who knows that his day will come.

2. *Taking the mound.* As always, his hustle on the field drew a mixture of cheers and laughter. People wanted to encourage his enthusiasm but couldn't help laughing at his skills. Wheeler's image of Faust

responding instantly to opportunity's tap suggests the modern-day relievers who race from the bullpen to the mound to psych out the other team. As for the "agent," only Wheeler mentioned it, and for all we know it was Wheeler himself wishing he could have captured the whole spectacle on film. Wheeler's image of Faust doffing his cap and using it to brush aside some dirt makes him sound like Mark Fidrych. "The Bird" was noted for talking to the baseball and for using his hands and cap to smooth the pitching-mound dirt, among other odd antics. Like Faust, he made some people nervous and did things that made people laugh at him, but he also became tremendously popular. Once he was established as a solid winner, his eccentricities made the fans love him more. When Faust reached the mound, the New York writers prepared to savor every movement he made.

3. *Pitching.* Of course, that was the key question: exactly what would happen to Faust once he had to throw the ball to a real opponent, not some easygoing fellow like Honus Wagner who would pretend to strike out? Was he a pitcher or wasn't he? Apparently he got the ball close enough to the plate to let the batters hit it. He got a break after Rariden powdered his double, when the pitcher bunted Rariden over. Sweeney also hit the ball well, but it was caught for the second out, and Mike Donlin may have been laughing too hard to hit the ball solidly. With a minimum of damage, Faust survived his debut. Charley Faust was no Charlie Brown. He did not get pulverized or even pounded, much less undressed. He told McGraw all along that he could pitch, and if McGraw had known that he would allow only one run, Faust surely would have gotten his chance sooner.

4. *At bat.* What were three outs to Faust? Nothing, not with his singleminded determination to show McGraw what a ballplayer he could be, given the opportunity. Notice that the Rustlers pulled the same stunt the Giants had that first day back in St. Louis, deliberately running Faust around the bases and getting him to slide home, this time through October mud rather than July-baked dirt. He even had to dodge fans to get to the plate. Ironically, although McGraw feared a travesty by putting Faust on the mound, in reality it was not a travesty until the Rustlers stayed in the field after the third out.

5. *Reactions.* The same old story, only more so. The reporters couldn't agree on the size of the crowd, but they agreed that Faust got

the kind of response Christy Mathewson usually got. This time, however, they stormed the field to celebrate Faust's quasi-official lurch
around the bases. Even the Boston players got into the act, as had players from other teams. The postgame dialogue was vintage McGraw-
Faust banter, with the manager trying to restrain his overeager
good-luck charm. Only one reaction to Faust was different this time:
McGraw had let him pitch. What made him relent? Wheeler's "young
cactus" quote aside, McGraw had been listening to Faust's pleas to
pitch for almost two months. He still enjoyed fending him off. What
impulse made him relent? Perhaps this running battle was not merely a
duet. The players had spoken up for Faust a couple of times earlier—in
August, when he threatened to abandon them, and in September,
when McGraw offered Charley to George Stallings in Buffalo. The
youngsters in the lineup were too intimidated by McGraw to make
demands, but the pitchers carried more weight, Mathewson in particular. Certainly Marquard and Ames believed in Faust, and if the pitching corps went to McGraw on Faust's behalf, he might have softened
momentarily to indulge them after their long summer of excellence.

Whatever prompted the change of heart, the result was that this
man Charley Faust, who only a few months earlier had been a home-
bound Kansas farmer, became a major league pitcher. Read the
accounts and feel Faust's exhilaration as he performed for the record
books for the first time. He experienced all the fears and joys any man
does on the threshold of realizing his dream, but without any awareness
of the absurdity other people sensed in the saga of this particular man
realizing this particular dream.

New York *Times*

Only three of the Giants' regulars played through the full game,
and outside of furnishing Rube Marquard with an opportunity to
loosen the kinks of his pitching arm, and making a full-fledged
major leaguer of Charley Faust, the session produced little of
interest to New York fans. Less than 1,000 fans—all belonging to
that species which would brave a blizzard to see a game—shivered
through yesterday's matinee. . . .

So when the ninth inning rolled around and the Giants were
dangling on the slim portion of a 4 to 2 score, McGraw decided to

give Charley Faust the chance which Charley dreamed about on his Kansas farm, and for which he has spent long hours warming up since he joined the Giants. Faust had been warming up for eight full innings, and when he answered the summons and ran in from the outfield he was given a cheer such as Matty will receive when he walks out against the Athletics next Saturday. Not so voluminous, but just as loud as the few fans could make it. Faust showed his peculiar wind-up and wore his uniform like a regular player. Four Rustlers faced him, and the quartet unloaded a two-bagger, a sacrifice hit on which Charley got an assist, a sacrifice fly, and a grounder to Fletcher which resulted in the third out. Faust was waiting to bat when Hartley made the third out in the Giants' half of the ninth, but the visitors obligingly remained in their places and gave Charley a chance to hit. He rolled weakly to Tyler and the latter purposely threw over Tenney's head. This was the cue for Faust to take an extra base, and when the ball was thrown over Sweeney's head Charley hustled to third, which he made after a long slide through the mud. Another wild peg sent Charley on a sprint homeward and the ball was thrown to Rariden in time to tag him at the plate.

New York *American*

'NUT' FAUST YIELDS ONE RUN
IN INNING AGAINST RUSTLERS

OFFICIAL JINX OF GIANTS PITCHES NINE INNINGS
AND ALLOWS ONLY ONE HIT

Charles Victory Faust, of Marion, Kansas, official Jinx of the Giants, made his debut as a big league pitcher at the Polo Grounds yesterday afternoon, working one inning, the ninth, against Boston. There were a few hundred half-frozen fans rewarded, getting a treat that money could not buy. When Umpire Finneran bulletined "Faust now pitching for New York," the crowd didn't believe it, but sure enough the famous "Nut" took the mound. His record in words and figures follows: Rariden doubled over Snodgrass's head. Tyler rolled to Faust, who threw the Boston pitcher out at first, Rariden taking third. This was some graceful fielding on the part of Faust. Sweeney flied to Murray, and Rariden scored after the catch. Donlin was tossed out by Fletcher.

The New York side was retired before Faust came to bat in his order, but Charley went in anyway, and tapped to Tyler for an easy out, but he went on around the bases anyway.

New York *Morning Telegraph*

FAUST IN ACTION AGAINST BOSTON

GIANTS' DARK HORSE DRAWS THE PITCHING ASSIGNMENT IN THE NINTH INNING AT POLO GROUNDS

Bats For Fourth Out

"For New York Faust now pitching."

The long delayed debut of McGraw's dark horse occurred yesterday. It was not against the Cubs, as Faust had hoped, nor was the game of any particular importance, but a debut is a debut just the same. Not even Mathewson in a time of stress ever got a more rousing hand than did the Kansas mascot when he trotted across the field to take his place in the box. With him he brought his ragtime wind-up, much to the delight of the spectators. He proved a surprise in that he was able to get the ball over the plate, or thereabouts, even though it did not hurtle across with any great amount of speed.

The Boston players did not let down in their efforts, but slugged away at the ball in regular fashion, but the dewdrop shoots proved puzzling and Faust was scored on only once. In the ninth there was an insistent demand that he be sent to bat, but as it was not his turn the umpire would not allow any such procedure.

After the third out had been made the rules were temporarily suspended and Faust came to the plate. He was unable to save the lost cause, for though he trickled a grounder down the first base line and ran ponderously around the bases while the Boston players juggled the ball, he was out at the plate as his famous hook slide left him some ten feet short of his destination.

He was surrounded by the entire crowd and only missed being carried off the field by rapid sprinting. . . .

In the ninth Faust made his entrance from deep center field, where he had been warming up furiously all afternoon. He set an example to his fellow players in the art of bowing. Most professionals when applauded snatch their cap off and then stick it back again with one and the same motion. Not so Charles Faust. He removed his cap and bowed half way to the ground before he took up the pitching burden. He threw two across the plate and they were both strikes, but Rariden then remembered his average and doubled over Snodgrass's head. The glory of Faust's pitching was dimmed at this point, for he was compelled to cut his long windup. All the Giant substitutes had come out from the bench and were giving the new recruit instructions. McGraw signalled him on each ball pitched. Tyler sacrificed and Faust got the assist. Sweeney sent a sacrifice fly to Burns, but Donlin was out on an infield tap to Fletcher.

New York *Press*

The big event of the day was the major-league debut of Charles Victory Faust, the demon jinx-destroyer of Marion, Kan. Charles V. was pressed into service in the ninth round, and gave a classy exhibition. Rariden, the Boston backstop, greeted Faust with a double, but Charles then settled down to his knitting, and retired the next three batters in order. . . . The Bostons scored their last run in the ninth against the hurling of Charley Faust. Faust made a neat bow to the fans before he entered on his duties and was greeted by roars of laughter.

New York *Sun*

The Boston tailenders beat the Champion Giants yesterday, the New York team including several substitute players. McGraw amused the fans by allowing his freak mascot, Charley Faust, to pitch the last inning. . . .

Although it was cold enough for football and the surface of the Polo Grounds was muddy the Giants played the Boston tailenders yesterday and were beaten. A crowd of 3,000 shivering fans paid to see the fun and were partially rewarded when Manager McGraw permitted Charley Faust, the Kansas farmer who has been the champions' mascot, to pitch the last inning. Faust, who takes himself seriously, gave a ludicrous exhibition of the box-man's art. He wound himself into knots and hurled up slow, dinky curves in a way that convulsed players and spectators.

The Bostons made a run off Faust and when they had retired the Giants in the final period the farmer was sent to the bat by Mc-Graw, who told him that only two men had been retired. Faust rapped a little grounder to Tyler, who purposely threw wildly to first. In turn the Boston basemen threw erratically in vain attempts to stop Faust's wild career around the paths. The fans had leaped out of the grandstand by this time, and Faust was compelled to dodge here and there as he galloped to the plate, where he slid head first in the soggy soil and was called out. It was the proudest moment of Faust's life, however, for he had pitched in a Giant uniform—a reward for his hypnotic influence over the New Yorks' rivals.

New York *Tribune*

FAUST RESCUES GIANTS

While a scanty crowd of two thousand spectators rooted and cheered Charles Victory Faust, the phenomenal jinx of opposing clubs made his debut as a big league pitcher with the champion Giants at the Polo Grounds yesterday afternoon. Faust twirled only one inning, and came too late to save the day, New York losing to Boston by a score of 5 to 2. The lowering clouds made a fitting background for his lightning speed and dazzling wind-up, but he was fighting for a lost cause. He made a game stand, and was compelled to battle uphill all the way, but he never lost his nerve in the crisis. Matty said after the game that the Kansas wonder's form was impressive. . . .

McGraw called Charley Faust out to pitch the ninth inning for the Giants. As a man the crowd rose to its feet, bellowing applause. Seldom has it been that even the crafty Mathewson or the brilliant Marquard has received such a reception. Doffing his cap and bowing right and left, the Kansas boy took his place on the rubber. "Shoot it down the groove, Charley," called Hartley from behind the bat as Rariden faced him. Faust wound up like a clock and put the first one right over the plate. "Strike!" called the umpire, while the crowd howled. "Two strikes!" was called after the next service. On the third ball, however, Rariden doubled to centre and took third when Tyler sacrificed, Faust making a clever play on the bunt. Sweeney whaled a long fly to Burns in centre field and Rariden scored. Mike Donlin, however, ended the inning by grounding out weakly to Fletcher.

New York *World*

In the ninth inning the game was turned into a burlesque. The Rustlers got another run.

FAUST'S DEBUT GENERATED quite an array of responses, from the blaring *Herald* to the oblivious *World*. The many "factual" discrepancies — the attendance, the count on Rariden, the outfielders, and so on — meant less than the shared truths of what the experience meant to Faust, the fans, and the other players. Only Heywood Broun addressed the critical question of how hard the Boston hitters tried against Faust, who tried his best, as always. Broun asserted that the hitters "did not let down" but were puzzled by Faust's "dewdrop shoots" (the most poetic euphemism yet for Faust's slow deliveries). They appear to have tried. The first hitter socked a double, the pitcher bunted, the next guy hit a well-used ball a long way and it happened to get caught, and Mike Donlin — a good enough actor to play a Confederate general in Buster Keaton's *The General* — made the third out. This sequence spared Faust from having to face the middle of the Boston order, and he succeeded in retiring the side in four batters.

How did Faust celebrate his triumph? With an extra slab of apple pie? With a surrogate for Lulu? Those are among the pieces of the Faust puzzle likely to remain missing. We don't know whether Faust read his press notices, or whether he could even comprehend what the New York writers wrote. He had all day Sunday to celebrate and to absorb what they wrote about him, with the Giants idle. On Monday they headed back to Brooklyn, where they had played on Thursday, and that's where Faust spent his thirty-first birthday. Did he play? No. Did he expect to? Well, two brief references give contradictory hints of an answer. According to John Wheeler, "It took a dozen restraining hands to prevent Charles Victory Faust from relieving 'Larry' Doyle when the latter hurt his ankle rounding first base in the sixth. He was so piqued when little Paulet was given the preference that he left the field before the close of the inning." Damon Runyon, though, reported that "the crowd clamored for Charley Faust to pitch the final inning, but Chas. is being groomed for jinx duty in the world's 'serious,' and blushingly declined to serve." There you go. Either he ran off and pouted because he couldn't pinch-run, or he coyly declined a chance to pitch in another game. Pouting would be the betting favorite, making it worth noting how much Faust wanted to run the bases again after nearly scoring a run against Boston.

The Giants split two games in Brooklyn, winning the first behind Hooks Wiltse and losing the second 2–1 in ten innings as Bert Maxwell pitched well. Faust remained idle, perhaps awaiting a second chance back at the Polo Grounds on Columbus Day. If McGraw had any plans to let Faust play, he again refrained from alerting the press and the public. Thus, after another day off on Wednesday, a crowd of no more than ten thousand assembled at the Polo Grounds on a sunny Thursday afternoon with no particular idea of what to expect. They got baseball and apple pie Faust-style, another slice of baseball history.

This time, Damon Runyon starred in the coverage corps, making solid contact with the journalistic hanging curve. Under the subheadline "Mascot Faust Furnishes Comedy for Many Fans at Baseball Burial," Runyon went to town on how the Giants closed their regular season.

C. Marion K. V. Faust, he pitched A Inning against Brooklyn, New York, and covered himself with glory and large patches of Mr. Groundkeeper Murphy's best blue grass and things. This makes C. M. Kansas V. Faust's second inning in organized ball and both of the same will be remembered when all hands have the long gray boys at the end of the chin.

The Giants, by the bike, lost two games to Brooklyn, the scores being 3 to 0 and 5 to 2, C. M. K. Victory Faust tallying one of the last two runs. Wicked William Dahlen, leader of the young men from the other end of the tunnel, played a bit o' shortstop for himself and friends in the second game, but after fanning desperately three times hand running William retired to the back of the grand stand and kicked himself in the same general vicinity.

Far be it from us to make any suggestions, but some people did say that William was trying to steal Charley Faust's stuff.

In addition to it marking the close, s'help us, of the almost perennial National League season, the nearly come back of Bill and the second appearance of Faust, it was otherwise quite a large, elegant afternoon. It was the Christopher Columbus day, so-called, which was invented by Charley Ebbets, of Brooklyn, especially for closing the N.L. season, although there are some people unkind enough to say that they doubt if the Brooklyn philanthropist would know Columbus if he met him at the pass gate.

Mr. Faust was not wholly content with the showing he made in the ninth inning, although he would have held the Dodgers hitless but for an error by Eugene Paulet, who is now viewed with suspicion by Chas. As it was, he hurled them back with a single smack (poetry) and stole two bases himself, not to mention the tally which he carried in himself by the nape of its neck. No, Mr. Faust was fretful, and aggrieved. Seen under the shower bath at the clubhouse by your correspondent after the game Mr. Faust said, quote:

"When the wires wing the word to Marion, K., to-night that Brooklyn was able to make a hit off the pride of the Jayhawker State, how will I look? Why—why—why! And also why! Words fail me at this juncture."

Charley relieved Bert Maxwell, the Birmingham bear who, in turn, had rousted Louis Drucke, of Waco, Texas, out of a job. Chas. wanted to go in prior to that time—some time prior, in fact. He would descend upon the pitching box every inning and announce to Cap. Doyle that this was the time. The captain would send him out to the high grass in centre field to warm up with Dick Hennessey, assuring the Kansas tornado that he needed more exercise.

A statistical shark has figured that the energy expended by Charles in warming up, running in from centre field every inning, lifting his hat to John T. Brush and winding up after he got in the box, would transport the entire wheat crop of Kansas six hundred miles if applied to wagon wheels.

Anyway, Charley finally finned in. Messr. Bill Brennan, the elegant umps, announced his name stammeringly, and the town of Marion was again on the baseball map. Grover Cleveland Hartley held mysterious consultation with Chas. before he started in on his celebrated wind-up, and Charley nodded understandingly. Zach Wheat bunted a ball right at Faust's extensive feet, but the wily Charles fell upon it with one hook and heaved the fleet Dodger out at first.

Some may argue that Messr. Klem overlooked a slight space of daylight, amounting to less than four yards between Zach's arrival at the bag and the hurled ball, but be that as it may, Zach was out. Daubert drove Fred Snodgrass over near the Harlem River after his fly, and then Paulet bobbled an easy toss on Daley's bounder, and Charley lost a no-hit game because Stark, the next man up, singled to left. Higgins forced Daley, Herzog making the play without assistance.

Faust was the first man up for the Giants in their end of the ninth, and young Master Dent almost hit him on the wrist with a pitched ball, so Messr. Brennan sent Charley to first. He stole second, and then stole third, busting into both bases standing up like a bombardier. The Dodgers saw him do it, too. Then Charley Herzog laid down a bunt over toward first, and Faust came booming into the plate with a noise like a patent harvester.

And the crowd did some whooping—some whooping, indeed!

Runyon's account captured the sense of farce which permeated this affair. Faust passed the afternoon as a (literally, if slowly) running joke in his repeated attempts to get in the game. Eventually, with one inning remaining in the season, John McGraw relented again, and he got to stay and pitch. Storming the mound was a far cry from his ceremonial entrance five days earlier. Runyon made him sound lucky to get the first two outs, but the other accounts pretended to give him credit for fooling the Brooklyn batters, as if he were a precursor of Rip Sewell, Steve Hamilton, and other perpetrators of assorted "blooper" pitches.

Faust's scoring a run was the greatest outrage of all, because the run counted; it made his postgame romp against the Rustlers seem legitimate. Heywood Broun made that historic fluke the opening theme of his coverage. The writers tried to outdo each other in accounting for Faust's pitching success, while portraying the run as crowd-pleasing burlesque.

New York *Morning Telegraph*

Marquard has won more games and Mathewson is considered by the dopesters as a more important principal in the world's series, but the fact remains that Charlie Faust pitched the last ball of the Giants' pennant-winning season. Larry Doyle and Josh Devore may be faster on the bases, but here again in black and white we find the records to show that Faust stole the last base and scored the last run.

Faust, no connection with the devil-dealing individual of that name, made several false starts before the time came for his entrance. On three distinct occasions he was summoned in from deep center field to take his place on the mound, but each time his ardor was restrained, and, led by Dick Hennessey, he went back to warm up again. The distance covered by Eddie Collins during a game, as computed by Hugh Fullerton, would fade into insignificance if any one would take the trouble to map out the route covered by Charlie Faust in his trips from the warm-up grounds to the bench and back to the warm-up grounds again.

Faust is splendidly equipped for pitching. He has an overhand and an underhand, a change of pace, a good wind-up and the most finished manners of any pitcher in the National League. It is to be hoped that McGraw will next year intrust to him the training of the recruits in the art of bowing. Faust was not scored upon and made one very nice play on a bunt. One of the stolen bases which was credited to him was a gift, but his steal of third was a dead on the level pilfer and a pretty one. He happened to catch Dent napping and fell into the base without opposition. The hook slide may be more effective, but the crawl slide as practised by Faust is a good deal more comfortable.

New York *Tribune*

Charlie Faust presided at the obsequies and ushered out the old season with much levity. About eight thousand "fans" took advan-

The score:—

BOSTON.

	AB.	H.	O.	A.	E.
Sweeney,2b	3	0	2	2	0
Donlin,cf.	4	1	3	0	0
Kirke,lf..	4	1	0	1	1
Miller,rf.	4	1	2	0	0
B'dwell,ss	4	1	1	2	0
Houser,1b	3	0	7	1	0
Tenney,1b	1	0	3	0	0
McD'ld,3b	2	0	2	0	0
In'rton,3b	0	0	1	0	0
Rariden,c	3	1	5	0	1
Tyler,p..	3	1	1	4	0
Totals	31	6	27	10	2

NEW YORK.

	AB.	H.	O.	A.	E.
Becker,lf	3	2	3	0	0
Devlin,2b.	4	1	1	3	0
S'grass,cf	4	1	5	0	0
Murray,rf	3	0	0	0	0
Burns,rf..	2	0	1	0	0
P'lette,1b.	4	0	9	0	0
Herzog,3b	3	1	1	1	1
F'tcher,ss	3	2	1	3	0
Wilson,c.	1	0	5	1	0
Hartley,c	2	0	1	1	0
M'quard,p	2	0	0	0	0
Drucke,p.	1	0	0	0	0
Faust,p..	0	0	0	1	0
Totals	31	1	27	10	1

Score by innings:—
Boston........ 0 0 2 0 0 0 2 0 1—5
New York... 0 0 2 0 0 0 0 0 0—2

Runs — Sweeney, Donlin, McDonald, Rariden (2); Becker and Devlin. Two-base hits—Bridwell, Rariden and Herzog. Home run—Donlin. Sacrifice hit — Tyler. Sacrifice fly — Sweeney. Stolen base—McDonald. First base on errors—Boston, 1; New York, 1. Left on bases—Boston, 6; New York, 6. Double plays—Tyler, Bridwell and Houser. Struck out—By Tyler, 4; by Marquard, 4; by Drucke, 1. Bases on balls—Off Tyler, 2; off Marquard, 1; off Drucke, 4. Hit by pitchers—By Tyler, 2 (Herzog and Fletcher). Hits—Off Marquard, 2 in five innings; off Drucke, 3 in three innings; off Faust, 1 in one inning. Umpires — Messrs. Finneran and Bush. Time—1h. 55m.

NEW YORK.

	AB.	R.	H.	BB.	SO.	PO.	A.	E.
Burns, lf........	4	0	1	0	0	0	0	0
Doyle, 2b......	4	0	0	0	3	4	0
Snodgrass, cf..	4	0	2	0	0	3	0	0
Murray, rf.....	3	0	1	0	0	1	0	0
Becker, rf......	2	0	0	0	0	1	0
Merkle, 1b.....	2	0	0	1	3	9	0
Maxwell, p.....	0	0	0	0	0	0	1	0
Faust, p........	0	1	0	0	0	0	1	0
Herzog, 3b.....	0	0	0	0	0	2	0	3
Devlin, ss.....	4	1	1	0	0	1	1	0
Hartley, c.....	4	0	0	0	9	1	1
Drucke, p......	1	0	0	0	0	0	0	0
Paulette, 1b...	2	0	0	0	0	5	0	1
Total	34	2	8	0	1	27	8	5

Two-base hits—Wheat, Hartley, Coulson. Stolen bases—Wheat, Coulson, Hummel, Faust, 2. First base on errors—Brooklyn, 2; New York, 7. Double plays—Dahlen and Daubert; Hummel and Erwin. Struck out—By Dent, 1; by Drucke, 3. Bases on balls—Off Drucke, 2; off Maxwell, 1. Hit by pitchers—By Drucke, 1, (Dent;) by Dent, 1, (Faust.) Hits—Off Drucke, 4 in 5 innings; off Maxwell, 4 in 3 innings; off Faust, 1 in 1 inning. Umpires—Messrs. Brennan and Klem. Time of game—One hour and thirty-eight minutes.

YOU COULD LOOK IT UP. Faust got his chance to pitch on October 7, then came back with a shutout inning five days later and recorded the final two stolen bases of the Giants' record total of 347.

tage of Columbus Day to get a last glimpse of the Giants before the real strife begins tomorrow. . . .

Charles Victory Faust, the man who made Kansas famous, was the feature of the second game. He did his best to rally the faltering cohorts of McGraw to victory, pitching one inning and scoring a run, but even a man with his superhuman endowments was unable to bring New York out ahead, alone and unaided. That Faust did not enter the struggle earlier was due to no fault of his own. He missed his cue to enter upon the scene three times, being a little previous on each occasion.

It took all the eloquence of Larry Doyle to persuade him that he had not warmed up sufficiently and that his arm would be ruined if he started too soon. At the opening of the ninth inning he declared that he was right and amid the cheers of the crowned heads and the flapping of the eagle's wings on the top of the stands he took his place on the mound. With his cartwheel delivery he was a terrible object to look upon, and except for an error by Paulette and a single by Stark the side was retired in order.

Charlie was the first man to bat in the ninth, and after rapping a two-base foul to left field was hit by a pitched ball and got a hit at first. Those who watched him steal second and third were unable to decide whether he resembled Nancy Hanks or Sosenby so far as stride went. A semi-squeeze play on a bunt by Herzog brought Faust home, and he did a beautiful spread eagle at the plate.

New York *Times*

Charley Faust, the Kansan brainstormer, pitched the ninth inning of the second game. Faust started to warm up for the critical test at noon, and by the time he was allowed to pitch he was somewhat tired, but was able to throw the ball almost fast enough to break a pane of glass. Charley pitched a one-hit game. He went to bat in the last half of the ninth inning, and Dent hit him on the wrist with the ball. Faust waddled to second and rolled to third and scored a run on an out. The crowd got excited about Faust's performance and cheered so long and heartily that Faust asked "Who's looney now?" Somebody told him he was all right, but they didn't know about the crowd.

New York *Sun*

Though the middle name of the paragon of mascots, Faust, is Victory, even the advent of that doughty reserve failed to turn defeat into victory in the second game. Drucke and Maxwell preceded Faust on the dais, but in response to urgent calls Faust was installed as pitcher in the ninth inning. His swing was a revelation to those who had not seen him before and his posture just before his windup, followed by sweeping convulsions of his arms, tearing the air into geometric tatters, so dismayed the Brooklyn batters that they failed to score in the inning in which they faced the sunflower phenom.

Faust's elbow ball, a forearm floater which came up airily as a soap bubble, so deceived Daley of the Brooklyns that that player fell flat when he missed it with a mighty lunge. The spectators were convulsed, though some of them did Faust the injustice of declaring that Daley was no slouch of a burlesquer. Umpire Brennan was so agitated that he covered his face with his hand and his chest pad shook violently. At the bat Faust took a position which proclaimed him an untamed demon, causing Pitcher Dent to lose his nerve completely and plunk the terrifying figure at the plate in the ribs. . . .

Snodgrass and Murray made hits in New York's half, the former giving a spirited exhibition of running in taking third while Dahlen was trying to grapple Murray's grounder. Barring Faust's whirlwind base running in the ninth, that was about all the pepper the Giants had.

Faust was hit in the ninth. From first he summoned Herzog to him for a conference. "I am going to steal second and third," said Faust, "and want you to sacrifice me home." No sooner said than done. Faust's trappy action carried him resistlessly from base to base—he was a regular Steve Philbin with the knee movement—and Herzog laid down the bunt on which he came home, a cross between a squeeze and a joke.

New York *Press*

Charles Victory Faust, the Kansas buffoon, twirled the ninth inning for New York, and gave the crowd plenty of amusement. Charley would have escaped without a hit had not Paulet muffed Daley's pop fly. . . .

The last New York run was a gift pure and simple. In order to amuse the crowd, Dent purposely winged Faust. The Kansan then was permitted to steal second and third, and he scored while Dent was throwing out Herzog.

New York *Herald*

In the second game Drucke started and then Maxwell went into the box and pitched awhile, followed for one inning by Faust, who had been insisting on going into the box for several rounds. . . .

Faust wore a path between the outfield and the pitcher's box in the second game trying to horn in. At last he got his chance in the ninth, and was reached for but one hit.

Philadelphia *Inquirer*

The second game was a farce. Charley Faust, the eccentric Kansan, pitched the last inning, which was pure burlesque. Faust was allowed to get on base, Dent hitting him. He was then allowed to steal second and third and scored on an infield out.

Brooklyn *Daily Eagle*

Charles V. Faust, the most unique character baseball has produced since the days of "Crazy" Schmidt, was sent out to the mound in the ninth of the second game after he had been warming up for four hours. Charles is indeed a strange character. He imagines himself a ballplayer and winds up and bats as if he were two or three ballplayers. The scientist who would undertake to describe the curves made by the arms of Charles as he prepares to hurl a ball would go down into history as Young Kid Isaac Newton. Charles reminds you of a mainspring that breaks when you are looking inside to see what makes the watch tick. He twists himself around the air in his vicinity as if he were giving an imitation of a pretzel. The show is well worth seeing. Still, Charles was not the worst ever. The rampageous Superbas reached him for one hit in one inning. . . .

The word was passed to Dent in the ninth inning to let Charles reach first, and show his ability as a base thief. Dent pitched Charles a couple of easy ones that had nothing whatever to do with pitching or the plate. Then, in an effort to walk the weird one, he shot Charles in the ribs with a mild inshoot. Charles reached first and started to steal right away. Erwin purposely made a low throw, but Charles failed to come up to expectations for he did not make one of those slides which have stirred up enough dust in the past to smother a caravan on a snowfield. It was hoped that Charles would steal third. He did, but he did it on the level. While Dent was wondering what to do with the next batter, Charles got a long lead and stole third in orthodox fashion. Again he accomplished his purpose with such ease and grace that he did not slide. The squeeze play is a great favorite with Charles, who showed that he was a dandy little squeezer when he came home in respectable condition when Herzog laid down a bunt. It was all a burlesque, but it was the last day of the National League season and the fans wanted to be amused.

SUPPORTING PLAYERS. Faust wouldn't look so good in the record books without the help of these two opposing pitchers. GEORGE "LEFTY" TYLER, left, had only six of his 127 career wins when he did Faust two favors: first, he bunted instead of swinging, then he let Faust hit the ball and run around the bases after the game was over. ELLIOTT "EDDIE" DENT, right, pitched in one dozen games in the majors, but worked just one inning after his only claim to fame, plunking Faust and letting him amass two stolen bases and a run scored. (National Baseball Hall of Fame Library & Archive, Cooperstown, N.Y.)

THE FANS WANTED to be amused. The players wanted to be distracted, wanted to laugh after a summer of listening to McGraw's tirades. McGraw wanted to get his way, but even more than that he wanted to win, and the players wanted to win, too, especially with the lingering bitterness over the stolen 1908 pennant. The writers wanted to win the battles for scoops and angles, and above all they wanted copy that would amuse their readers. How unlikely that so many interlinked desires and hopes could be satisfied by the addition of one person to the mix of personalities and forces already on McGraw's Giants. And how incredible that that decisive person was Charles Victor Faust, alias Victory Faust, the greatest jinx-killer of all time.

8
Bursting Bubbles

AFTER THE RIDICULOUS Columbus Day doubleheader, the Giants hardly had a chance to catch their breath before opening the World Series on Saturday, October 14. Meanwhile, their opponents, the Philadelphia Athletics, spent the lame-duck days sparring against an American League all-star team led by Ty Cobb and Walter Johnson. The Athletics tuned up for Christy Mathewson and the Giants by beating Johnson on Wednesday; on Thursday, the day Charley Faust mowed down the Superbas, the Athletics polished off Smokey Joe Wood and the all-stars one more time. The defending world champions were ready.

The 1911 Athletics fielded virtually the same team that had won the 1910 World Series by mauling the Chicago Cubs in five lopsided games. Manager Connie Mack, like John McGraw, built his teams around pitching, defense, and speed. When their teams met in the 1905 World Series, all five games were shutouts, with Christy Mathewson pitching three to bring the title to New York. The only Athletics win in the 1905 World Series was a shutout by Charles "Chief" Bender. Bender joined fellow Hall of Fame pitchers Rube Waddell and Eddie Plank in anchoring Mack's early Philadelphia teams. Bender and Plank were still around, combining for thirty-nine wins in 1910 and duplicating that total in 1911. The new ace was "Colby Jack" Coombs, a workhorse right-hander who pitched a staggering 690 innings in 1910–1911 (65 more than Mathewson). In 1910 he won thirty-one games, then capped his season with three complete-game wins over the Cubs in six days to lead the Athletics to their Series triumph.

In 1911 the new cork-center baseball increased run production in the American League by almost 24 percent, but the Athletics remained the team to beat. Coombs, for instance, gave up almost two more runs per game than in 1910, but he still won twenty-eight games because the Athletics led the majors in batting and runs scored. They outscored the Giants by more than one hundred runs and had a .296 team average, the highest of the dead-ball era.

Five Athletics regulars batted over .300, compared with two Giants (Doyle and Meyers). Among the five were outfielders Danny Murphy and Bris Lord, both of whom had flailed helplessly at Mathewson's deliveries in the 1905 World Series. The other three played the infield, the young nucleus of a team that also won pennants in 1913 and 1914 before financial pressure from the Federal League compelled Mack to sell his stars and exile his franchise to seven years in last place. First base belonged to John "Stuffy" McInnis, a twenty-year-old who took the job away from veteran captain Harry Davis in 1911. McInnis hit .321, launching a career that lasted until 1927 with a lifetime .308 batting average. Hall of Famer Eddie Collins starred at second base, hitting .365 in 1911, up from .322 the year before. He retired in 1930, fourth on the all-time hit list with 3,313. Shortstop Jack Barry was the offensive weak link but anchored the defense and ran well. He hit .265 in 1911, stealing thirty bases. Frank Baker played third base, having learned the position at the University of Maryland from a part-time coach named Buck Herzog—now the Giants third baseman. Baker's march to the Hall of Fame began in 1911, his first great year, when he hit .334 and led the league in home runs. This was the legendary "$100,000 infield," so-called because they were worth that much—$100,000, that is, for four players, a daydream figure in a day when the four best players in baseball didn't make that much in aggregate salary.

The Athletics needed every bit of that offense, for they spent the first two-thirds of the season chasing the Detroit Tigers. The Tigers didn't have much pitching, but they did have two Hall of Famers in their outfield. Ty Cobb had his best season ever, batting .420 and leading the league in everything except home runs. Sam Crawford hit .378 and tied Frank Baker with 115 runs batted in, second in the majors to Cobb. Managed by Hughie Jennings, John McGraw's teammate and best friend in Baltimore, the Tigers had won three straight pennants before being dethroned by the Athletics in 1910, and they came out firing in 1911, intent on reclaiming the title. Their sizzling 33–11 start gave the Athletics a skyward view of first place most of the summer. The last week of July—the same weekend that Charley Faust introduced himself to McGraw—the Athletics took four of five games from the Tigers in Philadelphia to get within a game of first. They passed Detroit the second week of August and poured it on, making the final margin of thirteen and a half games misleading. Like the Athletics, the Tigers scored well over five runs a game, keeping the defending champions at bay until Detroit's weaker pitching faded late in the summer.

The Athletics suffered a blow on September 25 when Tigers ace George Mullin hit Stuffy McInnis with a pitch, nearly breaking his wrist. Despite optimism that McInnis would be ready to face the Giants, the injury prevented him from throwing, limiting him to a token appearance in the World Series. With McInnis out, Manager Mack dusted off thirty-seven-year-old Harry Davis to play first base in the World Series. But Davis had hit only .197 during the season and didn't do much against Mathewson even in his prime. This key replacement accounted for the only perceived difference between the teams heading into the mid-October showdown. The Athletics could steal, too, led by Collins and Baker with thirty-eight apiece. Oddsmakers installed the Giants as a slight favorite, with no shortage of action reported.

How much faith did Giants fans have in their team? Ask Max Voll, a Harlem restaurateur quoted in the *Globe*: "One week ago I had $7,285.16 on deposit in my bank. I bet all but 16c. on the Giants. My wife is ripping mad. I am sleeping in the bathroom. But wait till the gravy comes in. Even the brewer is worrying about me, but he is Dutch and don't know baseball from pinochle. I bet my receipts for this entire week. I even sold my automobile to get money to bet. I have nothing left but my clothes, the 16c. and my business. . . . I have the best Restaurant in Harlem. I will bet my Cafe, Rathskeller and Restaurant that the Giants win the series. I also have a bartender who comes from Philadelphia and he thinks he knows baseball. I will throw him in as well if anybody wants to bet." Presumably Mr. Voll passed a long, chilly winter checking his clothes for loose change, lucky that he didn't lose his shirts.

The first-game crowd at the Polo Grounds totaled 38,281, many of them already boiling about the scandalous ticket distribution. Somehow, speculators snatched up thousands of tickets and were charging double face value (or more) across the street from the box office before it even closed. Prices escalated from there, counterfeit tickets flooded the market, and the scalpers cleaned up. Only the cheapest bleacher seats were withheld for day-of-game sale, leaving the average fan literally out in the street. Still, with the enormous new stadium finished at last and decked out in traditional bunting, everyone who helped fill the magnificent double-tiered grandstand felt glad for the chance to cheer the Giants on to victory in their first World Series game since Christy Mathewson beat Chief Bender 2–0 to end the 1905 World Series, six years earlier to the day.

John T. Brush and John McGraw evoked memories of that success by using the same ploy they did at the opening of the 1905 World Series. Once again, the Giants took the field wearing solid black uniforms—sinister and intimidating, a dark force that had stifled the Athletics once before and would do so again. Mathewson, the brightly shining star at the core of that force, wore the long gray ulster coat he had preserved from the 1905 uniform as he brought up the rear of the procession. In a more important echo of 1905, Matty pitched the opener, once again opposed by Chief Bender.

The Athletics got good news early as they finally broke the Mathewson hoodoo by scoring in the second inning. Frank Baker singled, advanced on a bunt and a passed ball, and scored on a single by the not-yet-doddering Harry Davis, the first Athletics run off Mathewson in twenty-nine innings. He didn't let them enjoy the breakthrough for long, holding them to four hits the rest of the way. The Giants tied the game in the fourth inning on an unearned run, Fred Snodgrass scoring from second base on an Eddie Collins error. In the seventh, doubles by Chief Meyers and Josh Devore put the Giants ahead 2–1, providing plenty of cushion for Mathewson. Retiring the final eleven Athletics, Matty gave Mack's men déjà vu. In two straight games, six years apart, Matty had beaten Bender 2–0 and 2–1, ending one World Series and beginning another.

"The Athletics as a whole struck me as being a wonderful ball team," declared Mathewson in the morning *Herald* (in a bylined column

FAUST relaxing on the dugout steps. He did his best work on the bench, predicting plays and cheering on the Giants to victory after victory. But his luck ran out in the World Series, when he was outmascotted by Louis Van Zelst of the Athletics. (Collection of Thomas Busch)

ghostwritten by John Wheeler and syndicated around the country), "a club which has had little trouble in winning the pennant in the American League and therefore perhaps lacking a little in grimness and fighting qualities. They had laughed their way to a championship in their league. . . . The Giants had to fight their way through the West to get the flag and they are used to fighting. We couldn't get a rise out of them yesterday." Matty claimed that the Athletics stole Chief Meyers's signals (something no National League team had been able to do) and that Harry Davis got his RBI single only because he knew a curve was coming. In the third inning, alerted to Mack's cunning, John McGraw had Meyers change his signals, and Matty befuddled the Athletics the rest of the way.

Of course, having Victory Faust on hand must have helped. "Charley Faust," noted the *Times*, "the Giants' 24-carat luck-bringer, didn't wear one of the undertaker's garbs. The other mascot, Dick Hennessey, didn't either. Arlie Latham looked like Hamlet." Wrote Damon Runyon, "It was an impressive sight as the big town boys trotted rapidly down the field and took their bench. With them was Charley Faust, the Kansas jinx, in the ordinary travelling uniform of the club." What did Faust do to mark this special occasion? The same as usual—he warmed up and willed the Giants to win. The *Tribune* contained the only description of Faust's pregame antics: "Charlie Faust gave the 'fans' in right field a sideache from so much laughing. Charlie was there, although he didn't have enough hair to braid. But on his chest fluttered a medal which is his dearest pride and joy. 'Red' Murray gave him the same as a mark of honor and esteem. The medal and Charlie flopped around chasing fly balls, and they had a delightful little time. The comedy, however, was denied to many who did not come equipped with field glasses."

The Athletics retreated to Philadelphia after the game, while the Giants spent the Sunday off day in New York. Sunday evening, most of them attended a testimonial at the New York Theatre. The gala affair was sold out, with many fans turned away at the door. The festivities featured several dozen vaudeville performers, including George M. Cohan and Lillian Russell. After several hours of entertainment, the fans got what they really wanted: a chance to celebrate their soon-to-be champions. Madison Square Garden announcer Joe Humphreys introduced the Giants one by one, and they paraded out on stage wearing tuxedos. Rube Marquard got the noisiest reception. According to the *Times*, Christy Mathewson was "too modest to appear," greatly disappointing the fans. Art Fletcher, Beals Becker, and Red Murray also missed the fun. Everyone else strutted around the stage, soaked in the adulation, brandished a silver trophy presented to the team, and spoke a few words to the crowd. Everyone, including John McGraw and Charley Faust. "For the first time in his life Charley Faust donned evening clothes, and didn't know just where to put his hands. He contributed his little piece, saying how sure he was that New York was going to beat the Athletics. Almost everybody believed him."

Monday morning at nine o'clock, the Giants boarded a train for Philadelphia and game 2. At one in the afternoon, they entered Shibe Park in their villainous black uniforms, led by mascot Dick Hennessey. "Charley Faust," wrote Sid Mercer, "hung to the flanks of the invading army and as soon as the Giants straggled on the field he began to doff his cap in response to the salvos of the multitude. Charley was clothed in a gray uniform, his medal, and a smile, and during the batting practice of the Giants he and 'Spud' Hennessey chased flies in the outfield. One line drive hit Faust on the shoulder and nearly put him out of business." The *Sun* noted that "during the lively practice the crowd laughed at the antics of the jinx killer, Charley Faust."

Game 2 saw another pitching duel between two Hall of Famers. The neophyte, Rube Marquard, took on the master, Eddie Plank, at thirty-five still more formidable than the Giants' young lefty. The last time he had faced the Giants, in game 4 in 1905, Plank lost 1–0 to Iron Man McGinnity on an unearned run. With that sour taste still in his mouth and 26,286 paying customers cheering him on, Plank held the Giants to five hits. Marquard gave the Athletics only four, but one of them made history.

The Athletics got an unearned run in the first inning, aided by a Red Murray error and plated on a wild pitch by Marquard. The Giants got the run right back in the second when Buck Herzog doubled and scored on a Chief Meyers single. Both pitchers settled into a dominating groove after that, with only one base runner between the second and sixth innings. In the sixth Eddie Collins sliced a two-out double to left field, bringing up Frank Baker. Mathewson's first-game scouting report said that Baker hammered fastballs and had trouble with curves.

Marquard had gotten Baker twice on curves already, but this time he and catcher Meyers became concerned that Collins would steal their signs. They conferred and decided that Meyers would signal for two fastballs and Marquard would throw two curves. One buckled Baker's knees for a strike; the other sailed outside for a ball. So far, so good. Next, Meyers signaled for the curve, but Marquard decided this was the perfect time to slip the high hard one past Baker. Baker drilled it over the right field fence for a two-run homer, and that was the ballgame. The Giants managed only one more hit off Plank, who struck out eight (including Josh Devore four times) to complete the 3–1 win that squared the Series at one game apiece.

"The fault was mine," conceded Marquard in the article that appeared under his byline in the New York *Times*. Most likely ghost-written by *Times* reporter W. W. Aulick (who could not get a byline of his own), the article detailed the problems with signals, Marquard's nervousness before his first World Series game, and his fatal sixth-inning hunch. "I will never give Baker that kind of ball again," he vowed, "and I expect to strike him out several times more before the series is over." For what it was worth, Marquard followed through by getting two strikeouts and a ground ball against Baker later in the Series.

Christy Mathewson, in the *Herald*, decided, "I don't think for a moment that 'Rube' intended to lay the ball over the plate for him, but he did it, and this cost us the game. . . . Aside from that one ball, Marquard pitched a beautiful game and deserved to win it." Mathewson discussed the sign-stealing issue, concluded that it was an ethical practice requiring frontier justice, and promised a new tactic the next time the Athletics put a runner on second base. "Some batter," warned Matty, "is likely to get beaned if he walks into the plate expecting one thing and meets another." He also accused the Athletics of the "bush-league" tactic of heavily watering the areas near the bases in order to slow down the faster Giants runners.

Matty got to test his resolve in game 3, pitching on two days' rest in front of 37,216 fans at the Polo Grounds. He faced a well-rested Jack Coombs, and the two squared off for eleven tense innings. The Giants managed only three hits but should have won the game, which instead consummated the legend of "Home Run" Baker. The Giants got singles by Meyers and Matty in the third inning to produce a run, then counted on Matty's usual whitewashing of the Athletics. In the fifth inning, the Athletics got the first two men on, but Matty shut them down. In the eighth inning, the Giants cut two Athletics down at the plate, one on a disputed call on which Meyers might have been late in tagging Jack Barry. Thanks to that out, Matty took his 1–0 lead to the ninth inning, and he got Eddie Collins for the first out.

Up stepped Frank Baker, who had led the American League with eleven home runs in 1911 but had no nickname yet. That changed on a two-one pitch, when he smacked a soaring line drive identical to his home run off Marquard the day before in Philadelphia. This one cleared the right field fence easily, tying the game. The Polo Grounds crowd, minutes away from celebrating another Mathewson victory, fell silent with shock. It was bad enough for Marquard, the untested youngster, to make a fatal mistake, but Matty? How could the peerless Matty give Baker a fat pitch in the ninth inning of a 1–0 game?

When the fans came to, Matty got razzed by some who had read his lecture on how to pitch to Baker and wondered why he didn't take his own advice. In his *Herald* column, Matty and John Wheeler scrambled to account for the lapse: "In the seventh," Matty explained,

> I pitched a fadeaway to Baker, and he hit the ball almost to the right field wall, where Murray caught it. I made a mental note and decided to feed him curves. When he came to the bat in the ninth I pitched him two curve balls. He missed one and the other was wide. The next I delivered was a curve over the outside corner, knee high, just where I wanted it, but Brennan called it a ball. I thought that he missed a strike and put me in the hole. The next one was a curve, and I didn't want to take any chances on not putting it over because it would get me in a three-and-one hole, so I laid it up better than I meant to, and he caught it on the end of his bat and drove the ball into the stand.

Here is how Rube Marquard's *Times* column began: "It was the hardest game to lose I ever saw, and Matty lost it the same way I lost the second game in Philadelphia. When he came back to the bench after Barry had been thrown out in the ninth inning, I asked him what it was. 'The same thing you did, Rube,' said Matty. 'I gave Baker a high, fast one. I have been in the business for a long time and have no excuse.'" Nice quote, except that it flatly contradicted Matty's own account. The problem was that, unlike Matty and Wheeler, Marquard and his ghostwriter did not consult on the column. Marquard didn't learn until the next day that he and Matty were feuding over their failure to prevent Frank Baker's metamorphosis into Home Run Baker, or that he had admitted after Baker's blast that the Giants "were a beaten team and they knew it when the score was tied." If he had read the column, he might have wondered what that *Times* writer was thinking of when he asserted that the Giants changed their signaling system because "we had just discovered how the Athletics were getting the signals. The little hunchback is the white-haired boy. He comes out with the batter to take back the bat he discards, and he is in a position to get a view of Meyers's bent knee into the glove. He then tips it to the coacher on the third base line, who gives it to the batter." A dubious theory at best— how could "the little hunchback" (Connie Mack's mascot, Louis Van Zelst) spot the signal after the first pitch? Not even Charley Faust could insinuate himself onto the field to steal a catcher's signs.

Neither Mathewson nor Marquard admitted to more than one bad pitch, leaving room to distribute the blame. The *Herald*'s headline read "Christy Mathewson Lays Second Defeat to Base Running Error in Tenth Inning." This play caused the real controversy of the 1911 World Series. Fred Snodgrass led off the bottom of the tenth by walking, and Red Murray sacrificed him to second. With Fred Merkle batting, a Coombs pitch rolled a few feet away from catcher Jack Lapp. Snodgrass broke for third, but Lapp recovered quickly and his throw beat Snodgrass easily. Seeing this, "Snow" went spikes-first into Baker, feet flying high. As Baker tagged him out, Snodgrass's spikes sliced through Baker's uniform and gashed his leg. This Ty Cobb–like viciousness earned Snodgrass a cascade of boos from his hometown fans. They had seen this before—in game 1, Snodgrass found himself heading for a sure out at third base and leaped high enough that his spikes cut Baker's forearm, causing him to drop the ball. A moment later, nailed at the plate on an attempted double steal, Snodgrass slid so hard that he tore off the catcher's shin guard. Nobody made a big deal of it until two games later when he spiked Baker again. "If it is part of the McGraw system of play," complained the Philadelphia *Inquirer*, "it is high time the McGraw system was being relegated to the dark ages where it belongs." Mathewson made no mention of the spiking in his column. Instead, he blamed Snodgrass for being overanxious. Snodgrass got too big a lead off second, so big that he had to double back toward second to avoid being picked off. He reversed course just as the pitch eluded Lapp, then had to turn again before heading for third. Mathewson felt that if Snodgrass had taken a normal lead, he could have broken for third right away and beaten the throw. This represented a by-product of their "acute overanxiety" at the plate, where each man tried to be a hero by swinging for the fences instead of chopping the ball as they normally did with great success. Combine overanxious batters and a trio of pitchers who totaled 693 career wins, and the Giants showed only thirteen hits for three games; Devore and Doyle, at the top of the order, had one hit apiece so far, while Murray and Fletcher were hitless.

The Snodgrass play cost the Giants a chance to win the game in the tenth inning, and they fell apart in the eleventh. With one out, Eddie Collins singled, and Baker smashed a hit off Buck Herzog at third. Herzog made what the *Times* called a "lurid" throw, his third error of the game, trying to get Baker, and by the time Merkle chased it down the runners were on second and third. Danny Murphy hit a grounder to shortstop, but Art Fletcher fumbled it and everyone was safe, Collins scoring. That made two errors on Fletcher, five for the left side of the Giants infield, the duo whose arrival in the everyday lineup in late July coincided with the charge to the top of the standings. Now they couldn't do anything right.

Harry Davis, Connie Mack's decaying captain, cashed in the mistakes with a run-scoring single, making it 3–1. That extra run made the difference, for the Giants got an unearned run of their own in the bottom of the eleventh. The game ended fittingly when Beals Becker, carrying the potential tying run, was thrown out trying to steal second. The 3–2 loss ended Mathewson's four-game hoodoo over the Athletics, who went home for game 4 sensing their title chances ripen after beating the Giants' two aces back-to-back.

Rain arrived in Philadelphia on October 18 about the same time as the ballclubs, but stayed longer. After that day's game was rained out, the writers found more time to stir up the Snodgrass-Baker controversy. Connie Mack and New York Highlanders manager Hal Chase called the spiking deliberate, yet Baker reportedly had no hard feelings. Snodgrass issued a statement defending himself, saying that Baker, despite having the ball in plenty of time to make a safe tag, chose to straddle the bag and drop to his knees "in such a position that he could not help getting hurt." According to Damon Runyon, "the ball players say that Baker is usually in the way of an incoming runner, and unless they whistle as they round the curves he has a hard time getting out of their way." Cobb and others had spiked him in the past, and he took this bloodletting in stride.

The Philadelphia fans bought only the notion that Snodgrass had tried to injure their star slugger. The Giants spent the rainy Wednesday hanging around the Majestic Hotel, where Art Fletcher nearly got into a fistfight with raucous fans. Occasionally the players ventured out into the city, where Snodgrass found himself booed and hissed by the brotherly citizens. The Giants had a lousy time until they attended an evening show, where nobody recognized them in the dim light. Meanwhile, John McGraw and Fred Merkle were in trouble with the National Commission. After Snodgrass spiked Baker in the tenth inning, Merkle walked and was thrown out trying to steal second, a call that he and McGraw had protested bitterly. Merkle bought a $100 fine for his trouble, while McGraw's angry comments on the way back to the dugout were overheard by the three members of the Commission, sitting in the box seats. They censured McGraw, warning him that another outburst would get him banned for the remainder of the Series and earn him a "heavy" fine.

McGraw had plenty of time to cool his heels as the rain continued, forcing another postponement on Thursday. "Snodgrass Hooted Out of Philadelphia," read the *Times* headline. After continued harassment of Snodgrass, McGraw sent his centerfielder back to New York. His absence led to a rumor that a fan had tried to shoot him. Another rumor had Baker rushed to the hospital with blood poisoning in his wounds. No, Baker was resting comfortably at home and expected to play in game 4.

If they ever played it. By the third day of rain, Shibe Park looked like a small lake. Chief umpire Bill Klem estimated that it would take more than one day of sunshine to dry out the field, and once they couldn't play Saturday, that meant two more days off, with Sunday games forbidden. After three intensely contested games, the players had to sit around letting their hostility fester. Even Charley Faust had trouble coping, according to two items by Damon Runyon. The first appeared after the second postponement.

A black curse has been pronounced against the house of Baker by Charles Victory Faust, who sits alone in his corner and mopes away the hours wondering what has become of his charm. They say that the tallow dips were kept burning late and at both ends up in Trappe, Maryland [Baker's hometown], last night, and that the good citizens clustered about the grocery store long after the curfew had rung, while they heard again and again the story of the strange doings of that Baker boy. In Marion, Kansas, however, there was a great deal of sadness over the fate of Charley Faust. McGraw is not worried. The thought being in sequence to the above shall not be taken to mean that he is not worried about Faust, or about Baker either, but that he is not worried over the series.

Next day, Runyon concocted a gibberish quote for Faust that poked fun at the whole controversy. "Charles Victory Faust arose above the level of his gloom this morning to give vent to a few words; then immediately ducked back under the surfacing of sorrow, as a whale lifts its nozzle from the deep, spouts, and submerges. 'The spiking of Marquard's fast ball and Mathewson's fadeaway by this fellow Baker was intentional beyond the shadow of a doubt,' said the ex-Jinx jabber of the Giants. 'It was the most cowardly thing I have ever seen in baseball.'"

On Sunday, October 22, with the teams idle for a fifth day, John Wheeler reviewed the Giants' "triumphal tour" on their final road trip in a long article in the *Herald* that featured one large chunk of Faust lore:

But the crudest product of the soil that ever affiliated himself with the Giants was Charles Victory Faust, of Marion, Kan. The first day that he blew into the Polo Ground his shoe tops and his trousers bottoms looked as if they had not associated for years and were drifting further apart. His trousers and coat were perfect strangers and on his head was a dinky little hat that would make a Dutch comedian's look sober. From out of the sleeves of his coat, which reached just below his elbows, dangled two red hands that resembled hams. Take this rough, uncut diamond and see what the Giants did to him.

They rallied him about his clothes. He began to realize that he was different from the rest — an unpleasant sensation — and he was the biggest "boob" that ever came out of Boobville. It wasn't long before he was having fuzz shaved off his face by a regular barber. He liked the treatment so well that he began to make up for lost time and spent all his spare moments in the shops. Two shaves and a massage a day was a temperate dose for him, and his face always looked like the shiny, waxed surface of a ballroom floor.

"Do you know," declared Charley one day in Boston out of a clear sky. "I think I'll have to get my shirts made to order? When I get them with the sleeves long enough they are too big around the neck," and he looked at his great dangling arms, that reached almost to the floor. He had just bought himself a new outfit and new shoes, which would have cost him as much as a suburban lot in New Jersey if he had to buy them by the acre.

Just one more thing about Faust. When he first came to the club he did not understand what it meant to tip a waiter. But he soon saw all the other players leaving their fifteen cents (the big league tip) after each meal, and now he carefully digs out a pocketbook and drops down the fifteen cents at his place. It won't be long before he discards the purse.

Early in the season the Giants spent a great deal of their time while traveling in playing cards, but when the race became so tight McGraw stopped all this, as it kept the men up at night. On the last trip many played hearts, a game not under the ban, while several of the athletes turned bookworms. Meyers is a voracious reader, consuming all sorts of deep works. Then there was the almost continual performance of Charley Faust's act in the smoking room, with Jack Murray as the manager. He likes Murray, and for the red headed outfielder alone will he work. His performance was greeted always with shouts and applause and demands for an encore.

That Sunday, the *Times* published a long article detailing the plans of many major leaguers to appear on the stage that winter. Rube Marquard had signed earlier to do a monologue, and Chief Meyers, who had performed with Christy Mathewson after the 1910 season, prepared to go on alone after Matty declined to return to show business. Three Athletics pitchers expected to cash in their successful season; Jack Coombs, Chief Bender, and Cy Morgan (who had some experience, billed as the "Minstrel Man of the Diamond") had signed during the summer to do an act called "Learning the Game," and after Coombs defeated Mathewson the asking price for the act went up to $2,500 a week. The *Times* listed others set to perform, including Mike Donlin and Joe Tinker. Home Run Baker, on the other hand, reportedly turned down many tempting offers made after his destruction of Marquard and Mathewson. He was willing to be spiked by Cobb and Snodgrass and anyone else who wanted a piece of him on the field, but he was unwilling to subject himself to the vegetable barrages of a vaudeville audience. "Last but not least," said the article, "among those who will break into vaudeville this year is Charley Faust, the eccentric Kansas farmer, who has been with the New York Giants' squad for several weeks. Faust will make his debut in New York."

While these winter daydreams filled the sports page, the rain continued to fall in Philadelphia throughout the weekend. On Saturday the Giants took a train back to New York, sick of being stranded in hostile territory. The players scattered to their homes, where they briefly spotted the sun but soon descended again into gloom. While the Athletics had commandeered an armory for indoor practice, the Giants had not worked out since Tuesday. Sunday night they boarded another train for Philadelphia. The *Times* reported that "the members of the team were so depressed by the weather when they took the train for Philadelphia last night that they looked more like a party going to a funeral than to play baseball for the world's championship." What a far cry from the rambunctious, rampaging final road trip. Only one thing encouraged them: thanks to the long delay, Christy Mathewson would be rested enough to tackle the Athletics in game 4.

On Monday, October 23, the sun shone upon Philadelphia for the first time in a week. The Shibe Park groundskeeper got the infield in decent enough shape to allow the Athletics to work out that afternoon, but it would take more sunshine Tuesday morning to burn off the outfield lakes enough to make a game playable. The Giants practiced Monday at Baker Bowl, home of the Phillies. While Mathewson and Marquard worked out with Chief Meyers, the other three pitchers—Ames, Wiltse, and Crandall—threw batting practice to the starved Giants hitters.

On Tuesday, October 24, they played. The one-week gap was the longest rain delay in World Series history (exceeded only by the 1989 earthquake delay), and no game in any other World Series was played as late as October 20 until the 1970s. Even before the rains began,

Garry Herrmann and the National Commission had announced that the regular season would end much earlier hereafter and would not include lame-duck weeks like the one that had occupied the Giants when they could have been playing the Athletics.

They played on a sunny, crisp day before 24,355 fans. The crowd arrived slowly and late, subdued after the one-week delay. "Charley Faust did his best," Sid Mercer assured his readers, "to cheer up the crowd. He borrowed the bandmaster's baton and conducted a rendition of Alexander's Ragtime Band. Then he fastened a miniature pennant to his belt and warmed up in front of the New York bench. He got a few laughs, but nobody paid any attention to him after Rube Marquard stepped out on the warming pan." Enthusiasm grew as the bleachers filled and the teams took the field, Fred Snodgrass leading his defiant teammates into a chilly reception sprinkled with cheers from New Yorkers who had made the trip.

After a week of frustration, the Giants got a quick jump on Chief Bender. Josh Devore led off the game with a single, and Larry Doyle ripped a line drive to right-center. Centerfielder Rube Oldring slipped on the wet grass, and the ball rolled to the fence for a triple. Fred Snodgrass fought off the jeering crowd and a Bender bender to hit a sacrifice fly, Doyle scoring to make it 2–0. In 1905, with the superhuman Christy Mathewson on the mound, the ballgame would have been over already. But this was 1911, only one game and one week after the Athletics defeated Mathewson to unmask him as human, mortal, and vulnerable. Two runs could no longer intimidate them.

Despite a full week of rest when he needed it most, Mathewson did not have his good stuff in Philadelphia. He fanned Baker to end the first inning with Collins on base, then escaped a leadoff double in the second thanks to a botched squeeze play by Jack Barry. He allowed another hit in the third, then met his Waterloo in the fourth. Baker led off with a screaming liner to left-center, which Devore just got his glove on while slipping down. Mathewson suggested that Devore also lost the ball in the crowd on this bright day. It went for a double, and Baker scored a moment later on a Danny Murphy smash, also good for a double. Next came captain Harry Davis, who had driven in a run in each of Mathewson's 1911 starts. Davis wasted no time here in tying the game up by slicing a double down the right field line. A groundout sent Davis to third, where he scored the go-ahead run on a sacrifice fly by Ira Thomas.

The Athletics scored again in the fifth inning. With two outs, Eddie Collins singled and scored on a long double to right by—who else?—Frank Baker. Next time up, with a runner on third and two outs (and Charley Faust warming up), Mathewson walked Baker intentionally and got Murphy, but it was too late. Once Chief Bender got the lead, he shut down the Giants on two hits over the last four innings. Their only real threat came in the eighth, when Josh Devore's single and an error put the tying runs on base. Bender got Red Murray—still hitless through four games—to foul out, and that was that. In the ninth, Fred Merkle doubled leading off, but Bender got the next three hitters. The Giants managed seven hits for the game, imprisoned in their team slump by Hall of Fame pitching. Even Mathewson conceded that "the Philadelphia team was the better ball club this afternoon for the first time in the series. . . . It was a case of too much Baker and Collins." In a syndicated column, Ty Cobb commented that "the Giants, when they were behind, seemed to make no extra effort to rally. . . . They seemed to go down in defeat with resentment." Cobb would have resented it, too, falling behind three games to one in the World Series despite Mathewson's having started three of the four games.

Back in New York on Wednesday, 33,228 rabid New Yorkers crowded into the Polo Grounds for game 5. John McGraw went with Marquard, of course, while Connie Mack bypassed game 2 winner Eddie Plank to go with game 3 winner Jack Coombs. Marquard lasted three innings. "It seems," his next column read, "that every time I go in someone makes a home run and breaks up the game. Oldring got me this time when I least expected it." That was in the third inning, when native New Yorker Reuben Henry "Rube" Oldring, four days after attending his sister's funeral (which he would have skipped if that day's game had not been postponed), drilled a two-out, three-run home run way into the left field bleachers. Now the Giants had an unaccustomed whiff of intimidation. They hadn't scored more than two runs in a game yet in the series, Coombs had just struck out three of them in the second inning, and suddenly they trailed by three runs in a game they had to win.

McGraw began his last stand by pinch-hitting for Marquard and substituting Red Ames, who hadn't pitched in two weeks. Ames, comfortable as always in the cool weather, gave McGraw four strong innings, allowing only two hits. The Giants did a little better against

Coombs, but not much. Larry Doyle made it to second base in the fourth inning and again in the sixth, but Snodgrass and Murray failed both times to score him. In the seventh, the Giants broke through with an unearned but much-needed run. Fred Merkle walked and made his way cheaply around the bases on an error, a groundout, and a sacrifice fly. Doc Crandall batted for Ames and drew a walk, but the "rally" ended when Josh Devore flied out.

The Giants stranded another runner at second base in the eighth inning and headed to the ninth trailing 3–1. Crandall stopped the Athletics, and the Giants needed two runs to save themselves. Coombs had limited them to five hits (eight over nineteen innings in two starts), yet the Giants rallied. With one out, Art Fletcher blooped a double to left field. Chief Meyers grounded to Jack Barry for the second out, but Crandall, who drove in twenty-one runs during the season, pounded a long fly ball to right center that went for a double, scoring Fletcher. "The crowd," said the *Times*, "was suddenly aroused from its lethargy. A howling, shouting mob of fanatics implored little Devore to do something. Josh was nervous and impatient. He waved his bat about in an aimless way and then brought it down hard against the ball, propelling a steaming grasser to left field. Crandall raced home with the tieing run, and people forgot all their manners and bringing up. Men and women who were perfect strangers suddenly became acquainted and slapped each other on the back with hilarious abandon." Their ecstasy faded as Devore was nailed trying to steal second, sending the second straight Polo Grounds game into extra innings.

In the tenth inning, the Giants got truly lucky for the first time in the series. Coombs beat out a bunt single but pulled a groin muscle straining to beat Chief Meyers's throw and had to leave the game. Eddie Plank warmed up hastily but didn't have enough time before the Athletics went out without scoring. Larry Doyle greeted Plank with a double just inside the line in left field. Fred Snodgrass bunted, and Plank tried to get Doyle at third base. This time the Giants had the jump, and Doyle slid in safely behind Baker. With nobody out, Red Murray had a chance to be the hero with his first hit of the series. He lifted a weak fly to short right field, and the runners had to hold.

That brought up Fred Merkle, a wonderful irony in light of what happened next. Merkle smashed a ball to right field on which Danny

Murphy made a great running catch, but his throw home was too late to catch Doyle, who scored the winning run. The crowd went wild—the Giants were alive! They went home blissful, unaware of exactly how miraculous the win was until the next day, when the papers carried the declaration of home plate umpire Bill Klem that Doyle never touched the plate. If the Athletics had appealed the play, Klem stated, he would have had to call Doyle out, ending the inning with the game still tied. That would have precipitated a riot exceeding the one in 1908 after the Cubs caught Merkle sneaking to the clubhouse instead of touching second base on a game-winning hit. This time, the Athletics failed to notice, mentally conceding the run even before Murphy made his running catch. The truth emerged too late for them to protest, Merkle got credit for knocking in the winning run, and the Series headed back to Philadelphia for game 6.

John McGraw had a tough time deciding on a starting pitcher. He went with Red Ames on the basis of his four shutout innings in game 5. Ames started off well, and the score was 1–1 to the fourth inning. Frank Baker and Danny Murphy singled, putting runners on first and third with nobody out. Two nightmarish plays later, the game was in flames. First, Harry Davis grounded to Doyle at second. Doyle glanced at Murphy running from first, saw that he had a double play, but hesitated an instant, then decided to cut down Baker with the go-ahead run. The hesitation cost him, as Baker barely beat his throw to give the Athletics a 2–1 lead. Then came, as the *Times* put it, "a hysterical outburst of loose playing by the Giants, which sent the whole team high into the azure." Jack Barry bunted. Ames fielded the ball near the first base line and threw it to Merkle. It never got to Merkle. It bounced off Barry's head and sailed into foul territory in right field. Red Murray retrieved it and tried to get Barry at second but threw the ball wildly. This time it crossed the foul line in left field, where Josh Devore fell down trying to snare it. "The crowd almost died laughing at the Giants," noted the *Times*; perhaps they were reminded of the way the Giants liked to send Charley Faust lumbering around the bases with those deliberate overthrows. Even Christy Mathewson admitted laughing when a fan hollered "nice head work!" at Barry after Ames's throw nailed him. Unfortunately for the Giants, this wasn't one of Faust's pregame romps. It was the World Series, and all three Athletics runners scampered quickly around the bases to score the runs that broke the Giants' backs. "Home Run Scored on a Bunt," the papers mocked.

The nightmare did not end there for the Giants. In the seventh inning, the Athletics exploded for seven runs against Hooks Wiltse. Two hits, an error, and four more hits marked the end of Wiltse and the Giants. McGraw sent Marquard in with runners on second and third, and Rube promptly threw a wild pitch. A disgusted Chief Meyers didn't even bother to chase the ball, letting both runners score. "Put Dick Hennessey or Charley Faust in," lamented the *Times*. "Perhaps they can stop this bombardment." Putting Faust in couldn't have hurt the Giants' chances at that point; they trailed 13–1 and wound up losing 13–2.

Thus the glorious 1911 season ended with the Giants giving up in a humiliating loss. The *Globe* printed a huge cartoon by C. H. Wellington titled "Napoleon's Return Had Nothing On This." The pagewide cartoon showed a funeral procession of five men with heads bowed, three in front of and two behind the funeral wagon, trailed by an endless army of fans. Heading the procession was a figure labeled "B. B. Scribe," harnessed to the wagon and beating a bass drum past which the tombstones loomed. Behind him slouched "C. Victory Faust" (with the "Victory" crossed out), a massive sackcloth draped over his shoulder, carrying a bucket of ashes and helping pull the wagon as drops of sweat poured off his face. Faust towered over the figure behind him, John McGraw, whose face was hidden behind a vessel of overflowing liquid labeled "Pitching Staff After the Blow-up." "Life's a fizzle anyhow!" muttered Wellington's squashed McGraw. Behind the wagon marched a top-hatted figure carrying a doctor's bag labeled "D. Crandall, M.D." and lamenting, "She was my dearest patient." Bringing up the rear of the Giants cortege was Chief Meyers, complete with headdress. His quote: "Ugh!" At the head of the hordes of fans, one carried a sign pledging, "The 'If' Squad will hold post mortems daily until further notice."

The "If Squad" had plenty to dwell on that winter, but there was no mystery about why the Athletics won the World Series. Their pitchers held the Giants to a team average of .175, short-circuiting McGraw's running game as the Giants stole only four bases in six games. Red Murray went hitless in twenty-one at-bats, and only Doyle and Meyers hit over .190. Connie Mack's offense didn't manhandle the Giants until the last game, but they got timely hits all along from their two Hall of Famers (Baker and Collins) and from Harry Davis. Finally, the Giants played atrocious defense, making sixteen errors, which led to ten unearned runs.

"The Athletics won," Mathewson concluded, "because they were the better team in the six games. If the Giants win the pennant next year they will be older and more seasoned. But what is the use of prophecies at this time? The season has just died. Let it rest." Mathewson was half-right on the prophecy: the Giants did win the next year, were indeed older and more seasoned, but they still lost the World Series to the Red Sox. In 1913, with virtually the same lineup, they got another shot at the Athletics and lost in five games.

THE END OF THE WORLD SERIES brought Charley Faust's joyride to a sudden halt at a puzzling crossroads. He had done everything he could to fulfill the prophecy, and according to baseball history he had succeeded by getting to pitch. Yet the World Series loss ruined his reputation as an invincible good-luck charm. In *Pitching in a Pinch*, Christy Mathewson wrote, "But, alas! Charley lost in the world's series. He couldn't make good. And a jinx killer never comes back. He is gone. And his expansive smile and bump-the-bumps slide are gone with him. That is, McGraw hopes he is gone. But he was a wonder while he had it." Midway through the World Series, the *Tribune* noted that "Charles Victory Faust was among those present. He has lost his powers but not his good humor."

Of the many odd places Faust landed during his eleven-week spree with the Giants, perhaps the most improbable was at the rim of the outfield in Shibe Park, warming up in the middle of game 4 of the World Series with Christy Mathewson on the mound. Damon Runyon wrote that "Charles Victory Faust pitched several world's series all by himself, warming up when the storm clouds broke for 'Big Six.'" When reality merged with illusion, when it no longer mattered whether Faust really thought he was going to rescue Matty as long as the players believed he belonged out there warming up, Faust's absurd power secured its greatest symbolic triumph. Two days later, the *Globe* crossed the "Victory" out of his name in its season-ending cartoon, and he wasn't invited to a dinner Saturday night at the Hotel Imperial at which the Giants were honored. The Giants did vote to "remember" Faust, along with Dick

Hennessey and trainer Ed Mackall, with an undisclosed sum when they distributed the World Series shares ($2,436 apiece to the losers). But they no longer invited him to dinner or to shoot pool.

Faust, stranded in the present, had no inkling of the historic significance of his major league career, which he didn't think was entirely history yet. He knew that his jinxing powers had let him down, but he also felt that McGraw had not given him a proper chance to pitch the Giants to the championship. He would have to work harder to get that chance next season. Now, as his summer adventures melted into a bittersweet blur, he faced his next adventure with typical gusto.

Vaudeville awaited his gleaming presence. The pennant had propelled him into the big time, and Willie Hammerstein made a spot for him at the Victoria Theatre of Varieties. No more out-of-town trials for Faust, unlike the Athletics pitchers, who played one week in Brooklyn and another in New Jersey before hazarding Broadway. No, Hammerstein had special plans for Faust. During the two-plus weeks between the end of the World Series and Faust's debut at the Victoria, Hammerstein turned him over to the notorious Loney Haskell, known to his peers as "That Rascal" and to one critic as "such a trying fellow." In an age of comedy duos, Haskell was a monologist, a rare solo comic, perhaps because nobody would willingly work with him. Apparently a cross between Fred Willard and Rip Taylor, Haskell took out an ad in the trade papers in 1911 announcing his "Last Season in Vaudeville — Everybody Glad." When not doing his own act, he would introduce other acts or even accompany them. Willie Hammerstein employed him to coach his more topical and clueless performers. Among his pupils were the Shooting Stars, the homicidal would-be chorus girls who succeeded in making bail but failed to remember their lines.

Haskell worked with an athlete in 1908 when Hammerstein signed the Italian runner Dorando, who had won a controversial marathon at the recent Olympics. The catch was that Dorando spoke no English, so Haskell simply "lectured" while Dorando stood on stage looking perplexed. At least Charley Faust spoke English, albeit with a German accent. Considering Faust's apprenticeship at the Manhattan and the road-trip performances, Haskell probably felt that this act had a chance. Especially since Haskell would also write it.

That may have been the mistake, though in any case Faust stood little chance as a big-time performer. The Victoria, for all its hokum,

THE DEATH OF VAUDEVILLE may have begun with the bizarre pairing of Faust, who didn't know better, with Loney Haskell, who should have. After the first performance at Hammerstein's, the following act went on strike, having glimpsed the end of show biz as they knew it.

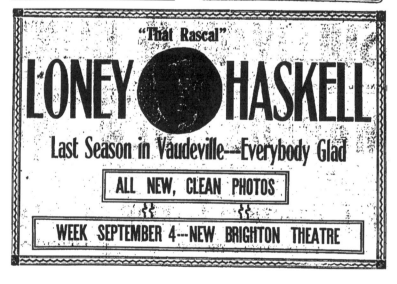

featured acts like Irving Berlin and Harry Houdini during the fall of 1911, and its patrons had some sense of what entertained them. Paying a dollar (for the best seats) entitled them to standards. The week that Faust played there, top billing went to McIntyre and Heath, the legendary blackface comedians. Together since 1874, they performed the same act for more than fifty years, lasting long enough to spurn the newest game, radio, and leave a gap later filled by "Amos 'n Andy." They were mainstays at the Victoria, heading the usual bill of seventeen acts. Faust appeared sixteenth at his debut, followed only by the Seven Picchianas, a tumbling act.

Faust's appearance received a burst of publicity in the two days before his November 13 opening. "'Baseballitis' will predominate at Hammerstein's next week," said the *Globe*, "where Loney Haskell will present Charley Faust, a 'Giant hero.'" The *Morning Telegraph* announced that "an extra added attraction will be Charley Faust, the Giants' mascot. Faust will deliver a monologue written expressly for him by Loney Haskell." The *Sun* also mentioned Faust as an added attraction, while one item in the *Times* termed him a "special attraction."

In fact, in the Sunday *Times* Faust's name appeared four times, including the brief mention above. In the "Acts Old and New on Vaudeville Stages" section, the *Times* made Faust's presence on the bill seem like more than an afterthought. "The novelty of the week at Hammerstein's Victoria will be the appearance of Mr. 'Charley' Faust, who made the Giants famous by being their mascot last summer. He has a monologue which, it is suspected, will contain something about baseball. Messrs. McIntyre and Heath will play 'The Man from Montana,' Miss Toots Paka and her Hawaiians will sing and dance and Messrs. Howard and Howard will appear in 'The Porter and the Salesman.'"

The *Times* also ran two large ads for the "entire change of bill" at the Victoria. A small ad listed the names of the acts, including "Charlie Faust (presented by Loney Haskell)." A larger ad described each act briefly, such as the Zoyarros, "Equilibrists"; Yvette, "The Dainty Singer and Violinist"; and Dick, Handwriting Dog. Faust's act required the longest explanation: "Charley Faust, The Man Who Helped the Giants Win the Pennant. Presented by Loney Haskell, That Rascal." On Monday, the day Faust opened, the *Times* had a tiny three-line ad for Hammerstein's with room for only the key attractions: "McIntyre & Heath, Howard & Howard, Charlie Faust and 15 other acts."

From the reviews, it appears that Haskell tried to incorporate Faust's baseball novelties into a more traditional piece of vaudeville shtick. A bigger house, a bigger stage, a bigger act, Haskell reasoned. The greater the lack of talent, the greater the smokescreen needed to disguise it. This was not like Dorando, where Haskell became the whole act. Still, by the time Faust opened, it was becoming more Haskell, less Faust, and all bad.

Faust's debut was nothing short of a disaster. The *Herald* published a full review of his act, under the headline "Giants' Mascot No Great 'Hit.'" The reviewer could hardly keep a straight face.

> Mr. Charles Victory Faust, no relative of the opera, appeared at Hammerstein's Victoria Theatre yesterday afternoon in what might be called his stage debut. . . . Even with this large chronometer space in which to operate he has to work fast to get it to the man in the front row before he reaches the door. There were some fast travellers in that audience.
>
> Mr. Faust, as every one will remember, is the personage who joined the New York Giants last summer because a fortune teller in Marion, Kan., told him that this was the way to become a great ball player. And when he joins something he is as hard to get loose as the paper from the wall. That is the way with him on the stage. It takes a lot of suggestion to get him off. He was down as the next to the last number on the bill. Perhaps that is a mistake or perhaps it is wisdom. Anyway, it's hard on the last number, for the eccentric product of Kansas did not exactly "knock 'em" out of their seats.
>
> An introducer supplied the audience with a key to Mr. Faust's act before he started, and then most of the spectators threw away the key and left. "Chipper Charley" wears a gray travelling uniform, such as the Giants wear on the road, and he does everything, from imitating railroad trains to Hans Wagner, and the beauty of it all is that you hardly can tell the difference between the two until the announcer points it out, of course.
>
> An unforeseen difficulty arose immediately after the star's entrance when they turned the spotlight on him. He has a peculiar weakness for manicures—no gender—and his nails were so brightly polished that they reflected the spotlight into the eyes of that part of the audience located in the front rows. This blinded

them, and they had to leave. The entertainment was in no way responsible. Mr. William Hammerstein said that he would have the new star's nails dulled of their glow right away.

Mr. Faust behaved as if he had taken a lease on the stage, and it looked for a few minutes as if there would be no evening performance. It looked that way until some one let the curtain go at the suggestion of the stage manager. Mr. Faust at the time was imitating Mr. "Ty" Cobb sliding into second base, the base being played by a sofa cushion and base line by a lot of splintery planks. Well, there aren't so many slivers in the boards this morning, but if Mr. Faust lasts the week out no doubt he will be able to open a lumber yard back in Marion. All he will have to do is to harvest the material from that portion on which he slides.

Imagine Faust's horror at learning that his precious polished nails had sabotaged his whole act.

The *Morning Telegraph* reviewer adopted a more succinct tone: "The conduct of a Hammerstein audience is a pretty fair barometer indicating public opinion. The Hammersteiners, by hurrying to the door as the act proceeded, showed clearly that New York has received an overdose of that elongated farmer person, Charles V. Faust."

The *Herald*'s concern about the act trying to follow Faust was not misplaced, judging by an item in *Variety:* "The Seven Picchianas, tumblers, who were scheduled to close the show at Hammerstein's this week, went on strike after the Monday matinee, refusing to continue unless their position was changed, as they declared it was impossible to follow Charley Faust. They were told to report earlier for the evening performance, but were finally persuaded to continue in the closing spot for Monday night on the promise that Tuesday they would precede the Faust turn." This concession spared the Picchianas, humble acrobats trying to make a decent living without some amateur scaring off their audience. It also gave the audiences one less reason to stick around once Haskell and Faust began orating.

The *Globe* also reviewed Faust's act, but not until Saturday, when the engagement was nearly over. Six days might have given critics time to mellow, but this one didn't pull any punches either. "The added attraction on the bill was Charles V. Faust, the New York Giants' mascot, presented by Loney Haskell. He should be called the Giants' joke.

Haskell precedes Faust with some incidental talk, explaining what he will do. You all know Haskell; he got the laughs preparing the audience for what they were to expect. Haskell told the truth. He said that Faust's act baffled description. Well, Faust appeared; that's all. It was pathetically funny, almost inhuman. The audience laughed, yelled, screamed. For the benefit of those who don't know, Faust is not one of the Giants. This is said in consideration for that team. What next?" Indeed, it would be tough to follow an act that was almost inhuman.

Clearly, the act was dreadful, but precisely how bad was it? This was Hammerstein's Victoria, after all, which once featured the Cherry Sisters, billed as "America's Worst Act," who performed behind a net to protect them from an audience that was encouraged to throw vegetables and other missiles. Was Faust worse than the Cherry Sisters or the Shooting Stars? Maybe, judging from the review in *Variety*, in which Jolo soberly related the particulars of the act's fourteen excruciating minutes:

> The act opens with a five-minute address by Loney Haskell, who diplomatically paves the way by asking you not to take Mr. Faust seriously. Finally the baseball enthusiast appears in field regalia. He attempts to sing the "Star Spangled Banner" and chuckles with glee while the stage hands march round him carrying small American flags. He follows this with a childish recitation about a mule. This in turn is succeeded by a monologue about the Giants. Concluding, he cavorts about the stage imitating a railroad train and the "mooing" of a cow, finishing with some illustrations of the various methods of pitching, batting and base-sliding of the various baseball celebrities. The majority of the audience did not participate in the "kidding" worked up.

No wonder they fled for the exits. By the time Faust got to his "A" material, those imitations of his fellow players that were fine-tuned during the road trip, the audience was out the door, driven away by Haskell's gratuitous "kidding." Butchering the "Star Spangled Banner" indeed! Faust was simply ahead of his time. In the 1970s he would have been a running gag on *The Gong Show*. In 1911, clearly out of his league, he did well to survive his week at Hammerstein's. No evidence has been found of further Faust appearances in vaudeville. Still, the blame should not fall entirely on his shoulders. Haskell hurt more than he helped, and it was Hammerstein who got the bright idea of expanding the act in the first place. He used Faust to put people in the Victoria's 1,350 seats. Once they paid, he didn't care when they left. He figured they'd come back.

They did not come back forever. Within a decade, movies and radio came along, and vaudeville's days were numbered. The countdown could have begun in 1911 with Charley Faust. Give the last word to *Variety*, where Jolo prophetically identified the Faust episode as a symptom of a larger problem. "Vaudeville must be desperate," Jolo warned, "when it will attach an 'act' of this sort to itself; also, vaudeville must be lifeless to endure it."

CHARLEY FAUST'S WHEREABOUTS for the next three months are unknown, a blank section of the puzzle. Having killed vaudeville, he had no special reason to stick around New York. Most of the Giants, led by Manager McGraw, went on a monthlong trip to Cuba, where they would play a dozen exhibition games. At some point Faust returned to Kansas, where he entertained his family and youngsters like Edwin Burkholder with tales of life in the major leagues. How many of them believed him, especially when he staked his claim to pitching greatness on striking out Honus Wagner in batting practice? Did he trot out his vaudeville act for the hometown folks? Did he go to San Francisco to look for Lulu? Wherever he went, he had time to think about what had happened to him and what it all meant. He lacked the perspective to savor his place in baseball history. In his solipsistic world, validation came only through fulfilling the fortune-teller's prophecy. He was supposed to pitch the Giants to the championship, and he hadn't—yet. Despite everything he had learned about behaving like a real major league pitcher, he hadn't proved that he was one—yet. He couldn't simply take the money and run, as any fool would today, feeling lucky to get away with as much as he did during his fifteen weeks of fame. Not Charley Faust, not the Human Blaster. He saw his glass half-full and doubled his determination to fill it in 1912.

9
The Sophomore Jinx

"CHARLEY FAUST, McGraw's comedian pitcher, reached the Spa today. He told Dahlen he was here to get into trim, and as he did not have any luck pitching right-hand ball last season, he intended turning around and passing up the pill with his left arm this year."

From this brief spring training note in the Brooklyn *Daily Eagle*, New Yorkers learned that Victory Faust was back. It was February 23, 1912, and players were starting to drift into the training camps. The Spa was at Hot Springs, Arkansas, and Dahlen was Bill Dahlen, the shortstop on the 1905 Giants who now managed the Brooklyn Dodgers. Several teams trained near Hot Springs; none expected Faust as an early arrival. He may have traveled to Hot Springs because it was easier to reach from Kansas than Marlin, Texas, where John McGraw isolated the Giants. Once there, he attached himself to Dahlen, his old rival from Columbus Day. Dahlen knew that he was a pitcher; hadn't he held Dahlen's team to one puny hit? Dahlen would give him a chance to develop his left-handed pitching, and once that was perfected he would be ready to show McGraw what he could do.

Faust joined the earliest arrivals at Hot Springs, which had experienced its best winter ever, with more than twenty-five thousand guests visiting the spas, and now prepared for its biggest case of baseball fever. By the end of February the Philadelphia Phillies and both Boston teams would arrive, but until then the daily intrasquad games featured minor league recruits and stray players from other teams who came to soak out their winter excesses in the mineral baths before joining their own teams. Dahlen kept everyone active. After rain canceled the February

25 scrimmage, the *Eagle* reported that "Manager Dahlen of the Trolley Dodgers gave his band of eight warriors a jog over the mountains both in the forenoon and in the afternoon even if it did drizzle at the time. Cy Seymour, Irwin et al. proved splendid 'mudlarks,' in fact 'Foam' Faust, the renowned New York Giant, is authority for the statement that the squad tore off some quarters in record time." A similar notice followed another rain-soaked day: "The pitchers and catchers worked out on the hotel lawn between showers and were a sprightly sight for the large colony of ladies at the Eastman, who were much obliged for the innocent diversion. The four catchers naturally worked with the twelve pitchers, aided and abetted by Charles Victory Faust, who was in full baseball costume and insisted upon taking a hand." When the local prosecutor refused to allow a Sunday game, the New York *Morning Telegraph* said that "the nearest approach to practise, to say nothing of playing a game, was this afternoon, when several of the heavyweight players put on heavy clothing and sweaters and visited 'Hell's Half Acre' about four miles out of town. Charley Faust threatened to put on his 'costume,' as he calls his uniform, and run out to the ball park and back, but after some deep thinking he changed his mind, saying that he did not want to 'worry my manager, Johnny McGraw.'" As early as February, Faust's eccentricity and his dedication to the Giants were already in midseason form.

It was a leap year, so the calendar sported an extra day, a perfect day for an extraordinary occurrence. On February 29, Charley Faust pitched a game! Representing a squad called the "All Nationals" against the "All Americans" at Whittington Park, Faust started the intrasquad game and hurled all eight innings. According to Thomas S. Rice in the *Eagle*, "Hub Perdue of the Boston Nationals twirled the entire route for the winners, while Charley Faust, Johnny McGraw's clown, worked for the losers. The players had a lot of fun with Faust and the Kansas rube also made a lot of fun for the bugs by his peculiar pitching antics on the slab and the way he raced and slid around the bases. Faust was presented with two hits and allowed to work in three pilfers. The two times he reached third he tried to swipe his way home, but was nipped each time in the last stride after a run up that was spectacular to a last degree." That sounded like a vintage Faust performance, much like his ninth-inning appearance in the final game of the 1911 season. Note that Rice focused more attention on the base running of Faust, who recorded the only stolen bases in the game. In this last of the weeklong exhibitions before the regulars hit town, the game turned into another Faustian farce, in the eyes of the Arkansas fans and Thomas S. Rice.

But it was no farce to Charley Faust. For him, this presented what might be his once-in-a-lifetime chance to pitch a whole game with real ballplayers. His team, the All Nationals, featured many major league veterans. His catcher was Oscar Stanage of Detroit, while the infield included Germany Schaefer of Washington (clownish himself, renowned as the player who stole first base), Charley O'Leary of Detroit, George Cutshaw of Brooklyn, and Barney Reilly, who played briefly with the Chicago White Sox in 1909. Cy Seymour, the thirty-eight-year-old ex-Giant, anchored the outfield, joined by Tex Irwin of Brooklyn and George Mullin, a good-hitting Detroit pitcher. Cutshaw made a couple of errors behind Faust but also hit two doubles and a single. Mullin had two hits, Faust was credited with two hits, and Reilly got the team's eighth hit against Hub Perdue, "The Gallatin Squash," a rookie who later won fifty-one games in the majors. They were limited to one run only by the All Americans' alertness in twice cutting Faust down at the plate.

With Faust that intense on the basepaths, you can imagine the energy he put into his pitching. No doubt he stuck to pitching right-handed, having had only a few days to develop a left-handed version of his crowd-pleasing windmill windup. According to the box score, he neither walked nor struck out a batter (Perdue fanned two), so he succeeded in putting the ball close enough to the plate for the batters to hit it. Yet they reached him for only seven hits and four runs. This suggests that either they were too busy laughing at Faust's deliveries to take smooth swings or they hit a lot of hard shots right at people. More likely both. To Faust, of course, it suggested quite the opposite—that he could pitch successfully against real players.

Who were these guys? Faust faced a lineup of varied talents and careers. Charlie Starr, a career minor league shortstop, led off and went hitless. Jim Burke, third baseman and manager of Indianapolis in the American Association, also took an 0-for-4 collar against the Kansas Zephyr. Batting third, second baseman Jim Delahanty of the Detroit Tigers (a career .283 hitter in 1,186 games in the majors) got a single in

SUPERBA RECRUITS SHINE AGAIN AT HOT SPRINGS

THE SCORE.

All Americans.						All Nationals.					
Name.	ab.	r.	h.	o.	a.	Name.	ab.	r.	h.	o.	a.
Starr, ss.	4	0	0	3	3	Schee'r, 1b	4	0	0	13	0
Burke, 1b	4	0	0	7	0	O'Leary, 2b	4	0	0	1	2
Dal'y, 2b	4	0	1	1	6	Mute'w, ss	4	1	1	0	4
James, rf.	4	1	1	1	0	Mullin, lf.	4	0	1	1	0
Riggs, cf.	4	0	1	1	0	Reilly, 3b.	3	0	1	1	2
Elliott, c.	4	1	1	3	1	Hermr'e, cf	3	0	0	4	0
Clarke, 1b	3	1	2	10	2	Erwin, rf.	3	0	0	0	0
Perude, p	3	1	1	2	4	Manage, c	3	0	0	2	2
And'n, lf.	3	0	0	1	0	Faust, p.	3	0	2	1	0
Total	33	4	7	24	19	Total	31	1	2	24	13

Score by Innings.

```
                      1 2 3 4 5 6 7 8
All Nationals .......  1 0 0 0 0 0 0 0—1
All Americans .......  0 1 0 0 0 1 2 0—4
```

Two-base hits—James, Cutshaw, 2; Mullin. Stolen bases—Faust, 3. Struck out—By Perdue, 3 (O'Leary and Erwin). Umpire—Mr. Van Syckle. Time of game—One hour 15 minutes.

Hot Springs, Ark., March 1—The so-called all-Americans and so-called all-Nationals completed their series at Whittington Park yesterday afternoon, and the followers of Ban Johnson won their third decision. The tally was 4 to 1. Hub Perdue of the Boston Nationals twirled the entire route for the winners, while Charley Faust, Johnny McGraw's clown, worked for the losers. The players had a lot of fun with Faust and the Kansas rube also made a lot of fun for the bugs by his peculiar pitching antics on the slab and the way he raced and slid around the bases. Faust was presented with two hits and allowed to work in three pilfers. The two times he reached third he tried to swipe his way home, but was nipped each time in the last stride after a run up that was spectacular to a last degree.

James, the Texas fence breaker, who was the batting hero of Wednesday's game, came back with another terrific drive to the right field wall for two bases. He bats left-handed, stands up fine and looks as if he is bound to hit. James yanked down one long fly, and for a windup whipped Erwin out at first on Tex's clean roller to right.

Cutshaw opened with two long doubles and came back with a stinging single to left. He made some tidy stops at short for the all-Americans, but spoiled an otherwise good performance by two low throws to first. Reilly got one hit out of three tries, and again fielded his position in nifty style. Seymour finally went hitless, but was there, with another sweet performance on the defense.

The game ended, the series, as the Superbas took possession of Whittington Park today. Saturday and Sunday the Dahlenites play the pick of the American League colony at present in Hot Springs. They will go against such stars as Garland Stahl, Bill Carrigan, George Mullin, Wild Bill Donovan, Jim Delehanty, Sam Crawford, Charley O'Leary, Tonneman, Fred Anderson, Germany Schaefer and Riggs, one of Bobby Wallace's recruits. The bugs are worked up over the games and two big crowds are expected.

LEAP YEAR DAY was the perfect occasion for letting Faust fulfill his fantasy of pitching a game. The box score made him look like a legitimate prospect, chiefly in his own eyes, and multiplied the force of his delusion that he could be a real pitcher.

four trips. The cleanup hitter, a much-touted Texas League slugger named Tony James, also got one hit, a "terrific drive" to the wall for a double, the only extra-base hit off Faust. Riggs, a St. Louis Browns prospect playing center field, got a single, as did Harold "Rowdy" Elliott, a catcher briefly in the majors in 1910 who resurfaced later in the decade for three seasons with the Cubs. Batting seventh, a first baseman named Clarke from Memphis managed two singles in three at-bats, the only man with more than one hit off Faust. Perdue batted eighth and singled once, while another pitcher, Fred Anderson, played left field and batted ninth. Anderson later spent three years with McGraw's Giants, winning fifty-three major league games. Faust held Anderson hitless.

This exhibition lasted one hour and fifteen minutes, more than enough time to cement in Charley Faust's mind the notion that he was well on his way toward becoming a legitimate pitcher. His two appearances in October, sudden and dreamlike, planted the seed of legitimacy. The February 29, 1912, complete game, more than an hour of sustained playing-field glory, fertilized the idea. It wouldn't have mattered to him who else played that day, but sharing the field with so many major leaguers, hearing their encouragement, feeling the fellowship of competition, made the event more convincing to his susceptible mind. Only five outs were recorded in the outfield (Tex Irwin, in right field, did not make a play all day); most of those guys pounded the ball into the ground, keeping Faust's infielders busy. He even made one putout himself. The score was tied 1-1 after five innings, and the sensation of being in a tight game heightened the illusion of a true pitching duel, exactly the kind of game he felt destined to pitch in someday for the Giants with the title on the line.

Charley Faust may or may not have felt like Christy Mathewson or Rube Marquard did in similar duels, and he may have considered the subsequent 4–1 loss a failure of sorts, so dedicated was he to winning. Yet the exhilaration of pitching a whole game fueled his baseball fantasies for a long time, making this episode the capstone of his delusion. After this, nobody could tell him that he couldn't pitch. They might laugh, but he knew better. He had all this evidence. Two innings in the majors with only one run allowed, now a solid effort through an entire game, provided all the proof he needed. Learning to pitch left-handed would simply make him twice as invaluable.

Oblivious to Faust's redoubled quest, the outside world continued to have fun at his expense. At Hot Springs he gravitated toward the most celebrated eccentric in the Brooklyn camp, Barney Reilly. Reilly, touted by the *Eagle*'s Rice as "a rara avis, a white-headed Irishman," graduated from Yale University Law School in 1910 and practiced law (his motto, according to Rice: "Let no guilty man escape—unless you are his lawyer!"). He hoped to resurrect a major league career that consisted of a .200 average in a dozen games for the White Sox in 1909. He never made it back, but he had looks, brains, and flair, capturing a fair amount of attention in Hot Springs.

On March 6 Rice carried an item reminiscent of Sid Mercer's offerings from the September road trip:

> Charles Victory Faust, himself a freak, has naturally cottoned to Barney Reilly, and visits Reilly's room for advice concerning the medicine he should take and the liniments he should use. Reilly has changed the remedy every day, and Charles Victor's room looks like a drugstore and smells like an automobile accident. He rubs liniments and ointments on his legs and arms hard enough to bring them out on the other side, and while those in the secret have expected to see the Kansas freak go up in the smoke or shrivel to a cinder under some of the applications, no such thing happens. In fact, he says he is much better since Reilly began to treat him, although what ailed him in the first place is not clear from the hearty manner in which he was going through the menu when the Brooklyn squad arrived.

The same day, the New York *American* described a rainy-day workout. "The spectacle of eleven pitchers and four catchers working out in front of a hotel was something new in Spring training. This, in addition to the antics of Charles 'Victory' Faust, who gave an exhibition of throwing out imaginary runners at second, and 'shadow batting' as he calls it, was greatly appreciated by the guests." Unfortunately for Faust fans, the *American*'s Damon Runyon made Marlin his March home that year, missing a front-row view of Faust's comeback.

Three days later, Faust caught the attention of the Arkansas *Democrat*, published in Little Rock, providing an intriguing piece of the Faust legend. "Charles V. Faust, the 'V' standing for Victory, has signed a contract of his own making with the New York Giants this year. Not having any paper handy when the spirit moved him, he wrote it on one of his cuffs and tore it off. Thomas J. Lynch, president of the National League, approved the contract, too. This is how it reads: 'I hereby do put my hand and seal to this contract to play baseball the seasons of 1911–1912 with the New York Baseball Club, National League. (Signed) Chas. V. Faust.'" Once he knew he could pitch, he apparently moved quickly to secure his rightful place on John McGraw's 1912 Giants, building on his 1911 success.

Within a couple of days, Sid Mercer, covering the Giants in Marlin, got wind of Faust's doings. On March 11 he mentioned Faust for the first time in 1912. "There will be one more mouth to feed here before the end of the week if Charley Faust travels on schedule time. Faust has now completed his course of training at Hot Springs, and is about to leave the Brooklyn team flat. He is an ambidextrous performer this year, and says he is the only pitcher and mascot who carries the punch in either hand."

Once Mercer picked up Faust's scent, it wasn't long before he came up with a scoop. "'Nut' Faust Writes Wishing Himself on McGraw," read the *Globe*'s headline above Mercer's report of a most impressive document: "Manager McGraw has received a letter from Charley Faust. The adult mascot has wished himself on the Giants again and is bound to join them. Following is a verbatim text of the letter.

> hot springs, ark., March 7—dear friend: i have been here now for two weeks there is an improvement i have pitched one game while here but did not put nothing on it because of the danger of injuring it. i throw a little every day and go through the mts which is the best way to get in shape there are two scouts after me but ill stick by you ill be here for another week at least but will report to you before you leave marlin or the last date you have in dallas it all depends upon the shape i am in i will be a transformed personality for i believe i can make things ripp i am warming up two of Dahlens pitchers i may want to catch or alternate if it is pitching or catching from your friend forever.
>
> CHARLES V. FAUST.

"McGraw is not pleased over the way Charley subscribes himself. He doesn't want to be Faust's manager forever. It will be noticed that periods and capital letters are foreign in Faust's system of letter writing."

Faust was all business in that letter. In his professional opinion, if he had pitched all-out, he would not have allowed those four runs, but in March he had to be careful in order to save himself for the late-season push toward redemption in the next World Series. Most signifi-

cant was the promise of being "a transformed personality" in 1912.
That's a fancy phrase for a man who couldn't punctuate. Was that an
embellishment by Mercer or a phrase dictated by aspiring lawyer Barney
Reilly as he helped his new pal Charley compose this appeal to
McGraw? Why did he say that? Presumably, he wanted McGraw to
appreciate that he was no longer the naive pest of 1911. This time
around he wouldn't bother McGraw with demands or pleadings to let
him pitch just because of what the fortune-teller said. There was no
need to do that any more, having gotten his chance to pitch in October.
No, this time he took his duties with the Giants more seriously and
would work hard to make himself an asset on the field. That's why he
was throwing left-handed and working on becoming a catcher as well.
Anything to help the team, and McGraw would have to realize that he
wasn't simply looking out for himself.

Naturally, Faust had no idea that declaring his unswerving devotion to McGraw would be bad news for "his manager." McGraw was
finished with Faust as soon as the Giants lost to the Athletics, and now
Faust wanted to horn in on a brand new season. A few days later, Mer-
cer mentioned trade talks between McGraw and George Stallings, the
Buffalo manager. "McGraw announced that as Stallings was going to
Hot Springs he would give him an option on the services of Charley
Faust, who is training up there. Faust is about to spread his wings and
land with the Giants again." McGraw had offered Faust to Stallings in
September when the Giants passed through Buffalo on their way to
Pittsburgh, a proposal quickly nixed by the players. Now McGraw tried
to unload Faust before the upstart could even get out of Hot Springs.

As it turned out, neither Stallings nor McGraw wound up with
Faust that March. Faust remained at Hot Springs longer than expected,
no doubt reluctant to report to McGraw until his expanded talents were
more polished and indisputable. He also had one major social engagement to fulfill. On March 6 the philanthropist Andrew Carnegie
arrived in Hot Springs with his wife and daughter for a week of recre-
ation. Noted the *American*, "Andrew Carnegie, who arrived yesterday,
has been invited to act as judge at a cakewalk next Monday night, in
company with Frank J. Gould, Mike Bowen, of Chicago, and Mike
McGreevy, of Boston. Charley Faust has already accepted the invita-
tion, and has volunteered to give his monologue." It is easy to imagine

Faust consenting to present part of his vaudeville act to a gathering of rich people headed by Andrew Carnegie; it is more difficult to imagine Carnegie consenting to witness it. Was there nobody in Hot Springs who knew Faust by more than reputation, nobody who had seen Faust perform his monologue and could warn Carnegie? There was no coverage of the cakewalk itself, so Carnegie may not have witnessed the man who had doomed vaudeville. Or he may have found this authentic American trailblazer the highlight of his week.

On March 22 Sid Mercer got a peek at another writing sample from Charley Faust. "McGraw received another series of thoughts by mail from Faust last night," Mercer disclosed.

> Charley now says that he will not join the team until the season begins, because he wants to stay in Hot Springs and keep boiling out. He always had a weakness for massage treatment, and the Turkish bath treatment at the Springs suits him so well that he would like to remain there indefinitely.
>
> "I have had offers from the Phillies, Pirates, and Boston Red Sox," wrote the adult mascot, "but I am going to stick with you. I know the club didn't treat me very well last year, but if I don't bat .300 and steal seventy bases this season I don't want a cent. If I had been allowed to pitch in the world's series we would have won it, but you didn't give me a chance, so all I could do was to coach the team. I will fiddle up about April 15 in New York, so no more until then."

This sounded more petulant than anything, sour grapes upstaging his usual claims. By not being treated very well Faust meant that McGraw had given him neither a contract nor a chance to win the World Series on his own. That was McGraw's fault, not Faust's, so he would give McGraw a second opportunity to give him his rightful chance to prove himself. Turning down offers from other teams, Faust flaunted his loyalty to McGraw in the belief that it would make McGraw more loyal to him. It almost made sense, did make sense in theory until he got carried away with the talk about stealing seventy bases (a boast that made perfect sense to him, given his five stolen bases in three games to date). Mercer added more Faust hype on April 8: "Charles Victory Faust takes his pen in hand to state that he will be along soon with a big surprise. Faust admits that he was a big sensation as a right-handed pitcher, but claims that he is now a 'southpawer,' and so good that he hates to talk about himself. His only fear is that he may make Matty and Marquard look like third raters and 'dutch' his popularity."

OVER IN MARLIN, TEXAS, John McGraw set about conditioning his men for the 1912 campaign. Bad weather limited the number of games they could play, but the hitters caught up during the annual barnstorming tour back to New York. In a bylined article in the New York *American*, McGraw pronounced his Giants the team to beat in the National League:

> It is a club of youngsters, and the hard race of last year was enough to try old, experienced men, let alone boys of just a few years in baseball. It was a valuable experience for my men, and I look for the profit to show in 1912.
>
> Every man of my regular line is coming, instead of going. The infield is one of the youngest in point of age that ever figured in a successful championship fight, and the same can be said of my outfield. Instead of decreasing in the speed which was such a factor for us last year they should all be increasing and advancing in every other department of play. . . .
>
> My pitching department will certainly be no weaker than last year and I have every reason to believe that it will be much stronger. Marquard should have another great year, and I may have found a good man in Tesreau. . . .
>
> No expert handicapper can figure on the disappointments and accidents of a season, or how the luck will turn. Claiming titles before they are won has never been one of my failings. I can only say that with an even break in luck the Giants should be a better team this year than last.

The Giants opened the season on April 11 in Brooklyn without Charley Faust, but they didn't need him as they pummeled the Dodgers 18–3, handing Rube Marquard an easy win. Jeff Tesreau lost his major league debut the next day, and by the time the Giants reached the Polo Grounds for their April 18 home opener, they had three losses in six games, a subpar start against Brooklyn and Boston, the league's weaklings. "Added features to-day," wrote Sid Mercer, "will be Charley Faust, disguised as a ball player; the Giants in spotless white for the first time since last October; C. Jeff Tesreau, the mastodon of the mound; etc." Look who got top billing.

The opener was postponed, however, following confirmation of news first received days earlier: the *Titanic* had struck an iceberg and sunk, killing more than fifteen hundred people, including John Jacob Astor and a number of other prominent New Yorkers. The Giants and the Yankees quickly scheduled a benefit exhibition game for Sunday, April 21, and the Giants opener was moved back a day to the 19th. At that, the populace remained too stunned by the disaster to stage its yearly overflow of the Polo Grounds bleachers. The Giants prepared for a crowd much larger than the eighteen thousand who attended on a cold, somber day with the flags flying at half-mast. "The bout will go on as originally advertised," Sid Mercer assured his readers. "Harry Stevens has shaved the 'hot dogs' and has the ice cream cones ready. Harry always prepares for any kind of weather. Charley Faust ate a planked steak for breakfast at the Hotel Braddock this morning and announced that if McGraw allowed him to pitch the opening game it would be a record event. And so it probably would, with the Dodgers making all the hitting and scoring records."

Before the opener, Christy Mathewson was presented with an automobile by adoring fans, and he repaid them by subduing Brooklyn on thirteen hits, winning 6–2. One spectator who did not share in the fun was Charley Faust. According to Sid Mercer, "Charley Faust mourned the fact that there were not enough of the new bed-tick uniforms to permit him to disguise himself as one of the team. The only adult mascot wandered through the grandstand disconsolate and watched the game from a high perch. He says he is not ready. Neither is McGraw." The *Times* contrasted Faust's status with fellow mascot Dick Hennessey's. "There was much applause for little Dick Hennessey . . . when he took the field and played at first base. Little Dick improves with age, and when he grows up, watch out for a good ball player. Charley Faust of Kansas sat in the grand stand and envied the players for all the attention they were receiving. Faust hasn't been fitted for his uniform, and so it looks as if his days with the Giants were over."

Despite the bittersweet day, Charley Faust would never concede that his days with the Giants were over. This refusal of McGraw's to give him a uniform had to be a temporary obstacle like all the others he had overcome. Two days later, he did don a Giants uniform—at the benefit game for families of *Titanic* victims. The *Times* mentioned him only in passing. "Charley Faust was resurrected for the occasion and did his bit." In the *American*, Damon Runyon elaborated a bit. "Charles Victory Faust, of Marion, Kan., arrayed in one of the Giants' discarded World's Series uniforms, and looking like an elongated Gloom, obliged with a little left-handed pitching and base running before the game, to the intense delight of the crowd." That may have been Faust's only New York display of left-handed pitching; at least it was the only time he received publicity for performing the stunt. Still, his familiar base-running antics probably brought more delight to the crowd of 14,083, which contributed nearly $10,000 to the *American's Titanic* Relief Fund.

That evening, the Giants went to Philadelphia while Faust stayed in New York. Two days later the *Times* found him at the Hilltop watching the Yankees play his old hoodoo, the Athletics. "Charley Faust looked Baker over yesterday and says that the slugger is going back. His average is about .600 or was up to yesterday." Faust disappeared from the newspapers for a couple of weeks after that outing. Meanwhile, the Giants took the National League by storm. Having seen Faust at the Polo Grounds opener, they won eight of their next nine games before leaving on their first western trip of the season. They left without Faust. Sid Mercer reported, "All the other athletes, with the exception of Jack Johnston and Billy Thompson, are making the rounds. Charley Faust is not with the party, as he has not signed his contract. In justice to Faust it can be positively stated that he is not a holdout. He would sign if somebody would let him." That condition never changed.

If Faust secretly hoped that the Giants would struggle without him on their road trip and desperately seek his aid when they returned, he did not wish hard enough. Incredibly, the Giants outdid their record from the September charge to the 1911 pennant. This time, they won seventeen of nineteen games and returned to New York at the end of May solidly in first place with a 28–6 record. Leading the way, Rube Marquard already had ten wins without a loss. Sid Mercer saw it coming back on April 25, after Marquard won his third start of the season. Marquard

> ought to compile a wonderful record this year if the Giants continue to bank runs for him as they did in his first three starts. . . . The Giants say that Marquard has obtained possession of George Wiltse's famous watch, which always brings good luck to its wearer. The story goes that many years ago Wiltse fell into a swamp and came up with a gold watch. He lent it to his friends, and for a long time Christy Mathewson was alleged to carry it. Anyhow, the Giants used to get runs whenever Matty pitched. Leon Ames never was allowed to pack the charm, and consequently he lost many well-pitched games because the team failed to score behind him. And now the champions allude to Rube as "Watch" Marquard. Rube doesn't care what they call him as long as they spot him those runs. . . . Marquard has never been able to get going in the spring, and the way he has started this year is very encouraging to Manager McGraw, to whom this reward of patience is most welcome.

On the road trip, McGraw needed patience about as little as Marquard needed runs. The left-hander pitched six complete games, winning comfortably by scores of 6–2, 10–3, 4–1, 3–0, 6–3, and 7–1. He kept it going through June, when he won eight more games on his way to the all-time record of nineteen straight victories in a season. No longer in Christy Mathewson's shadow, Marquard became the most feared pitcher in the league and the toast of New York. He didn't need patience either, as runs, wins, and fame followed his every step.

The man who needed patience was Charley Faust. Only one newspaper mentioned him during the western trip. Sid Mercer, discussing an opening on the Giants' twenty-five-man roster, stated that "Several candidates for the empty berth are in the offing. One is Bugs Raymond, but he stands little show. Charley Faust has announced his willingness to run on an independent ticket, but the chances are that the vacancy will not be filled until Southpaw Robertson reports next month after his graduation from college." Raymond would be dead by September and Robertson never made it to the majors, so Faust might have been the cream of that crop.

Late in the trip, when the Giants reached Philadelphia, Mercer commented, "It appears that Charley Faust has gone and left the Giants flat. Either that or he is showing exclusively at the Polo Grounds." Faust was at the Polo Grounds when the Giants returned, only to see the Cardinals bust up their third nine-game winning streak of the season. He could have told himself that it was the Giants' own fault, that they lost because they wouldn't give him a uniform and let him play like they did in 1911, but that didn't help his overall outlook. It must have been difficult for him to comprehend that his extra efforts to improve himself had not been rewarded by McGraw. Everything was topsy-turvy; the Giants won without him, and when he did watch them play they lost. On top of that, he felt the sting of the fickle press. "Despondency note," the *Times* said tersely the next day, "Charley Faust is back." Sid Mercer wrote that "Charley Faust has retired as a pitcher, and now wants to sign as a catcher. John Whalen has offered to use his influence to get Charley a job as dog catcher." Times were getting tougher for the former jinx destroyer even as they got sweeter for his team.

June began with the Giants leading the National League with a 28–7 record. When the month ended, they stood at an incredible 50–11 and led the second-place Pirates by fifteen games. The pennant race was over before it was halfway done. The Giants won ten of fourteen at home the first half of the month, then headed to Boston, where they launched their longest winning streak of the season, sixteen in a row. Charley Faust, who attended the Polo Grounds games without participating, left New York the same day the Giants did but did not head to Boston. That news arrived in a detailed report by Sid Mercer, which stands as the last thorough accounting of Faust's career.

GOOD THING GIANTS HAVE LEAD, FOR CHARLEY FAUST HAS JUMPED

Those who predicted a dull finish in the National League this season had better hedge. For Charley Faust has gone and left the Giants flat, and has joined the Cubs to make the race close. No more will he put on his blue suit and don his ambidextrous glove for the entertainment of the low-brows. No more will he wind up like an eight-day clock to provoke the merry guffaw—not unless he comes back with the Cubs.

The Giants went away from here last night. They had nothing on Charley as he eloped the previous evening, and when last seen was headed toward Philadelphia. Carrying a big grip, he strolled sadly away from the Polo Grounds after Monday's twilight finish. Dick Fuller, who will be remembered as the former keeper of the notorious Bugs Raymond, accompanied Faust as far as the elevated station. Charles had a big grip in one hand and a lot of gestures in the other.

The Best Adult Mascot stopped at the Hotel Braddock and bade some of the Giants a last farewell before settling his accounts and trudging on his way. To them he confided his notion of joining the Cubs.

"Chance needs pitchers," he declared, "and McGraw won't give me a chance. I've got my arm in shape now and the Cubs need me so I'm going to Philadelphia to-night as they leave for Chicago to-morrow night."

"Does Chance know you are going to join his team?" inquired Larry Doyle.

"Well, I haint spoke to him about it yet," replied Charley, "but I'll fix it up with him when I get there. I'm ready to sign and ready to pitch. Them's my middle names."

Not long ago a suspicion lodged in Faust's mind and refused to be dislodged. He centered much heavy thought on it and finally decided that McGraw was discriminating against him to favor Mathewson, Marquard, and some others. So he decided he was wasting time in New York. He wants to try himself on a western team and picked the Cubs.

Charley has not signed a contract since he put his signature to a collection of words written on a soiled collar. When the collar went to the laundry Faust automatically became a free agent. He flirted with the Brooklyn team, but finally rejoined the Giants. He did not travel with them, simply playing the home stands.

"I've been patient with Mr. McGraw," he told one of the Giants, "but I don't think he likes me any more. They made me pay 75 cents to get into the park Monday, so I guess they don't need me as a pitcher. My arm is fine and I bet I can beat any of 'em now."

Faust is one of the most peculiar "bugs" that baseball ever had. It was so hard to discourage him when he first showed up that he worked himself into a locker at the Polo Grounds. Later he was regarded as a mascot and made several trips with the team.

Unlike the average "bug," he bothered nobody. He flocked by himself and never spoke unless spoken to. His one big delusion was that he was a great pitcher. He learned the pitching grips from a baseball guide and never had any real experience. McGraw permitted him to pitch part of one game against the Brooklyn team last fall and he got through fairly well.

While the club paid Faust's expenses on the road, he took care of himself at home. It cost him several dollars a day to live here, the most expensive part being a daily massage and special electric treatment of his arm.

Faust came from a little town in Kansas, and according to the Giants he had some property. He spent several weeks at Hot Springs during the training season, and always had money. It was said that he sold a piece of his property for $1,500 and he received a draft for $500 at regular intervals.

No other baseball freak ever got so much publicity or so much consideration from the managers or players. Visiting players let him strike them out in practice, which only added to his delusion.

"As long as Charley's property holds out he will stick in the league," said one of the players recently, "but when he goes broke he may have to drop back to the minors."

The Cubs went west from Philadelphia last night. There is no account of a stowaway, and as Charley has not been seen around his accustomed haunts in Harlem the supposition is that he has joined himself to Frank Chance.

THE ARTICLE BEGAN like a eulogy and maintained a note of finality throughout. Mercer summarized Faust's exploits and made a balanced judgment of his character. More important for us, he provided the only glimpse into the details of Faust's separation from the Giants. Let's look at this colorful mixed bag of puzzle-pieces.

1. John McGraw finally came up with a hint that even Charley Faust could take. When he had to cough up six bits to get into the Polo Grounds, his patience with McGraw ran out. "I don't think he likes me any more," he concluded, getting the picture clearly except for the "any more" part. Reluctantly, he made plans to abandon his manager.

2. Not that he couldn't afford to pay his way in (it was the principle). Back in September, Cincinnati reporter Jack Ryder had claimed that Faust "had money" and that Faust's father owned five hundred acres of prime land. As the eldest child, Charley might have had some land that he could sell without his father's consent. Records from that period were destroyed in a flood, so there is no definitive answer to the money question. Mercer's explanation would account for Faust's ability to support himself in Hot Springs and later in New York during the first two months of the season, when McGraw refused to subsidize him further.

3. If Faust felt bitter toward McGraw, he retained his affection for the players, stopping to say goodbye and share his latest scheme with them. Aside from Larry Doyle's pertinent question, a hint of reality which Faust brushed aside, their consensus reaction probably would have been "Thanks for showing up when you did, thanks for leaving now, and good luck."

4. He wanted to pitch, felt ready to pitch, and chose the Cubs because "Chance needs pitchers." Frank Chance, that is. Chance certainly had no idea he needed Faust, if only because Faust had not yet mentioned it to him. This was not the first time he had offered his services to another team. Early in his tenure, he "flirted" with Brooklyn, as Mercer put it. His claim of offers from teams in Hot Springs was probably self-promotion, but then again his whole career was sheer self-promotion, with an occasional boost from sympathetic teammates and hungry writers. Anything could happen in Chicago. Trailing the Giants by eleven games, they might take him on as a jinx-killer and let him pitch later. If it happened once, it could happen again, and you couldn't tell him otherwise. You could hammer him over the head for a few months and get him to admit the possibility that it might not happen right away, but he would bend no further. When you think about George Stallings, a man reputedly more superstitious than McGraw, missing out on two chances to acquire Charley Faust, it makes you won-

der how he managed the "Miracle Braves" to the 1914 National League pennant without him. With Faust, he would have needed no miracles. With Faust, Mercer suggested in his opening, the 1912 Cubs had a shot at making a pennant race and avoiding a "dull finish" after the Giants' torrid start.

5. While still giving credit to Faust's jinxing power, Mercer declared that "his one big delusion was that he was a great pitcher." Mercer cited the players—including Honus Wagner, the best hitter in the league—who had allowed Faust to strike them out in batting practice, a charade "which only added to his delusion." This is vital to understanding Faust's fate. If he had accepted that he was not a great pitcher but simply a man who got lucky for a few months, he might have been more content with his career while it lasted.

6. An ambidextrous glove? We can only imagine what it looked like; not even Barry Halper's collection at its zenith included a genuine Charley Faust–model ambidextrous glove. How many times did Faust entertain the lowbrows with this glove in order for it to appear so prominently in Mercer's opening lament? Add the ambidextrous glove to the list of Faust novelties, alongside the fall-apart slide and shadow batting. We can only guess how many more inventions would have flowed from his original genius—given the opportunity.

Mercer followed up the next day with an update on the Faust defection. "Private advices from Chicago announce the arrival of Charley Faust with the Cubs. Charley has decided to offer himself to the big convention as a compromise candidate. A hustler like Faust ought to be considered. His record is without a flaw. The Giants were in second place when he joined them last summer. They won the pennant and Charley remained with them long enough this season to insure another championship. Speaking of wood, how about Charley for presidential timber?" Why not? He could have grabbed the lowbrow vote against Woodrow Wilson.

Mercer's scoop about Victory Faust's having left the Giants to join the Cubs had one serious oversight—it did not happen. The fond farewell, the thoughtful postmortem on a punctured career, proved premature. On June 27 Faust showed up again at the Polo Grounds. Right on cue, the Giants overcame a 3–0 deficit in the eighth inning that afternoon to extend their latest winning streak to nine games. "If you are superstitious," mused the *Times*, "maybe you will think that the return of Charley Faust to the Giant bench had something to do with the Giants' ninth-inning victory. Charley is just like the taxes, you can't duck him. He has been absent for some time, and when asked where he had been, Charley said that he had been visiting the Hazel family over in Nutley, New Jersey. They are friends of his and come from Kansas, too." Where else but Nutley would friends of Faust live?

"Officer, he's in again!" cried Sid Mercer in the *Globe*. "Charles Victory Faust, repelled by the Chicago club because of his former services to the Giants, is back on the job. Charley almost caught on with the Cubs last week. When he mentioned his little idea to Frank Chance the Cub manager replied 'No.' If he had said 'Yes,' Charles would have gone. Faust will remain with the Giants until some club that needs a hard-working and faithful mascot comes along and makes him an offer. He can give the best references. Here is a guy who dispersed the Jinx tribe, won a pennant for the Giants, and set them far in front of the next race. Charley thinks that maybe [Boston manager] Johnny Kling will give him a tumble." Note how directly Mercer explained Faust's failure to win Chance over, and how he credited him with putting the Giants so far ahead already in 1912. If only Faust could get over the idea of having to pitch.

The Giants, 47–11 when Faust rejoined them, kept winning under his vigilant and envious eyes. They ended June and began July by sweeping five games from Boston, including Rube Marquard's eighteenth straight victory, in which he almost blew a 7–0 lead against a team that already trailed them by thirty-two games. After Boston, seventh-place Brooklyn came to town for a July 3 doubleheader, which the Giants swept. Marquard won the opener 2–1, his record nineteenth consecutive victory. When they won the nightcap 10–9, the team's sixteenth win in a row, their record peaked at 54–11. Next day, the Dodgers stunned the July 4 mob at the Polo Grounds by sweeping a doubleheader. Then the teams went to Brooklyn for two days, the Giants taking both games. So the Giants were 56–13 when they departed on their second western trip of the season, scheduled to begin on July 8 in Chicago against the 40–27, second-place Cubs.

Several good things came to an end in Chicago. The Giants' bulldozing of the National League ceased when the Cubs took three out of four. The Giants won only the second game, as Christy Mathewson outdueled traditional rival Three Finger Brown, 5–2. In the opener, Rube Marquard's winning streak ended. The Cubs knocked him out with a trio of two-run innings, beating him 7–2. "Rube pitched better ball than the score indicates," the *Times* consoled his swelling legion of fans. Losing the last two games shoved the Giants into a mediocre road trip during which they won nine games and lost eight. Granted, they had avoided any sign of struggle until July, but once obstacles appeared, turmoil seemed to set in on all sides.

For the first time in almost a year, doubt and discord permeated the Giants. The cause of this calamity was, well, Charley Faust. He materialized when the Giants reached Chicago—when and how is unknown, but on his own—and tried once more to secure a place on the team of his destiny. Once again he got the heave-ho, and this time he took it personally. If Mercer was right that Faust harbored a theory about McGraw discriminating against him, this final rejection triggered his impulse to act on that theory.

He struck back first the best way he knew how, by using his jinxing power. After the Giants were subdued 3–0 in the third Cubs game, Sid Mercer explained why. "Charley Faust claims that New York's bad luck yesterday was due entirely to the spurning of his services as mascot and pitcher. Charley is still free agenting in these parts and will accept any and all offers. He claims to have put a jinx on the Giants, and is mighty unpopular with them just now. Faust must be a vindictive cuss when he won't even allow a team to score a run."

After the Giants lost the final game, they headed for St. Louis, while Charley Faust again veered away at a tangent. The *Times* reported that "Charlie Faust, who last year traveled with the New York National League ball team as their 'mascot' but who Manager McGraw would not allow with the team this year, is in Cincinnati to appeal to the National Baseball Commission to take up his claim that the management of the Giants owes him a year's salary. It is not likely that there will be any official action by Chairman Herrmann, as Faust was not classed as a ball player." Faust figured that he would get justice from his old pal Garry Herrmann, who had summoned him to his hotel room back in September for a command performance of his vaudeville monologue.

The same day, July 12, Damon Runyon penned his last words about Charley Faust, an original character who had caught his fancy that first summer in New York. In this sympathetic and humorous article, Runyon suspended judgment until a final wry comment.

FAUST CLAIMS CREDIT FOR GIANTS' VICTORY

"If it hadn't been for me maybe the Giants wouldn't have won the pennant last year. There was a jinx after 'em, and I chased him out of camp. I delivered 942 speeches in the smoking room of the Pullmans under the tutelage of John J. McGraw while I was with the Giants on their last trip around the ring last Fall, and I'm entitled to a year's pay."

Thus Charles Victory Faust, the celebrated Kansas squirrel fodder, who arrived in Cincinnati to-day to present a claim to the National Commission for a gigantic sum of money which he claims is due him from the Giant management.

"I signed a two years' contract on a dirty collar with Mist' McGraw," continued Charles. "We didn't have no paper. I changed my pitching from right to left handed to help him out this season, and now he won't allow me with the team. I spent some weeks at Hot Springs at my own expense training under Bill Dahlen and 'Dutch' Schaefer, but I never deserted Mist' McGraw."

Faust joined the Giants one day last year at St. Louis, and thereafter they were unable to shake him. He put in a brief career in vaudeville after the season closed. Charles comes from Marion County, Kansas, and has—or is able to get—money, but not from McGraw. His theory is that he is a great pitcher, and was permitted to pitch an inning or two in regular games by McGraw. Mostly, however, he was considered a jinx dispeller.

Pressed for information as to why he fell down in that capacity in the world's series, Mr. Faust was strangely silent to-night. It is not likely that Chairman Hermann will take any official action, because Charles was not classed as a ball player—a suggestion which may hurt his feelings, but which is, unfortunately, true.

ONCE CHARLEY FAUST landed in Cincinnati, Jack Ryder of the Cincinnati *Enquirer* picked up the trail:

> Charles Faust, the Giants' mascot, took a run over from Chicago yesterday to consult the National Commission regarding his future. He says that Chicago wants to sign him, but that McGraw insists on covering him up and won't give him his release. As President Herrmann was quite busy when the bug came into his office he turned Charley over to Brownie Burke, who is an expert on the mascot business, and had a long talk with Faust. Brownie then wrote President Brush of the Giants a letter, explaining Faust's position, and recommending mercy for him as a brother mascot. Faust attended yesterday's game as Brownie's guest, and left last night for St. Louis to join the Giants. He has never been signed to a New York contract, but has been kidded along so steadily by the players that he thinks he is a real ball player and is being abused in not being allowed to go with the Cubs, who would not have him around. It is a sad case, and Mr. Herrmann will take the matter up with President Brush to-day and advise that Faust be sent about his business.

Faust himself must have sensed that his case was in sad condition when the man who relished his performance last September now handed him off to Brownie Burke, the Reds' teenage mascot.

Faust's whirlwind week in the Midwest brought him next to St. Louis, where Sid Mercer filed the most alarming update yet on Faust:

> The only stir in camp yesterday was caused by the arrival of Charles Victor Faust from Cincinnati, bearing tidings from the National Commission. Faust left Chicago Wednesday night and spent the next day pestering Garry Herrmann. He has been officially declared a free agent, but he will not sign with a minor league club. He put in a claim against the New York club for a year's salary, then hopped on a train and came over here Thursday night.
>
> Last night he doubled back on his trail and went back to Chicago to join the Cubs, whether they like it or not. If Charley Murphy finds Faust as persistent as the New York club found him, he may get after McGraw for unloading the mascot on the Cubs.

McGraw and many of the players argued with Faust yesterday, trying to persuade him to go back to his Kansas farm from here. No use. They might as well have talked to a paving stone. The poor deluded jayhawker's case is pathetic now. He surely is a determined cuss. The idea that he is the greatest pitcher in the world and worth thousands of dollars is rooted in his head more firmly than ever. The Giants get nervous now when he hangs around, as they fear he may become violent one of these days.

"All I need is the signs to win," said Faust yesterday. "I've got all the rest down pat." Nothing can shake his belief that there is a conspiracy to keep him out of the league. He refuses to work his way up through the minors, because he says that he doesn't have to prove his ability that way. He admits that he is the greatest pitcher.

McGraw says that he cannot take Faust on because Charley accepted $10 advance money from Charley Murphy last winter. Faust admits this and says he confessed to Garry Herrmann. He figures, therefore, that the Chicago club is entitled to his services, and so he went there last night to give himself up. If Charley doesn't get placed pretty soon he may pull some stuff that will cause him to be placed in durance vile.

Why this sudden note of paranoia consuming both sides of the dispute? Mercer had often discussed Faust's notion of a conspiracy to prevent him from pitching, understandable in light of the innumerable dodges John McGraw had invented to fend off Faust's pestering. Now, however, the Giants were physically afraid of Faust. Why? A clue can be found in an unattributed 1914 article in the Faust file at the National Baseball Library. It reads, in part,

> There is no telling how far he might have gone had not a well-meaning Chicago friend of McGraw taken to relating to the Little Corporal the manner of the taking off of the elder Carter Harrison, mayor of the Windy City.
>
> The Giants manager was warned that the assassin, another boob, had for years been kidded by Cook county politicians, who predicted for him a gorgeous future that would carry him through the mayoralty to the governorship of Illinois and finally to the

United States Senate and perhaps the presidential chair. But after a while the boob "got wise" and killed Mr. Harrison.

Until then McGraw enjoyed the antics of his clown just about as thoroughly as the next man. But almost immediately he discovered in the Faust eye a look of wickedness and smoldering fire and all that sort of thing, until the notion that one morning he might awaken to find Faust bending over him and operating on his jugular vein with a safety razor blade kind o' took hold of him. Faust wasn't intensely popular with his chief after that.

That certainly tallied with Mercer's statement that the Giants "fear he may become violent one of these days." If McGraw shared the warning with Mercer and other writers, they were discreet enough not to liken Faust to an assassin but rather to confess a vague unease around him. Mercer noted that Faust's idea of pitching greatness was "rooted in his head more firmly than ever," but the notion of Faust's violent potential must have gripped McGraw and the Giants with equal force or they would not have tried so heatedly to persuade him to leave the team and return to Kansas. Was their fear justified?

Carter Harrison was a successful businessman who turned to politics in his forties. First elected a county commissioner in 1871, he put in two terms as a Congressman before being elected in 1879 to his first two-year term as mayor of Chicago. After four terms as mayor, he left office to travel around the world and write two books before returning to Chicago, where he ran again for mayor in 1891. He barely lost but, liberal and popular, won the office again in 1893. Widowed, he planned to remarry in the fall, but ten days before the wedding, on October 28, 1893, Harrison was murdered, shot three times by Patrick Eugene Prendergast, a young man admitted to the mayor's home as a visitor. Prendergast escaped the scene but surrendered to police a half-hour later, telling them, "I worked hard for him during his campaign for the Mayoralty, and he promised to make me Corporation Counsel. He was elected, but he failed to keep his promise, and I have shot him because he didn't do as he said he would."

During questioning, Prendergast changed his motive, charging that the mayor had reneged on his promise to elevate the city's railroad tracks. Indeed, two days earlier Prendergast had confronted the mayor's secretary, W. A. S. Graham, at a restaurant, telling him, "If he don't elevate the tracks I will kill him. I will shoot him dead." Graham knew Prendergast as one of what the New York *Times* termed "the small army of cranks that day in and day out deluge the Mayor's office with recommendations and propositions and suggestions of all kinds." When Prendergast angrily repeated his threat, saying, "Unless he does it, he is a dead man," Graham changed the subject, tried to calm Prendergast down, and forgot about it. Nor did Graham pay much attention on the morning of October 28, when a letter arrived from Prendergast urging "immediate action" on elevating the train tracks. Graham set the letter aside about the same time that Prendergast was purchasing the pistol he used that evening to make good his threat.

The key to Prendergast's crime was that he was commonly regarded as a harmless crank. Graham watched Prendergast bang the table so hard that dishes rattled while he threatened the mayor without "imagining for a moment that Prendergast cherished any thought of murder in his heart." When Prendergast went to the mayor's home, he gained entrance from a maid who knew him. She went to summon the mayor, who had retired after dinner with instructions to admit visitors. Meeting Harrison in the hallway, Prendergast said nothing before shooting him. Sometime after that, word reached Graham that Prendergast was not harmless after all.

When John McGraw heard this tale, naturally he could imagine his friends sitting around at his wake talking about the signs that should have warned them Charley Faust was about to inflict more than a baseball jinx on his former manager. No wonder, then, if he detected a wicked glint in Faust's eyes the next time they met, and every time after that. How much of this description of Prendergast also applied to Faust? "He is a smooth-faced, hollow-cheeked, weak-looking young man, the most prominent feature of his face being a protruding under lip. His whole appearance indicated a depraved and vicious mind. His nose is sharp and crooked, and his hair, cut short, sparsely covers his misshapen head." McGraw knew the type, and he could see clearly now that he no longer wanted to be anywhere near this Faust character.

The day after Sid Mercer denounced Charley Faust as "pathetic," Faust put another curse on the Giants and headed for Chicago to try his luck with Chance. The hoodoo-hampered Giants played a doubleheader in St. Louis, and Rube Marquard lost both games! This was the same Cardinals team Marquard beat five times in a row after Faust joined them in 1911, then twice more during his 1912 streak. After winning nineteen in a row, he lost three times in the week after Faust jinxed the Giants, twice to the Cardinals. Unbelievable. In the opener, he relieved in the eighth inning of a tie game and gave up the winning run in the bottom of the ninth. He started the second game and allowed eleven hits, trailing 3–2 when he left after seven innings. Just when he seemed blessed with invincibility—what a terrible time for his talisman to leave town and put a curse on them!

After a third Giants loss to the Cardinals, Sid Mercer noted that "Charley Faust, who is here in Chicago trying to persuade Frank Chance to sign him, has apparently been vindicated. The Giants believe that Faust put the Kansas curse on them when he ducked out of St. Louis. When the team started west Faust predicted that it would not win the pennant if he lost his job as mascot. The day Faust appeared in Chicago the champions won and the day after he showed up in St. Louis they won again. Then Faust got in his deadly work." Rube Marquard, the chief beneficiary of Faust's jinx-killing, now found himself the victim, caught in the crossfire.

The day Faust left, Marquard's 1912 party ended. After his 19–0 start, he went 7–11 the rest of the season.

On the other hand, perhaps Marquard considered himself lucky at this point that Faust had merely cost him a loss of points on his winning percentage rather than a loss of blood. On July 19 Sid Mercer wrote, "Nothing has been heard from Charley Faust for two days, and the boys hope that they have seen the last of him. Charley announced in Chicago that he was going to start something soon. He declares he has so much speed that the catcher has to give him two signs for his fast ball, and he positively declines to waste his talent in the minor leagues. Faust is no longer a mascot, he's a menace." If Mercer said Faust was a menace, he was a menace.

The Giants rebounded to win three out of four games in Pittsburgh before traveling to Cincinnati. Charley Faust got there a day ahead of them, as usual. According to Jack Ryder, "Charley Faust is holding on. He showed up here yesterday and interviewed President Herrmann, who assured him that the Giants did not care to hold him, and that he is free to sign with any other club desiring his valuable services. Faust remained here in the hope of persuading McGraw to allow him to stick with the Giants and put on his beloved uniform again. Tough about this poor fellow." Ryder pitied Faust even more the next day. "Charley Faust practiced with the Giants in citizen's clothes, not being able to obtain a uniform. It seems about time to call off this joshing of the poor fellow and let him go about his business. The stall that they cannot get rid of him is a joke. No one is allowed on the playing field without the consent of the manager of the team." Ryder's comment suggests that when the Giants saw Faust again in Cincinnati, they realized that they ought to humor him some more and hope for the best, rather than risk antagonizing him.

Ryder and Mercer certainly differed on how tough it was to get rid of Faust. Ryder seemed to think the Giants could dismiss him any time they wanted, but the New York writers knew better. On July 23, after Christy Mathewson beat the Reds for the umpteenth time, Walter Trumbull of the *Times* reported Faust's umpteenth attempt to resume his career: "Charley Faust, the eccentric Kansan who was mascot for the Giants last season, is still sticking to the New York club and refuses to be shaken. He is at the ball park every day and, although Manager McGraw has not given him back a uniform, he practices with the players every day. Every chance Faust gets he talks with Chairman August Herrmann of the National Commission, begging him to take some action in his case. Faust now wants a year's salary from the Giants. Herrmann has told him repeatedly that he has nothing whatever to do with his case, but this doesn't in the least affect Charley's frequent appeals for aid."

The Giants returned to New York from Cincinnati, surviving the so-so road trip with a solid grip on first place. This time, Charley Faust did not return with them, nor did he hop freights and get there in time to greet them. On July 25, while the Giants hosted the Cubs at the Polo Grounds, Sid Mercer carried an item that downplayed what was in fact momentous news: "Charley Faust has disappeared again, and it is understood that he has gone back to his Kansas farm. Faust hung on as long as he could, but evidently he tumbled to himself at last. The Giants are glad that he went quietly. He had repeatedly threatened to start something, and the players were a bit uneasy."

It took another week for Mercer to get the full story. The next Faust news arrived on August 1—one year to the day of Mercer's first report of "the Kansas phenom's" debut weekend in St. Louis. "Manager McGraw has a letter from Charley Faust, who is back on the farm at Marion, Kan. Somebody told Faust to go home and make the club send for him, as Hub Perdue did with the Boston club. Charley went home ten days ago and now writes McGraw to inquire why the summons has not been sent. Perdue, by the way, has again quit the Boston club." Hub Perdue, of course, began 1912 as Faust's mound opponent in that exhibition game in Hot Springs. A hotshot rookie on a last-place team (he went 13–16 in 1912, leading the team in wins), he had fled the team that spring, holding out for a better contract, waiting until Johnny Kling got desperate enough to summon him. The ploy worked, as it has many times in baseball history. Finally someone on the Giants twisted it around to fit into Faust's brain, convincing him that McGraw, once deprived of Faust's talents, would appreciate them doubly and quickly send for him.

So Faust returned to Kansas exactly one year after leaving there. He expected only a short interlude, as indicated by the letter to McGraw, written within a week of his retreat. Meanwhile, the Giants began their home stand by losing three straight to the Cubs, reducing their lead to nine games and making New Yorkers fret. Then came six straight wins, four over the Reds, followed by three straight losses to the Pirates. In the midst of this new roller-coaster ride came the first sign of Faust's hoped-for scenario. Sid Mercer wrote that "Dick Hennessey, official mascot for the Giants, has an assistant now, but still the Giants lose. It looks as if Charley Faust will have to be recalled."

On August 12—the first anniversary of Charley Faust's arrival at the Polo Grounds—the Giants finally got around to raising their 1911 National League pennant. After a parade, some speeches, and a serenade by a brass band, the Giants went out and lost to the Cardinals for the second time in three days. This chopped their lead over the Cubs to the smallest margin since April, leaving the Giants squarely in a pennant race. Sid Mercer reacted predictably as the Giants left New York that night for a showdown in Chicago: "The Giants took with them a large company of players and almost players, one mascot, the tender and not-to-be-toyed-with lead of six games and one-half over the Cubs, and the satisfaction of having just floated a pennant from their own pole. There was talk of wiring for 'Charley' Faust to join on in Chicago as, since he left the club flat on its standing, and put the gypsy curse on it, the boys have been dropping a lot of contests. Perhaps the insinuation of Faust into the company for a little pinch mascoting might do the club a lot of good."

Poor Mercer couldn't help himself. No matter how pathetic or menacing Faust had gotten, Mercer found himself wishing in print for the return of the benign Victory Faust who had fun on the field, helped them win every day, and generated more copy than problems. Did the players feel that way? Even after Mercer called Faust a menace, the players let him practice with them in Cincinnati. Even after McGraw insisted that he go back to Kansas, they found a way to send him back there with hope. Within weeks, their confidence shaken by inconsistent, uninspired play, they wanted to believe that turning things around again was as easy as having an infallible jinx-killer like good old Charley on hand. They did believe that he could work jinxes in all directions despite the World Series failure. After all, from the day they met him to the day they ran him off, they won more than 80 percent of their games. With Faust working his powers directly, they won more than 90 percent of the time, an incredible feat seemingly beyond the range of coincidence. Rube Marquard went 33–3 during that stretch, with Faust absent for two of those losses. Take that stretch away and you have a pitcher with a career record below .500 who would never have made the Hall of Fame. Three losses in a year, then three losses in the week after Faust jinxed the Giants? Marquard opened this August series in Chicago by getting knocked out in the fifth inning of a 5–1 loss. Do you think Marquard wanted to see Faust warming up one more time to spur him on to victory?

The Giants lost two of three in Chicago, and their lead trembled at five games as they traveled to St. Louis. There Sid Mercer filed his penultimate Faust scoop. "Charley Faust, the noted jinx-dispeller, failed to show up here as advertised. The day the Giants left New York McGraw received a letter from Faust, who stated that he would leave his Kansas farm and join the team in St. Louis. He thinks his professional services as mascot are needed. But somebody failed to come across and Faust is still missing." We don't know how many people were aware of the letter—that is, whether the players eagerly anticipated another St. Louis rendezvous, or dreaded it, or knew nothing about it—but knowing Faust's determination, they would have expected him to be there when he said he would be. In fact, he never did meet them again, in St. Louis or anywhere else.

They went ahead without him and rebounded from their midsummer doldrums to win the National League pennant by ten games over the second-place Pirates. As far as is known, Charley Faust's name found its way into the New York newspapers only once more in 1912 after the missed return to St. Louis. That came on September 13, and naturally it arrived courtesy of Sid Mercer: "Charles V. Faust, the well-known adult mascot, horns in from Marion, Kan., with a novel proposition. He is willing to do the world's series by long-distance telephone from Marion for any paper that will pay the tolls. This offer ought to be investigated. Many ball players have signed for the series, but no mascots have been engaged." One more nugget, one last Faustian innovation, one final and original but no less futile effort to land another gig with or near his beloved Giants. To Sid Mercer, he horned in like any far-flung correspondent, at an amusing and safe distance from the Giants and their welfare. Mercer, remembering Faust's juicily absurd comments on Home Run Baker during the 1911 World Series, would have loved getting fresh material from Faust, especially if he remained in Kansas. That didn't happen either. And the Giants, with little Dick Hennessey as mascot, lost the World Series to the Boston Red Sox.

For better or worse, Charley Faust's career with the New York Giants was over. Persuaded by a fortune-teller to join the Giants, he found renown in New York before being dispatched back to Kansas. Entering the scene as an anonymous rube, a subject of ridicule, he had his run of the National League for the better part of a year until meeting a minor legend's demise—doubted, disdained, and finally discarded. Nobody mentioned him during the World Series; nobody summoned him when the Red Sox went ahead three games to one. If they didn't need him then, he was gone, even by his own standards.

However desperate Charley Faust felt in those final flailing weeks, however pathetic his case had become, there is no denying him his glory. Even though the Giants did not become world champions, they won almost every game he saw, so he did everything he could to fulfill the fortune-teller's prophecy, which was the single motivating force behind his actions. And he succeeded in the one area which impresses any fan: he got his name in the record books. All the record books. In some, he's on the same page as Hall of Famer Bob Feller, a fellow Corn-belt fireballer. More than a dozen pitchers performed in the major leagues without ever retiring a batter, saddled with a lifetime earned run average of infinity, doomed to envy Faust's listing in the encyclope-dias. His ERA of 4.50—one run in two innings—equaled the pitching record of Ted Williams, among many others. Capping his achieve-ments, he contributed two stolen bases to the Giants' all-time record of 347.

For the average baseball fan, the bottom line is all that matters. Faust got into a couple of games; he has statistics in the record books. Many highly touted athletes never achieved that much. That he did it with no discernible athletic talent makes it all the more amazing. The sad irony is that we can savor Faust's triumph more than he could. The extraordinary drive needed to overcome that dearth of major league skills prevented him from basking in his glory, would not allow him to be content with a partial victory, refused to relent in the face of all fur-ther obstacles. Even after the Giants exiled him, shunned him during the pennant drive, and shut him out of the 1912 World Series, he did not give up.

10
After the Fall

NOT MANY DETAILS are known about Charley Faust's life after the summer of 1912, and that is just as well. We know enough to understand what happened to him and to guess why, but little about how it unfolded or how he experienced it. The available pieces of evidence point toward the dark part of the Faust puzzle.

He did not stay long in Kansas. His dismissal from the Giants proved his uselessness in his father's eyes, and he headed for California by the end of September. He may have hoped to launch the third part of his quest, the search for Lulu, but in any case he wound up not in her reputed hometown of San Francisco but in Pasadena. In a letter to August Herrmann written in 1914, Faust said that he arrived in Pasadena on October 7, 1912, on the eve of the World Series opener and two days before his thirty-second birthday, and he worked as a carpenter's assistant there through Christmas. He listed several jobs held in the Los Angeles area during 1913—wheeling cement for foundations, putting up steel lathes, gardening—before he moved in November, 1913 to Seattle, where his brother George lived.

In between jobs, Faust apparently spent much of his free time lobbying Herrmann and John McGraw to return him to his rightful place as a fully qualified member of the New York Giants. This did not come out until later; the running joke had long since run its course, and nobody cared to publicize it. A 1914 article said that "not until this year were the Giants rid of Faust, for he made repeated trips to New York in an effort to get back with the baseball club." If this is true, McGraw may have silenced the writers, hoping that Faust would go away if nobody paid attention to him. Leave the crazy person alone and he might not kill you. The newspapers didn't mention him during the season, and even Sid Mercer managed to drag Faust's name into print only once in all of 1913. He got it out of the way early, too, reporting on January 6 that "John J. McGraw is out in St. Louis this week uplifting vaudeville and dodging Charley Faust & Bro."

After that, Mercer remained silent on the subject of Charley Faust. So did Damon Runyon. Ironically, Runyon's rival in the Quirky Literature corner of posterity, Ring Lardner, did write something about Charley Faust. In his famous short story "My Roomy," published May 9, 1914, in the *Saturday Evening Post,* Lardner wrote about an eccentric, wild-eyed outfielder named Elliott, who considered his talents wasted on the Boston team. Elliott wanted to play for John McGraw and the Giants and was on the verge of persuading McGraw to trade for him after his pinch-hit home run beat Christy Mathewson. But he blew it when he "went crazy" the next day at the Polo Grounds. Sent up to pinch-hit again against Mathewson with the game on the line, Elliott swaggered over to McGraw to ask, "If I whiff, will you get me on your club?" McGraw said yes, Elliott whiffed on purpose, and before he could blink, he was exiled to the minors. Back at their hotel room, the narrator watched his despondent roomy read the notice telling him he had been sold to Atlanta of the Southern League. "Thought you was goin' to get on the New York club?" the narrator asked Elliott. "No," he said. "I got turned down cold. McGraw says he wouldn't have me in his club. He says he'd had Charlie Faust—and that was enough for him."

In some ways, the Charley Faust story followed its usual pattern in 1913. Faust put a lot of effort into trying to get John McGraw or August Herrmann to give him a chance to pitch. The Giants won another pennant and lost another World Series to the Athletics, earning the losers' share for the third straight year. McGraw and Herrmann managed to duck the Faust issue, and Faust grew more restless on the West Coast, eager to fulfill the rest of his destiny.

One must sympathize with Herrmann in this ongoing charade. The Giants asked for their aggravation by stringing Faust along in the first place, but Herrmann was an innocent bystander. All he did was invite Faust to perform one time, and the guy thought they were buddies for life. Faust was not the only thorn in Herrmann's side. As the chairman of the National Commission and the owner of the Cincinnati Reds, he was besieged regularly by aspiring ballplayers of varied ability. Take the Faust-like scribblings of Arthur Tillmann of Greenville, Ohio, who peppered Herrmann with letters early in 1914. "While pitching is not my favorite position," he conceded early on, "I am sure that I can make my services reign supreme. I can twirl winning ball, am a heavy hitter, and am fast on the bases. If I did not think that I could do you justice, I would not be asking you for your earnest consideration." Advised to pay his way to spring training, he replied to Herrmann that "while I like to play ball, I do not feel that I can devote my life to that profession but I would like to help Cincinnati win a pennant and a world's championship, then I am through." His next letter boasted and confessed more. "I have played no professional ball but will try out for shortstop against any, or as many as you may have for that position, no one excepted. I know what I can do and will play in the major leagues or not at all. I am saying what I mean and mean what I say." Many others— sandlot wannabes and average fans with stars in their eyes—wanted a chance to be in the major leagues. For Herrmann, the only sane policy was to humor or ignore them and hope they would go away. That included Charley Faust.

On February 21, 1914, the New York *Times* published a remarkable article, a page 9 non sequitur that was vintage Faustiana in its insistence on poking fun at its subject:

> Charley Faust, who was at one time a mascot for the Giants because there was no logical way of preventing it, made himself acquainted with James E. Sullivan, Secretary and Treasurer of the A.A.U. yesterday. That was because Mr. Sullivan didn't see Charley first. Faust sent in his card to Mr. Sullivan yesterday, and when he saw the words "Member of the New York Base Ball Club" on the card, Charley was invited into the inner sanctum of the Warren Street office.
>
> The next time Faust calls on Mr. Sullivan he will not see him by means of a card; he will need a ladder.
>
> Faust went to the A.A.U. because somebody told him that his name ought to be in the record book for climbing a mountain in California. Charley believes everything anybody tells him. Last Fall Charley was told that if he climbed a mountain in record

time he would receive a medal. That appealed to him, so he climbed a mountain with much speed. He came all the way from California to get the medal and to see that his record was placed on the A.A.U. record book.

The only record that Charley is known to have made is getting easy money from the Giants when he was a mascot. In 1912 the club carried him all over the circuit and he was quite a novelty. Now the New York Club is having an awful time trying to make Faust understand that he is no longer a novelty.

Mr. Sullivan yesterday listened to Faust a few minutes and then began to move uneasily in his chair. For a while he didn't quite "get" Charley, but then it dawned upon him that perhaps Faust was conversing through the big hole in the side of his hat. Mr. Sullivan was right; that's just what Charley was doing.

To please his caller, Mr. Sullivan took down a book and after perusing the pages said that he could not find Faust's mountain-climbing record. Mr. Faust didn't know at the time that Mr. Sullivan was looking through the telephone directory to get the number of the Aquarium or the Zoo.

Faust left Mr. Sullivan quietly, saying that he would climb the mountain again, so as to verify his record.

Mr. Sullivan would like to know who sent Faust to him.

That strange meeting—Charley Faust again crossing paths with one of the most influential men in the country—occurred on February 20. Faust immediately headed west, arriving in Cincinnati the next day. He met with August Herrmann again and accomplished as much as always, namely making a nuisance of himself. At the train depot, waiting for the train that would return him to Seattle, he wrote the letter to Herrmann listing his various jobs around Los Angeles. In this letter, by the way, Faust did not do what he did in the letter he wrote to John McGraw from Hot Springs in March 1912, when he reportedly used no capital letters. Somebody had introduced him to capital letters, and he came to like them as much as manicures. In the February 1914 letter, he capitalized every single word, though he continued to end sentences without periods. He had to draw the line somewhere.

In Seattle, Charley Faust lived with his younger brother George at the downtown Ellis Hotel. How he passed his days is unknown, but the restlessness stayed with him. His destiny tugged at him, the nagging sensation that perseverance had gotten him his first chance and would get him another. If he gave up, if he stopped pushing, the chance wouldn't come. He could never accept that.

Inevitably, he snapped. On June 3, 1914, the Portland *Oregonian* published distressing news, under the headline "Noted Pitcher-Buffoon Is in Toils Here, Is Belief." The folks in Oregon knew all about the Kansas Zephyr's New York exploits. "Can it be," began the article,

> that the original Charles V. Faust, erstwhile clown and pitcher buffoon of the New York Giants, is under arrest here in Portland under a charge of insanity?
>
> Surely no policeman would have the temerity to arrest the original, blown-in-the-bottle Charles?
>
> But, whether or no, Charles Faust, said to be from Seattle, is impaled in the County Jail en route afoot to New York City, where he says he is booked to pitch in the world's series this Fall.
>
> Faust walked here from the North and was arrested by Patrolman Nutter at the Hoyt Hotel. He will be examined as to his sanity.

The Portland *Evening Telegram* carried a similar notice later that day (their headline: "Says He Is Walking to N.Y. To Aid Giants"). "Held for examination for sanity, a man giving his name as Charles Faust and who says he is walking to New York to pitch for the Giants in the world series this Fall, was arrested at Sixth and Hoyt streets last night by Patrolmen Nutter and Gouldstone. Faust says he is from Seattle and his rambling talk caused the arrest. The Faust that was once with the Giants acted as a buffoon until McGraw tired of his antics."

Walking to New York? If so, he was taking the scenic route, for Portland is south and a bit west of Seattle, 175 miles by highway. It took Faust days to walk there, and he could have had no hope of reaching New York. Maybe some instinct told him that the Giants desperately needed him; it was around this time that George Stallings's "Miracle Braves" began the astonishing run that allowed them to keep the Giants out of the 1914 World Series. Did something tell Faust that he had to get back to New York, no matter what? If he could somehow have reached New York with his jinxing powers rejuvenated, would the

Giants have let him save them, reversing the Braves' miracle and capping the comeback with a World Series championship? He could have gotten there—if he had no money, he could hop trains, as he did the first time he found them—that is, if he still knew what he was doing. Instead, walking to New York via Oregon landed him in a jail cell one night and in a sanity hearing the next day, as reported in the *Oregonian*.

CHARLIE FAUST SENT TO SALEM

Real New York Mascot Goes to Asylum Mentally Unbalanced

That the Charlie Faust, who was yesterday committed to the State Insane Asylum by Judge Cleeton for an indefinite period was none other than Charlie Faust, the quaint character formerly with the New York Giants, is beyond question.

When searched at the county jail Faust had a telegram from his brother in Marion, Kan., the town which produced the original Charlie. In addition, he was out at the ball grounds on Sunday and worked out with the Los Angeles players, Harry Wolter and long Tom Hughes both recognizing him as the former mascot for McGraw.

He was picked up on the street Monday and examined as to his sanity. It was decided that while Faust wasn't a dangerous character, it would be better to watch him for a time, at least.

Two years ago Faust had more advertising over the National League circuit than any of the stars. His eccentricities and belief that he was a real pitcher gave the sport writers subjects with which they filled columns of space. Faust was actually worked in one or two games by McGraw, but only after the game had been either won or lost by a decisive score.

It was this same Faust, who was told by McGraw to go and warm up. Imagine the New York leader's surprise to come on him a little later, lazily lolling in the sun.

"I thought I told you to warm up," said Mac.

"Well, I can't find any warmer spot," replied Charlie, seriously, looking around to see whether there was a furnace in sight.

Faust walked here from Seattle, having gotten there from San Francisco by boat.

EIGHTEEN NEW PATIENTS were admitted to the State Insane Asylum at Salem, Oregon, during the first half of June 1914. They constituted a fair cross-section of the population except for two qualities: all were men and only three were married. They ranged in age from a sixteen-year-old with epilepsy to a senile eighty-one-year-old. The largest group—five—were in their thirties, including Faust, then thirty-three. Only two of the eighteen were born in Oregon; two others were born in Maine, three in New York, and the rest in places like Russia, Sweden, Montana, and Kansas. Their initial diagnoses included paranoia, melancholia, manic depression, dementia praecox (or, as it is now known, schizophrenia), psychasthenia, and general paresis (insanity resulting from untreated syphilis). Faust was the only one listed simply as "dementia"—"severe impairment or loss of intellectual capacity and personality integration," in the clinical language of the time, from the Latin for "out of [one's] mind." The cause was unknown. He wasn't like the epileptic from Nebraska who had been kicked in the head by a mule; there was no simple explanation for the phenomenon of Victory Faust except that it had something to do with baseball.

The admissions log also listed each new patient's occupation. Again, there was quite a variety. Most common was laborer, with five. There were two ranchers, a lawyer, a student, an upholsterer, an electrical engineer, a salesman, and a sawmill worker. Two patients listed no occupation. Then there was Charles Faust. Across from his name, under Occupation, the log reads "Prof. Ball player." Never mind that he had spent the past two years as a laborer. In his mind, he was a professional ball player, a free agent between winning streaks. He was Victory Faust of the New York Base Ball Club, plodding toward his destiny, and he didn't care who knew it.

On July 20, one month and seventeen days later, Charley Faust was released from the Salem asylum, heading for Seattle with "friends." The friends may have been ballplayers who agreed to rescue Charley from his confinement and return him safely to his brother. Or his brother may have fetched Charley himself. The ledger page listing his discharge included thirteen entries for July, seven of them women. One column reads "Mental State When Discharged." Of the thirteen patients released in July, five were described as "Recovered." Five others were "Much Improved," while two were merely "Improved." Then there was Charley Faust, singled out as "Not Improved"—the only patient to flunk out of the asylum all month.

How do we know that forty-seven days of some kind of treatment did not improve Charley Faust's condition? Because when he was discharged, he still gave his occupation as "Prof. Base-ball player." The doctors realized that there was nothing they could do for him. If John McGraw, one of the greatest minds in baseball, couldn't convince Faust that he was not a ballplayer, what chance did someone with three college degrees have?

Once free, Charley Faust resumed the crusade to restore his career with the Giants. On August 6, back in Seattle, he sent a fresh telegram to August Herrmann. It read: "Your honor, I Charles Victor Faust of Marion Kansas I have been residing at Ellis Hotel 504 5th Ave. Seattle Wash. Since last time I seen you at Cincinnati on Feb. 21.1914. I sent telegrams to Mr. McGraw asking to forward ticket for myself and brother but he refused so I wish to see if your honor will forward me two tickets over Great Northern and Big Four from Seattle to Cincinnati. I will sign what is right what I told Mr. McGraw when I first went there and your honor will do right to me. Yours truly, Charles Victor Faust." That feeble plea set Faust back $1.10, a sum he used to spend daily on manicures and massages in his glory weeks with the Giants. Now it bought him nothing but more silence from the other end and more frustration in his deluded mind.

News of Faust's confinement reached New York before the end of June, judging by two unmarked clippings in Faust's file at the National Baseball Library. The articles give oddly different versions of Faust's beginning as well as his talents. How can we blame recent writers for getting the story wrong when the reporters couldn't get it straight even when Faust was alive? One clipping bears the headline "Charlie Faust Sent to Bughouse League."

> Charlie Victory Faust, once mascot of the Giants, has been found insane by the authorities in Portland, Ore. He joined the Giants in 1911, spurred on by the belief that he was a great pitcher. Faust told McGraw that in a dream a voice had commanded him to offer his services to the Giants and that he had no peace until he left his farm in Kansas in compliance with the bidding of the voice.

No sooner had the volunteer been allowed to take a place on the bench with the team than the fortunes of the Giants began to rise. Moreover, Faust showed an extraordinary ability to predict plays.

But his mania grew, and fearing that the big rawboned countryman might do somebody an injury McGraw tried to lose him at the end of the 1912 season. Not until this year were the Giants rid of Faust, for he made repeated trips to New York in an effort to get back with the baseball club.

The other clipping lacks a headline but contains more facts:

Charley Faust, once the most remarkable mascot ever carried by a big-league ball club, has been found insane by the authorities in Portland, Ore., and is confined in an asylum there. Faust attached himself to the Giants while the then prospective champions were playing a series in St. Louis, back in 1911, and was not finally completely ditched until last winter.

A native of Marion, Kan., Faust was told by a fortune teller that he could become the greatest pitcher the world has ever known if he would join the Giants. Three times she told him this, adding that when he had established himself he would meet a girl named Lulu, marry her and become the father of future generations of baseball stars.

Faust confided all this to McGraw one day in St. Louis in 1911, and on the strength of it was invited to practice with the boys that afternoon. A great big, raw-boned, simple-minded yap, Faust took it all very seriously. Even to beating his way to the Giants' next stop and then back to the East with them. And as the Giants immediately plunged into a winning streak that carried them into first place, some of the more superstitious players really grew to look upon Faust as a jinx-killer.

Faust couldn't play ball, of course. But he could and did predict plays and the results of series and all that sort of thing. And the advertising he received made him everywhere a drawing card strong enough to make it worth the club's while to more or less officially adopt him as its mascot and pay his expenses on the road.

He lasted through the season of 1911, but lost most of his standing with the players when he misfired on the world's series.

Again in 1912 he bobbed up nuttier than ever, but still a jinx dispeller. There is no telling how far he might have gone.

The reporter then reveals, in a passage quoted earlier, the crucial connection in McGraw's mind between Faust's persistent nagging and Carter Harrison's assassin.

Faust wasn't intensely popular with his chief after that. It took a long, long time to flag him, but he was finally dumped overboard, to drift west to the Pacific coast. The club received a letter from him a while ago in which Faust declared that he had lost faith in McGraw and the Giants and would seek his fortune elsewhere, but recommending a younger brother, who was "even better" than Charles himself. C. Victory was in Los Angeles then and nothing further was heard from him until yesterday, when word was flashed east that he had gone hopelessly out of his head and been placed under restraint.

That pretty much cemented Charley Faust's reputation in New York. On his best days, he was nutty. Back in Seattle, Faust stewed, never giving up. In October he saw a familiar face, fanning his hope. The story appeared in *The Glory of Their Times*, courtesy of Fred Snodgrass:

That fall I joined a group of Big Leaguers and we made a barnstorming trip, starting in Chicago and going through the Northwest and down the Coast and over to Honolulu. In Seattle, who came down to the hotel to see me but Charlie Faust.

"Snow," he said to me, "I'm not very well. But I think if you could prevail on Mr. McGraw to send me to Hot Springs a month before spring training, I could get into shape and help the Giants win another pennant."

But, unfortunately, that never came to pass. Because Charlie Faust died that winter, and we did not win the pennant the next year. Believe it or not, that's the way it happened.

Not quite. Snodgrass placed this final encounter with Faust in the fall of 1913, killing him off that winter. That all-star tour took place in 1914, and it passed through Seattle on October 29. Snodgrass was joined on the National League squad by fellow Giants Art Fletcher and George Burns. Burns played the outfield, while Snodgrass played third

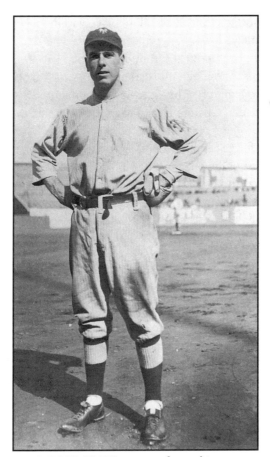

FRED SNODGRASS was one of several impressionable youngsters in the Giants lineup in 1911, his first as their full-time centerfielder. Luckily for us, Faust made a strong impression on Snodgrass, even though many of the details were murky by the time he passed the tale along to Lawrence Ritter. (National Baseball Hall of Fame Library & Archive, Cooperstown, N.Y.)

base and went hitless that day. Oddly, both starting pitchers were named Bill James. One of them, conveniently nicknamed "Seattle Bill," hogged most of the attention from the Seattle papers, which found no reason to mention Charley Faust.

When Faust told Snodgrass, "I'm not very well," did he mean physically or mentally? It would have been the first time he admitted being subpar, unless you count the time he complained of arm weariness after the Giants tricked him into carrying a suitcase full of iron from the train station to the hotel. This time he meant it.

Within weeks, Charley Faust began the final misadventure of his life. On December 1, 1914, he was confined at the Western Washington Hospital for the Insane. Located at Steilacoom, a small, isolated town southwest of Tacoma at the southern tip of Puget Sound, it was the first mental hospital in the Pacific Northwest. The land originally housed a fort, built in 1849 to protect settlers from Indians and abandoned in 1868. The first twenty-one patients arrived in 1871, after the state purchased the buildings. From there the asylum flourished, growing to a peak of three thousand patients in the 1950s and gaining some notoriety as the institution which for many years housed the actress Frances Farmer.

When Charley Faust was admitted, there were 1,475 patients, of whom roughly half returned to society. Overcrowding was always a problem, with new wards filling up almost before construction was finished. Two days after Faust's arrival, the hospital's director, Dr. William N. Keller, announced plans to transfer at least two hundred of those patients to another facility. Mental health care was relatively primitive, but the hospital at Steilacoom was known for its innovative methods. The longtime director, Dr. A. P. Calhoun, believed in making the facility as self-sufficient and beautiful as possible. To that end, he advocated work therapy, involving patients in maintaining a working farm, building roads, and so on. Dr. Keller took over from Calhoun in October 1914 and continued to improve and expand the grounds and the treatment. By the end of 1914 the hospital even built so-called "tubercular cottages," frame dwellings which afforded maximum exposure to fresh air, the newest idea in treatment of tuberculosis. The cottages were erected just in time, for that winter brought a major tuberculosis scare, the disease first found in cattle and soon spreading among people.

Charley Faust contracted tuberculosis, and it killed him. He may have had it when he saw Fred Snodgrass in September and told him that he didn't feel well. Or he may have caught it after he reached

Steilacoom. Unfortunately, there are no available records of his admission, of the circumstances leading up to his confinement, or of any diagnosis of his condition. He may or may not have been housed in one of those new cottages, and he may or may not have been treated for insanity. We don't know. All we have is the death certificate, in which Dr. Keller stated that he tended the patient (a "laborer") from December 1, 1914, until his death from pulmonary tuberculosis on June 18, 1915.

Although we have no direct description of Charley Faust's existence at Steilacoom, certainly it must have been hellish. Increasingly ravaged by the disease, he got no mental comfort either, alone and forgotten, facing the truth that he would never rejoin the Giants. Consumed by his delusion of pitching greatness, he never could find a middle ground on which to balance his life. He could not sit back wistfully and think "Gee, it was nice of Honus Wagner to let me strike him out that time." His mind did not work that way. Instead, it said, "Gee, if McGraw would only give me another chance, I'd strike Wagner out every time!" Nobody at Steilacoom could understand that. When he told them about fanning Wagner or pitching left-handed at the Polo Grounds benefit for the *Titanic* victims or performing his vaudeville act for Andrew Carnegie, they merely counted it as further evidence of his dementia.

How could they know how vividly he had lived it all? However barren the rest of his existence had been, he had a richer life in his year with the Giants than many people have in a lifetime. Nothing in his young life prepared him for it, and nothing that happened afterward could match it. The best he could hope for was to relive it, and he hoped too hard for that, partly because he had a short memory and needed fresh reminders. Whether driven by the need to fulfill the prophecy or by some realization that he never had it as good as he did when he was with the Giants, his feverish attempts to rejoin them wound up separating him further from reality. Ironically, all the things people did years earlier to humor his desire to be a pitcher—letting him strike opponents out in batting practice, letting him pitch those two innings after the pennant was clinched, letting him pitch a whole exhibition game as a February 29 afterthought—ultimately ripened into a debilitating delusion. His most glorious moments became the signposts of his insanity. Did they happen? How could any of them have happened? Yet they did. Of course he wasn't a pitcher, yet you can look up his major league career in the record book. He did better—on paper—than a lot of pitchers in the encyclopedias. That was a fact, but he had nothing to fall back on when he could no longer prove it.

The Tacoma *Daily Ledger* published the following item, datelined June 18, 1915, from San Bernardino, California. The headline read "Real Baseball Bugs Play National Game."

> Taking to the fine points of the pastime like a duck to water, 200 inmates of the Patton Insane asylum "rooted" like real fans for both sides in the first baseball played here today in which the "Cubs" defeated the "Giants" by a score of 11 to 6. The teams were made up from inmates of the institution.
>
> Dr. J. A. Riley, superintendent of the hospital, announced after the game that a series of games would be played.
>
> A game has been arranged for next week between the physicians of the county hospital and the patients to afford the doctors an opportunity to study the effect of the game on the patients.
>
> "The inauguration of baseball here is simply in accordance with the generally recognized theory that entertainment is helpful for patients," said Dr. Riley.

Alas, someone finally created the league in which Charley Faust could have starred, and it came too late for him. Asylum ball debuted in San Bernardino the same day that Faust died in Washington. You know he would have looked at that clipping in the Tacoma paper and thought, "Gee, if I'd been there to pitch, the 'Giants' would've won." And he would have been right.

Charles Victor Faust was buried across the street on the property of the Western Washington State Hospital for the Insane, in a field in what is now a county park along Steilacoom Boulevard. A baseball field is nearby. The grave is marked only with a small stone numbered 1395. You can walk right over it and not know it is there, just as you can read about the 1911 baseball season without coming across Victory Faust. But if you look more closely, you will see that grave number 1395 sits on the crest of the most gradually sloping mound, a perfect resting place for an eternally striving pitcher.

DYING IN ISOLATION, Charley Faust quickly moved into obscurity, a forgotten fluke in baseball history. Every generation or so his strange story surfaced, each time sounding more ludicrous and improbable, his reputation increasingly dependent on half-remembered rumors. Fred Lieb recounted the Faust legend at least twice, first in 1930 and again in 1957. Inevitably, he misstated the details of Faust's career two different ways. In 1930 he wrote:

> Among famous Spring bloomers we also might include Charley Faust, who, 19 years ago, wished himself on the Giants. Charley imagined himself the greatest pitcher in the world and McGraw just couldn't get rid of him. He managed to get to the bull pen one day and the Giants pulled out a game with a great late-inning rally.
>
> Thereafter, the Giants decided Charley was lucky and whenever the McGraw men were behind, they sent Charley to the bull pen to warm up. It used to act like magic and ball players, naturally superstitious, came to regard Faust as the best mascot in the league. McGraw drew a contract with him on the back of a collar.
>
> However, Charley begged for a chance to pitch. Finally he got it on the last day of the 1911 season, Columbus Day, when the Giants played Brooklyn. It was a game which didn't count one way or the other, and McGraw permitted Charley to pitch the ninth inning.
>
> The Brooklyn players, enjoying the burlesque, struck out with wild swings at Charley's dinky curves. When New York had its turn at bat, Faust was intentionally passed and permitted to steal second, third and home, coming into each base with a great gust of dust.
>
> After Baker smacked Marquard and Mathewson for home runs in the World's Series games a few days later, Charley Faust solemnly shook his head, and said it was all McGraw's fault for not pitching him.
>
> "Baker might have hit me for singles, but he never could have hit my curves for home runs," said the eccentric pitcher. Charley died a few years ago in an insane asylum.

In 1957, as the New York Giants prepared to abandon the Polo Grounds and head west, the *Sporting News* published numerous articles recounting Polo Grounds history. In one article, Lieb selected the ball-park's most historic, tragic, and humorous incidents. For Lieb, the most historic event was John McGraw's 1902 debut as Giants manager; the most tragic was the Giants losing the 1908 pennant because of "Merkle's Boner."

"Perhaps the most comical incident ever seen at the Polo Grounds," Lieb wrote this time,

> came on Columbus Day, 1911, when Charley Faust, who imagined himself a great pitcher, was permitted to pitch and go to bat in the ninth inning. The Giants had long since clinched John McGraw's third pennant, and the Dodgers, the holiday opponent, were anchored in seventh place.
>
> Faust had joined the Giants in midseason as a good-luck charm, and for this game McGraw signed him to a Giant contract on the back of a collar. In Faust's only National League inning, he struck out three Dodgers, all of whom took furious swings at his dinky delivery.
>
> When it came Faust's time at bat, the Dodgers enabled him to get on base, after which Charley stole second and third with grotesque slides. His two steals are among the 347 registered by the Giants that year, a modern major league record.

Curious that Lieb credited Faust with three stolen bases the first time and only two the second time, as if he looked up the records before writing the later story. Forget that he twice ignored Faust's earlier appearance against Boston, or that he stuck by his earlier fable that Faust struck out the side. At least he got the stolen bases straight the second time.

That's about as much as Edwin Burkholder got right in his 1950 article on Faust in *Sport* magazine. This article, which put Faust back on the baseball map, contributed much Faust lore, unfortunately most of it dubious. Consider, for instance, Burkholder's account of Faust as faith healer:

> In late August, the team was on a Western trip. At Cincinnati, George Wiltse suffered an injury to his hip, and McGraw had to pull him out of several games. The Giants couldn't afford to lose his services, so McGraw sent him to Youngstown, Ohio, to have

Dr. Reese, called "the bonesetter" by the club, look at his hip. Dr. Reese couldn't do much good, and Christy Mathewson suggested that McGraw have Charley use his strange power on Wiltse.

The entire club stood outside the door of Wiltse's hotel room as Charley walked in. Wiltse was on the bed, writhing and moaning. Charley walked up to him and said: "Shucks, George, there ain't a thing the matter with you." Charley touched the hip and Wiltse relaxed and looked up at Charley, like a man might stare at a ghost. He got off the bed, walked out of the door without a limp. "The minute Charley touched me," he announced to his teammates, "the pain left. I feel fine. There isn't a damn thing wrong with my hip now."

Which sounds more likely—Charley Faust healing Wiltse's hip by the laying on of hands, or Charley Faust rubbing liniment all over himself because Barney Reilly told him it would strengthen his arm? What was Burkholder thinking? Perhaps the most telling portrait of Faust by a nonjournalist was the interview John "Red" Murray gave in 1934. It was Murray who acted as Faust's impresario during the long road trip in 1911 when he honed his vaudeville routine (only to see it discarded in favor of Loney Haskell's nonsense). That may have qualified Murray as the closest thing Faust had to a friend on the team (as distinct from the friendly treatment the players gave him when they kept winning). Murray's interview, "as told to Harry Markson," included comments about Bugs Raymond, Sherry Magee, and Christy Mathewson, but two-thirds of it was devoted to Faust:

> But it remained for the season of 1911 to produce baseball's greatest laugh and oddest character, and it was occasioned by the advent into baseball of one Charley Faust, who joined our team during midseason, of his own accord.
>
> The Giants were playing in St. Louis at the time, and Arthur Devlin and myself were in the clubhouse before the game. A big, lanky, six-foot rube breezed in and said to us, "I'm a pitcher." We asked him where he had pitched and he said, "I'm from Kansas and I've pitched in Ohio."
>
> We sized him up at once for some fun and told him to get into his uniform, which he brought along. It must have been a boy's outfit, for he was a sight. The pants came only as far as the half-

way mark between his waistline and his knees, and he looked as if he had been through a shrinking process with his uniform on.

Devlin sent him on the field and tipped off Roger Bresnahan, the Cardinals' manager, what it was all about. Bresnahan shook hands with Faust and ordered him to start playing ball. Well, he couldn't any more play ball than a ten-year-old child. The fellows joshed him but he took it all.

The first thing the boys did was to have Charley start running bases, under the St. Louis sun that was hitting above 100 in the shade. The poor fellow ran from base to base, slid when told to, and finally passed out of the picture near first base from the heat, exhaustion and the bruises of sliding. Some of the boys got nervous then and thought that maybe they had carried it too far. But Charley came to and sat on the Giants' bench during the regular game.

He told Manager McGraw that he was a pitcher and the leader of the Giants signed him for the season, then and there. McGraw really kept him for the entertainment that he furnished and the good humor that it put the boys in, on the field.

His hands were the largest I had ever seen. They must have done farm work at one time. When the game was over and the boys went into the showers, what a sight poor Charley was as he stripped. His body, legs and arms were skinned and bruised from the base sliding, and he looked like a piece of raw meat. What a sight he was, and how he must have suffered! When you do not know how to slide bases and besides, wear no pads, such as ball players wear, then and only then can you realize what the poor devil went through sliding bases in St. Louis in midsummer.

VALUE AS CLOWN CAUSES McGRAW TO CARRY FAUST WITH GIANTS

We kept Charley with us the rest of the season, paying his expenses and giving him a salary besides. He travelled with us wherever we went and on the same trains and in the same Pullmans. And what tricks the boys did play on Charley. I'll never forget them. In fact, some of them are unprintable.

Charley sat on our bench during the rest of the season, in uniform, and practiced with the boys on the field. All the players and fans everywhere knew him and he was a standing joke in the base-ball world. However, he nevertheless sat in uniform on our bench during the World's Series that year. McGraw kept him that one season and then let him go.

The funniest incident in connection with Charley's sojourn with the Giants that year occurred in New York one day, when we were playing Boston. After the regular game, it was announced that Charley Faust would bat for Doyle. The crowd waited and the Boston team took the field, as Faust went to bat. He couldn't hit 15 pitched balls, though McGraw stood nearby, coaching him. Finally, McGraw ordered him to bunt, and he did, starting for first and sliding into that bag, under McGraw's advice, who ran along with him to first base. He then stole second, again on orders from McGraw, who ordered him to slide and stood over him as he slid into the bag, yelling directions. With McGraw at his side, he stole third, sliding into that bag as the Giants' manager yelled "slide!"

He was now perched on third base and the players and crowd roared. All the way over from first to third, McGraw had kept right behind him. Again he was ordered to steal, this time, home, and he left third and started for the plate, McGraw right behind him. As he neared the home plate, McGraw yelled "slide" and the poor fellow did. The Boston catcher and Faust came together in a mix-up four feet from the home plate, the Boston man's hands around Faust's neck and Faust struggling to reach home. As he finally con-tacted the plate, the umpire bent over him and yelled "Out!" Faust looked up feebly, murmured "No" and then collapsed.

I am glad nobody but the players saw his body when he stripped for the showers. It was pitiful. I do not know if another such character is living today. In the clubhouse after the game, McGraw told him that he was released because of his wretched playing, and the man cried like a baby. He asked some of us to intervene for him and we told him we would, and assured him that McGraw would keep him. He was kept. Lanigan's Baseball Records list him as a member of the 1911 Giants.

THERE IS NO INDICATION that Murray's account of Faust dented the American consciousness. For decades a copy of it lan-guished unnoticed in Murray's file at the National Baseball Library. It would have perpetuated an image of Faust quite different from Burk-holder's—pathetic in his abilities but nobler in his suffering. Instead, it was Burkholder's article that was reprinted in *Reader's Digest*, spreading the Faust name further. In 1955 *TV Reader's Digest* presented a thirty-minute dramatization of Faust's career based on Burkholder's account. Lee Marvin starred as Faust in a cast that also included Lee Van Cleef. This teleplay, titled "How Charlie Faust Won a Pennant for the Giants," caught the eye of a California banker named Fred Snodgrass. Years later, when Lawrence Ritter interviewed Snodgrass for *The Glory of Their Times*, Snodgrass said, "I'll tell you this story about a character in baseball which was written up in the *Reader's Digest* and later televised when the *Digest* was putting on those television plays and I happened to see it twice on television and, of course, they changed the story a little bit in the end to make it a little bit more adapted to television, but the true story is what I'm going to tell you now."

Ritter's book brought a whole generation of ballplayers back into the limelight, with Charley Faust there, too, lurking on the fringe, wait-ing to be given a chance to regain his rightful place in baseball history. From this point, it took only a dozen years for Thomas Busch to do the first serious research on Faust, and only another dozen years after that for the research to begin on this book. That adds up to glacial progress for some seventy-five years after Faust died, decades during which his reputation lay dormant. As late as the 1980s one historian referred to Faust as "somewhat apocryphal," a vague phrase which indicated that the facts of the Faust case had become obscured by their very improba-bility.

One observer who got the gist of Faust's experiences was novelist E. L. Doctorow. In *Ragtime*, Father takes his son to the Polo Grounds, where Faust catches their eye during the game:

> On the Boston side the boy who picked up the bats and replaced them in the dugout was, upon second look, a midget, in a team uniform like the rest but proportionately minute. His shouts and taunts were piped in soprano. Most of the players who came to bat first touched him on the head, a gesture he seemed to invite, so that Father realized it was a kind of good luck ritual. On the Giant side was no midget but a strange skinny man whose uniform was

ill-fitting, who had weak eyes that did not align properly and who seemed to shadow the game in a lethargic pantomime of his own solitude, pitching imaginary balls more or less in time to the real pitches. He looked like a dirt eater. He waved his arm in complete circles, like a windmill turns. Father began to watch the game less than he did this unfortunate creature, obviously a team pet, like the Boston midget. During dull moments of the game the crowd yelled to him and applauded his antics. Sure enough, he was listed in the program as mascot. His name was Charles Victor Faust. He was clearly a fool who, for imagining himself one of the players, was kept on the team roster for their amusement.

At the end of the chapter, Father's son catches a foul ball and is cheered by the crowd.

For one instant everyone in the park looked in their direction. Then the fool with the weak eyes who imagined he was a player on the team came up to the fence in front of them and stared at the boy, his arms and hands twitching in his baggy flannel shirt. His hat was absurdly small for his abnormally large head. The boy held out the ball to him and gently, with a smile almost sane, he accepted it.

An interesting note is that this poor fellow, Charles Victor Faust, was actually called upon to pitch one inning in a game toward the end of this same season when the Giants had already won the pennant and were in a carefree mood. For a moment his delusion that he was a big-leaguer fused with reality. Soon thereafter the players became bored with him and he was no longer regarded as a good luck charm by Manager McGraw. His uniform was confiscated and he was unceremoniously sent on his way. He was remanded to an insane asylum and some months later died there.

Doctorow captured the average fan's response to Faust and the tendency of crowds to lose interest in games when Faust was cavorting on the sidelines. He remanded Faust to an asylum too hastily, yet created haunting images of an insane mascot parading his foolishness before a harsh, uncaring world (contrasted with a child's fleeting kindness). Glossing over Faust's positive achievements, Doctorow instead focused on the symptoms of his insanity, embellishing and inventing for his fictional purposes just as the New York reporters who saw Faust in action did for the advancement of their journalistic careers. Everyone has taken a turn doctoring the Faust legend, a story so remarkable that its truth transcends the inaccuracies of any particular telling.

For the final word, we have a simple statement of that truth from a man who was there front and center. Historian John Holway approached Rube Marquard during the 1979 Hall of Fame induction weekend at Cooperstown. Marquard, the last living member of the 1911 Giants, was ninety-two years old at the time. Confined to a wheelchair in a nearly fetal position, he spoke so softly that Holway had to lean close to hear him. When Holway asked him about Charley Faust, the reply came slowly but with a smile on the contorted face. "When he was with us," Marquard told Holway, "we won. When he wasn't, we didn't."

Bibliography

Books and Articles

Alexander, Charles. *John McGraw*. New York: Viking, 1988.

Burkholder, Edwin V. "The Curious Case of Charley Faust," *Sport* 8, no. 6 (June 1950).

Burns, Ken, and Geoffrey Ward. *Baseball: An Illustrated History*. New York: Knopf, 1994.

Busch, Thomas S. "In Search of Victory: The Story of Charles Victor ('Victory') Faust," *Kansas History* 6, no. 2 (Summer 1983).

Carter, Craig, ed. *Daguerrotypes*. St. Louis: Sporting News, 1990.

Clark, Tom. *The World of Damon Runyon*. New York: Harper and Row, 1978.

Cooley, Clara. *The Western State Hospital*. Fort Steilacoom, Wash., 1964.

DiMeglio, John. *Vaudeville, U.S.A*. Bowling Green, Ohio: Bowling Green University Press, 1973.

Doctorow, E. L. *Ragtime*. New York: Bantam, 1975.

Durso, Joseph. *Casey & Mr. McGraw*. St. Louis: Sporting News, 1989.

Emery, Edwin. *The Press and America*. Englewood Cliffs, N.J.: Prentice Hall, 1972.

Fleming, G. H. *The Unforgettable Season*. New York: Simon and Schuster, 1981.

Gilbert, Douglas. *American Vaudeville*. New York: Whittlesey House, 1940.

Greenberg, Eric Rolfe. *The Celebrant*. Lincoln: University of Nebraska Press, 1983.

Hind, Noel. *The Giants of the Polo Grounds*. Dallas: Taylor, 1988.

Johnson, Allen, and Dumas Malone, eds. *Dictionary of American Biography*, vol. 4. New York: Scribner, 1931.

Lardner, Ring. *Ring Around the Bases.* New York: Scribner, 1992.

Lieb, Fred. *Baseball As I Have Known It.* New York: Grosset and Dunlap, 1977.

Lowry, Philip J. *Green Cathedrals.* New York: Addison-Wesley, 1992.

Mathewson, Christy. *Pitching in a Pinch.* New York: Grosset and Dunlap, 1912.

McGraw, John. *My Thirty Years in Baseball.* Lincoln: University of Nebraska Press, 1995.

McLean, Albert F., Jr. *American Vaudeville As Ritual.* Lexington: University of Kentucky Press, 1965.

Mote, James. *Everything Baseball.* New York: Prentice Hall, 1989.

Neft, David S., and Richard M. Cohen. *The Sports Encyclopedia: Baseball.* New York: St. Martin's Griffin, 1996.

O'Connor, Richard. *Heywood Broun: A Biography.* New York: Putnam, 1975.

Okkonen, Marc. *Baseball Uniforms of the 20th Century.* New York: Sterling, 1991.

——. *Baseball Memories, 1900–1909.* New York: Sterling, 1992.

Reichler, Joseph L. *The Baseball Trade Register.* New York: Macmillan, 1984.

Ritter, Lawrence. *The Glory of Their Times.* New York: Macmillan, 1966.

Robinson, Ray. *Matty: An American Hero.* New York: Oxford University Press, 1993.

Seymour, Harold. *Baseball: The Golden Age.* New York: Oxford University Press, 1971.

Snyder, Robert W. *The Voice of the City.* New York: Oxford University Press, 1989.

Stark, Benton. *The Year They Called Off the World Series.* Garden City Park, N.Y.: Avery, 1991.

Stein, Charles W., ed. *American Vaudeville As Seen by Its Contemporaries.* New York: Knopf, 1984.

Stein, Fred. *Under Coogan's Bluff.* Glenshaw, Pa.: Chapter and Cask, 1978.

Weiner, Ed. *The Damon Runyon Story.* New York: Longmans, Green, 1948.

Newspapers

Arkansas *Democrat*
Boston *Globe*
Brooklyn *Daily Eagle*
Chicago *Daily News*
Chicago *Daily Tribune*
Chicago *Record-Herald*
Cincinnati *Enquirer*
Marion County *Record*
New York *American*
New York *Globe*
New York *Herald*
New York *Morning Telegraph*
New York *Press*
New York *Sun*

New York *Times*
New York *Tribune*
New York *World*
Philadelphia *Inquirer*
Portland *Evening Telegram*
Portland *Oregonian*
Seattle *Post-Intelligencer*
Seattle *Times*
Sporting Life
Sporting News
St. Louis *Post-Dispatch*
Tacoma *Daily Ledger*
Topeka *Daily Capital*
Variety

Player Files

The following individual player files were examined at the National Baseball Library in Cooperstown, New York: Red Ames, Beals Becker, Al Bridwell, Doc Crandall, Eddie Dent, Art Devlin, Josh Devore, Mike Donlin, Larry Doyle, Louis Drucke, Steve Evans, Art Fletcher, Grover Hartley, Buck Herzog, Arlie Latham, Rube Marquard, Christy Mathewson, Bert Maxwell, John McGraw, Fred Merkle, Chief Meyers, Red Murray, Bill Rariden, Bugs Raymond, Wilbert Robinson, Fred Snodgrass, Lefty Tyler, Art Wilson, Hooks Wiltse.

Index

Alexander, Grover Cleveland, 73, 156
American League, origin of, 25–26
Ames, Leon "Red": cold-weather pitcher,
  3; "Ames Hoodoo," 18–21, 39, 72;
  nicknamed "Kalamity," 20; vs.
  Chicago, 35, 53, 148–49; disdained
  run support, 75–76; turned season
  around in Boston, 107–8; in "Frame of
  Fame," 108; testimonial to Faust's jinx-
  ing powers, 108; and lucky tie, 115,
  119, 148–49, 152, 160–61; in *1911*
  World Series, 200–202
Arkansas *Democrat*, 217
Atwood, Harry, 84–85, 104
Aulick, W. W., 13, 191
Aviation, early history of, 84–85, 104–5

Baker, Frank: beat Marquard in World
  Series, 190–91; beat Mathewson,
  became "Home Run" Baker, 191–93;
  spiked by Snodgrass, 193, 194–95; crit-
  icized by Faust, 196, 257; vaudeville
  declined by, 198; key hits in World
  Series game 4 by, 199–200
Baltimore Orioles, 25–26, 33
Barry, Jack, 185, 202–3
Becker, Beals, 73, 125, 194
Bender, Chief, 184, 187, 197, 199–200
Berlin, Irving, 207
Bernard, Edward George, 63
Black Hand, 120
Blanck, Max, 16–17
Boston *Globe*, 109–10

Boston Rustlers. *See* New York Giants
Bresnahan, Roger, 1, 29, 60, 260
Bridwell, Al: felled by malaria, 1, 42, 44;
  traded to Boston, 2, 55–56; in Atlanta
  brawl, 16; conspicuous errors by, 20,
  53; hitting stats of, 33
Brooklyn *Daily Eagle*, 182, 212, 213. *See
  also* Rice, Thomas
Broun, Heywood: on Polo Grounds, 11,
  29; critical of McGraw's tantrums,
  36–37; quip about Brooklyn, 38; praise
  of Mathewson, 65–66; on Faust, 77,
  86, 99–100, 171–72, 174, 177–78
Brown, Mordecai "Three Finger," 12,
  34–35, 39, 64, 82–83, 231
Brush, John T.: at Opening Day, 18; and
  Baltimore Orioles, 26; let Yankees use
  Polo Grounds, 27; and Donlin, 40; and
  Faust, 68, 86; saw Atwood, 85; and
  McGraw, 103, 133, 161
Brush Stadium, 45, 52
Burke, Brownie, 136, 233
Burkholder, Edwin V., 61–63, 141,
  258–59, 262

Carnegie, Andrew, 219–20
Chance, Frank, 34, 37, 52; linked with
  Faust in rumors, 226, 227, 228, 230
Cherry Sisters, 130, 210
Chicago Cubs, 12, 34. *See also* New York
  Giants
Cincinnati *Enquirer. See* Ryder, Jack
Cincinnati Reds. *See* New York Giants